# Praise for The Passionate Life: Creating Vitality and Joy at Any Age

I love good books, because they are born from real and personal stories. Where someone doesn't tell me, they invite me. They show me ways to "come alive and start living." Mara invites us to appreciate and grasp what is already within. And she's not just a teacher; she's a guide who walks with us. The book may be an invitation to women perhaps, but after reading the book, I can tell you I definitely want some of what she's talking about: the permission to live out loud, in our power, in the light, every day. Count me in. It's down-to-earth. Thank you, Mara. And I agree, the best is yet to come.

~ Terry Hershey, inspirational speaker and author of fifteen books, including *The Power of Pause: Becoming More by Doing Less.*

Dr. Mara Karpel is firmly fixed in her "zone of genius" in this amazing book, which is the ultimate road map to energy, inspiration, and purposeful living. Dr. Karpel fearlessly proclaims: out with the old paradigms, in with new! Here is everything one needs to make the golden years truly and radiantly golden!

~ Ana Brett and Ravi Singh
Authors of *The Kundalini Yoga Book: Life in the Vast Lane*

In *The Passionate Life: Creating Vitality and Joy at Any Age*, Dr. Mara Karpel gifts us with the wisdom of dozens of experts in the fields of peak performance, lifestyle, spirituality and aging, just to name a few. She highlights the essence of many best selling books and weaves their expertise together through personal stories and lovely narratives. I will return to this book whenever I need a reminder of possibilities

in life. Most compelling is her unwavering candor about her own life journey. As a repeat guest on her radio show, *Dr. Mara Karpel & Your Golden Years*, I've been blessed to get to know Mara over the past two years. As I reader of her book, I feel honored by her continual invitation to deepen our friendship through her personal stories. Dr. Karpel is a treasure to her clients, and Mara a gift to her listeners and now her readers.

~ Tresa Leftenant, CFP, author of *Reinventing Her: Helping Women Plan, Pursue, and Capitalize Their Next Chapter*, founder of *My Financial Design*, Registered Investment Advisor, and National Speaker.

*The Passionate Life* is an excellent roadmap to help others discover their passions and live their purpose no matter their age or setbacks. Dr. Mara Karpel has put together a masterpiece that I recommend everyone to read.

~ Quentin Vennie, Author of *Strong in the Broken Places: A Memoir of Addiction and Redemption Through Wellness*

Mara is a living embodiment of what it looks like to live a purpose driven life: energetic, bright-eyed, and joyful. Fortunately, for the rest of us, Mara's purpose is to help each of us find our own purpose. This is a book about how to get out of our own way and reconnect with that inner voice and ask: By what measures do you want to define yourself? What truly drives you? All answers lead toward living a happier, healthier, more passionate and purpose driven life.

~ Steve Kane, Certified Yoga Instructor and Facilitator of "The Art of Happiness"

Dr. Mara Karpel shows us that a life full of happiness, meaning and vitality can be found at any age. She shares empowering and inspiring stories from experts on a wide variety of topics, including relationships, nutrition, stress management and spirituality (to name a few). Dr. Karpel offers life-changing, but also practical, strategies that will lead you through a journey of self-discovery. Living a meaningful life often requires us to step outside of our comfort zones, question societal norms, and even face a bit of adversity—this is part of what makes life rich and varied! Dr. Karpel addresses this beautifully and provides tools to help you make your dreams a reality even when you are faced with challenges and setbacks. I highly recommend this book to anyone who is looking to create something new, or who simply wants to experience more contentment and appreciation for the life they are currently living!

~ Dara Kelly, M.S., OTR/L, RYT500
Occupational Therapist, Certified Yoga Instructor, and
Transformational Energy Mentor

Creating a state of mind and body well-being begins every moment, and we have a choice each time we sit down for a meal to start the journey. Dr. Mara offers an outlook on where we strive to be with personal wellness in a very genuine style, sharing with us some of her own experiences along the journey to health. As a chef and culinary educator, I enjoyed the *Food for the Soul* section and appreciate that she outlines how food affects our mood and, more specifically, how adding plant-based foods to our diet can improve our mind and body wellbeing. With the added support of the experts she has interviewed, Dr. Mara offers great guidance and the valuable steps toward a greater health and overall wellness––no matter our age.

~ Chef Chad Sarno,
Chef, Author, Culinary Educator and
Co-Founder of Wicked Healthy

# The Passionate Life

*Creating Vitality and Joy at Any Age*

**Dr. Mara Karpel**

Published by Best Seller Publishing®, Pasadena, CA
Best Seller Publishing® is a registered trademark
Printed in the United States of America.
ISBN: 978-1-946978-87-5

This publication is designed to provide accurate and authoritative information with regard to the subject matter covered. It is sold with the understanding that the publisher is not engaged in rendering legal, accounting, or other professional advice. If legal advice or other expert assistance is required, the services of a competent professional should be sought. The opinions expressed by the authors in this book are not endorsed by Best Seller Publishing® and are the sole responsibility of the author rendering the opinion.

Most Best Seller Publishing® titles are available at special quantity discounts for bulk purchases for sales promotions, premiums, fundraising, and educational use. Special versions or book excerpts can also be created to fit specific needs.

For more information, please write:
Best Seller Publishing®
1346 Walnut Street, #205
Pasadena, CA 91106
or call 1(626) 765 9750
Toll Free: 1(844) 850-3500
Visit us online at: www.BestSellerPublishing.org

**Disclaimer:** The information contained in this book is based upon the research and personal and professional experiences of the author. It is not intended as a substitute for consulting with your physician or other health care provider. Any attempt to diagnose or treat an illness should be done under the direction of a health care professional.

Artwork by: Mara E. Karpel
Cover Photography by: Fox Aguilar

Dedicated to those who dare to dream – at **any** age –
The world surely needs you right about now.

*"Youth has no age."*

~ PABLO PICASSO

# Table of Contents

# Foreword

You don't have to look far these days to notice that a million pretenders and their cousins have jumped shamelessly on the bandwagon of investigating optimal ways of ameliorating the human condition. Nor is it difficult to see those who devote their time to playing the social media self-promotion game rather than actually being of service to others. And these are the ones everyone flocks to.

Until, the next one comes along.

The irony, aside from the intense disingenuousness required to behave that way in the world, is that hardly anyone receives any lasting help. Not because what's being offered is necessarily flawed—most of it's merely derivative of other things, or a rehash, or even a straight lift and is good enough to work with—but because most people rarely actually put the techniques into practice. And that's exactly why the public appetite for the next new thing is so constant: nothing works unless you use it.

But when someone comes along who is genuine—who actually cares about the people they're helping more than they care about making a face for themselves, or who has devoted years to studying and developing their skill sets, rather than setting up shop after doing a couple of weekends' worth of seminars, and who is imbued with the timeless wisdom of the ancients, along with the generosity of spirit to communicate that wisdom clearly, free of mystification, and who will help others most rather than merely make themselves appear great and knowledgeable—it comes as a breath of fresh air in an otherwise toxic environment.

Dr. Mara is elegantly understated, humble, and modest, and genuinely so, not as a ruse so people will comment in how lovely she is, but because she really is lovely.

Kindness exudes from her.

But she doesn't trade on it. Instead, she offers a perfectly sound schema culled from decades of experience, which if followed properly will help enormously.

However, what's exciting here is the subject matter of this wonderful book.

In this ever increasingly unhinged reality, in which all the familiar structures are morphing or coming off their moorings, it makes sense once you've gone fifty orbits or more round the sun that you stop driving yourself mad trying to conform or keep up—and you instead grab the adventure while you still can, and with all your wealth of experience and knowledge, go forth and have a total ball.

The good doctor tells you how and encourages you in the softest, kindest, and wisest way to claim the ride now and gain the full value of existence you were born to enjoy.

I'm proud to be the one to leave you in her good hands now.

~ Stephen Russell, "The Barefoot Doctor"
Author of *Barefoot Doctor's Handbook for the Urban Warrior: Wayword Taoist Survival Technique* and *The Message: Vision for a New Golden Era*

# Prologue

A few years ago, during an esoteric discussion with a family member regarding "happiness," my relative told me about a lecture that she had attended with a famous rabbi. During the rabbi's discussion about the meaning of life, he said something to the effect, "Happiness is like sand. Each day, we need to continue to pick up the grains of sand to create our happiness." That quote, whether or not I've mangled it, has stuck with me and has put a frame around the moments of my own life.

In my profession as a psychologist, as well as my personal life, I've come to see that happiness is a choice. And this choice requires us to behave in ways, whether outwardly or inwardly (our thought habits), which support the happiness choice. It's obvious from all of the money spent on self-help books, workshops, pharmacological aids, and psychotherapy, that most of us wish to achieve these, often elusive, experiences of joy, vitality, and *happiness*. I've spent much of the more-than twenty-six years of my career looking for the answers, the grains of sand, in order to help my clients and, honestly, myself, to create happy, more fulfilling lives. Having specialized in working with older adults for a good part of my career, even adults nearing the century mark, I know that this pursuit to feel joyful and purposeful never ends, unless one has become depressed and has given up on life.

I began to write for various newspapers and publications several years ago in order to spread any information that I had learned along the way. Writing turned out to be good therapy for me. It helped me to distill events of my own life and lessons that I had learned, leading me to a clearer understanding and better use of those lessons. Once I started writing, I couldn't stop.

Then, I turned fifty and launched my radio show, *Dr. Mara Karpel & Your Golden Years*, all in the same year, 2012. On this program, I've had the privilege of interviewing experts of various fields, making up the different components that contribute to the "grains" of joy and fulfillment. Having their words of wisdom and expertise to add to my own exploration, I felt that I had to write a book about it, almost as if I had no choice. And, so, in 2014, I began the remarkable journey of becoming an author, and I've integrated excerpts from many of the interviews from my show into the content. While this book, in many ways, is a culmination of lessons learned, grains of sand, about the choices that can lead to more healthful and joyful living at any age, it is in no way all-inclusive about such a vast topic. Therefore, it is the first in a series. I promise there will be more.

I've enjoyed every minute of this public exploration, even the tougher and more emotional, raw, moments that have consisted of digging deep within and putting my heart out into the open. It is my deepest hope that my having taken this public journey will help you to realize that you're not alone with some of the struggles you might be dealing with in your own life. In addition, I hope that there will be some new lessons you might learn from my own on my path, as well as reminders of some lessons you already knew, that will help you in picking up your own grains of joyfulness and vitality and in making the choice to do it over and over again.

With all my love,

*Mara*

# Introduction

Many of us suddenly find ourselves in our fifties, when we discover that a half-century of our life has gone by, and we haven't made time to pursue what it is that calls to us from our soul's desire—or to live a fuller and healthier lifestyle. Or, perhaps, we haven't figured out yet what it is that we truly desire. We've been too busy raising a family, taking care of elderly parents, partners, children, or working at the career that we first pursued when we were in our twenties.

Yet, it's not too late to follow our dreams. It's also not too late to create a healthy life for the next half-century, in order to feel vibrant, energetic, enthusiastic, and satisfied on physical, emotional, and spiritual levels. With this book, *The Passionate Life: Creating Vitality and Joy at Any Age*, I composed a guide to navigate through this time of our lives in order to transform it into the satisfying, happy, and healthy life that we so crave. I share my own personal stories of growth and learning, along with my years of experience as a clinical psychologist. Additionally, I include information that I've learned from the many knowledgeable guests that I've interviewed on my radio program who are all experts in their fields of study within the realm of mind and body health throughout the lifespan. Everything in this book is something that I need to remind myself about, daily. Some of these recommendations are ones that I am in the process of implementing more and more into my own life. Some I've been practicing for years.

One of the guests on my show, Tresa Leftenant, wrote the book, *Reinventing Her: Helping Women Plan, Pursue, and Capitalize Their Next Chapter*. I **love** this word that she uses for her inspiring guide for women to get on track with financial health at any age, reinvention. I feel that I've *reinvented* myself in one way or another and usually out of necessity, multiple times in my life. Now in my fifties, I'm choosing to reinvent myself from a place of passionate desire to live my purpose—on purpose. I believe that this purpose in life is dynamic in that it changes as we go through life, and as we build a variety of skills and expertise in different areas. My purpose, now, is to share information about creating a happier and healthier life, throughout our journey through life and into old age, with as many people as possible, rather than only to the individual clients that I see in my practice.

What I do not do in this book is tell you that there are ways that you should think, ideas that you must believe, or foods that you have to eat or avoid. I will merely present the information that I've found to be helpful, both personally and in my practice with clients, so that you can make an informed choice. I urge you to do more research on your own. It's a very confusing world, especially when you get into nutritional advice. It's important to find out as much information as possible in order to make informed choices. I'm also not going to tell you that you're a bad person or faulted in any way if you choose to follow some of these suggestions and end up slipping into old habits. It's part of being human. Humans are creatures of habit and it often takes several efforts in order to break old habits. The Buddhist teacher, Pema Chodron, wrote, "Nothing ever goes away until it teaches us what we need to know." Perfection is not necessary and, in fact, *having to be perfect* is rather unhealthy.

Like many of us, I've accepted that I'm a work-in-progress, sometimes getting off-track from my own advice, letting old, less-than-healthy, habits of caring for myself, take over my thoughts and behaviors. Sometimes, we all need to check in with ourselves to see if we're awake and aware, or just going on autopilot, eating without being mindful of the food-choices that we're making, for example, or mindlessly playing old tapes of thoughts and beliefs that don't serve life well. It becomes easier and easier to get ourselves back on track if we come from a place of passion and a desire to create a happier and healthier life—and not from a place of self-chastisement.

I believe, that if you're reading this book, you feel that same burning passion to leap forward in all areas of your life, to feel good physically and emotionally, and to move right into your "golden years" with joyfulness and healthfulness. Maybe you have been successfully walking this path for many years and just want some more information to tweak the twists and turns along the journey. Or you could be thirty-five and want to plan ahead to avoid unnecessary challenges— and live the best life possible. If you're in any of these categories, congratulations!

Wherever you are in life, I'm excited to share all that I've been learning on my own journey! And I'm thrilled that you've decided to use this as one of your guidebooks along your own exciting trek! Just remember that wherever we each are is a perfect place to start. Whatever has happened on our different paths has brought us all to this point together, and I welcome your company as we join together on this joyful and healthful journey. So, without further ado, ándale! Let's go!

## Part I

# Follow Your Dreams

Having a dream and passionately following it – No
matter our age and – no matter how scary it may feel,
Gives our life direction and meaning.

# Part I

# Follow Your Dreams

*"Don't die with your music still inside you.
Listen to your intuitive inner voice and find
what passion stirs your soul."*

~ Dr. Wayne Dyer

My dad was usually a practical man. He taught my brothers and me to play it safe, always have a back-up skill if "Plan A" doesn't work out, and always be pragmatic, looking at all the pros and cons before taking a risk. It was good to have that message, since I was the one of my parents' three children, born with my head in the clouds. Dad and I often took walks together, when I was a child and later whenever I visited on vacations from college, graduate school, and after moving away. He liked to walk fast, and he liked to talk while we walked, and I focused on keeping up with his pace while catching my breath. Dad would to speak about practical things, asking my plans for my next move in life and making safe suggestions.

Yet, there was another side to him that he shared with me. Frequently, he would excitedly ask me what I would do if I could do anything I wanted, what would I do if I won the lottery, or where would I love to travel. "Just let your imagination run wild," he'd say, with a smile on his face and a twinkle in his eye. Over the years, he used that expression more and more. His desire for me to play it safe seemed to transform to faith in my ability to do whatever I chose to do along my path. He became more excited by risks that I took in order to follow my dreams. To this day, when I get bogged down in the daily grind of life and forget about the bigger picture of the path I'm on toward fulfilling my dreams, I can hear his voice as a whisper through the trees, "Just let your imagination run wild."

Early on, while practicality still seemed to be his driving force, I followed my dad's advice, embarking on my college education with the plan to obtain my degree in civil engineering. It was safe. In 1984, with this degree, I was almost guaranteed that, as a woman, I would garner a high-paying job. However, in my second year of college, I began working in a peer-counseling center. I counseled just one student, but was able to convince him that suicide was not the answer. It was then that I knew that my dream was to become a clinical psychologist. I have realized this dream and have been working as a psychologist for over twenty-six years.

Since receiving my doctorate in 1992, I have reinvented myself several times in this career, discovering new paths that I wanted to take or that would help me to better support myself. Some reinventions were out of desire and some were out of need. Now, I find myself at another turning point in my life. "Just let your imagination run wild," I hear louder and louder, carried to me on a breeze through the leaves on the trees, lining the sidewalks and gracing my backyard. The years that I've worked at my chosen career have been very rewarding, but I now see that I've been living in what Gay Hendricks describes as my "Zone of Excellence."

Hendricks wrote in his book, *The Big Leap: Conquer Your Hidden Fear and Take Life to the Next Level,* "In the Zone of Excellence are the activities you do extremely well...You're reliable there, and you provide a steady supply of all things that family, friends, and organizations thrive on...This zone is a seductive and even dangerous trap...The temptation is strong to remain in the Zone of Excellence; it's where your own addiction to comfort wants to stay."

According to Hendricks, there's a better way to live—what he refers to as the "Zone of Genius." When we're in the flow of following our true calling, we're in the Zone of Genius. This is where we feel excited, fulfilled, and that our life has meaning. We are following our dreams.

My Zone of Genius at this juncture is to share, in a more creative way, what I've learned about building a happier and healthier life, throughout our journey from youth, through middle age, and into old age, with as many people as possible. I'm excited to be following a new dream now, as letting my "imagination run wild" has often taken the back seat at different periods in my life. I've discovered, too, that it continues to take awareness not to slip back into my Zone of Excellence.

Perhaps, in the course of raising your children or earning a living, your own dreams have gotten lost in the shuffle. You're not alone if you've been diverted from your path toward pursuing your dreams or even figuring out what you want to be *when you grow up*. It's easy to get drawn into "life-as-usual." But this may actually be the ideal time to discover what your *bliss* will be for the next chapter of your life and to *follow it*—no matter your age.

# Chapter 1

# Dreams Continue
# No Matter Our Age

*"You can get what you want
or you can just get old."*

~ Billy Joel

A commonly held perception is that dreaming and following our dreams are for the young. However, logic points to the contrary. After we've had life experience, raised our family, or worked at the career calling us in our youth, we often have a much better idea about what we would now find fulfilling and what gifts we have to offer—or at least, a gut feeling that there's something more.

Many of us have tuned out our call to this Zone of Genius by age forty. When we do this, we end up "getting loud, repeated alarms… in the form of depression, illness, injuries, and relationship conflict," writes Hendricks. Not pursuing our Zone of Genius can cause what he refers to as *diseases of un-fulfillment.* "When people are not expressing their full potential, they often get illnesses that have vague, hard-to-diagnose symptoms…Chronic fatigue syndrome and fibromyalgia are good examples. I've seen both illnesses disappear when people began to break out of the sub-Genius zones and move toward fulfilling their true potential."

# REINVENT YOURSELF!

*Tresa Leftenant, author of Reinventing Her: Helping Women Plan, Pursue, and Capitalize Their Next Chapter and Founder of My Financial Design*

I use the word "reinvention" because there are many times in our lives where we are forced to undergo change. Things happen to us. We go through divorce or we have a new child. It doesn't have to be a negative thing. It can be any kind of life event that causes us to look inside and reflect on what we really want. Then, there's that choice of consciously making our life better. There are a lot of aspects to reinventing ourselves and I describe this process using the Four Pillars of Reinvention in my book.

Here's Pillar Number One: Giving up what we *should* do for what we were *born* to do. Some of the "should" messages, like, "You should marry a wealthy man," or "You should always wear pink," don't necessarily help us. I invite people to really look at their life and ask, "Where am I living from old-fashioned ideas about what a life *should* look like?" That really causes us unhappiness and pain in a lot of ways. Investigating those beliefs is how we can begin the reinvention. We start to see

▶

▶ things that we are good at and those things that make our hearts sing. There are many of those things for all of us. Reinvention is really about discovering what we were born to do and to unhook ourselves from that "should." What an exciting life that is when we truly commit to it!

"When we start to live our own story, that's when we come alive; we really start living," stated Kathy Sparrow, leadership expert and founder of *Writing at Your Edge*, when she appeared on *Dr. Mara Karpel & Your Golden Years*. "Embracing our edge is being willing to step outside of our comfort zone or that familiarity zone, that place where we settle with 'Well, this is as good as it gets,' even when our hearts are yearning for more." Once we start to "lean into it," as Kathy puts it, momentum builds and life begins to feel more meaningful and interesting. "The edge is that place where we become bigger than who we have been and our horizons expand," she explains. "If we can just lean into our edge—that place just on the other side of fear, where we feel excited and a bit frightened at the same time—and be willing to discover more about ourselves—life can become quite an adventure."

# DEFINING SUCCESS!

Quentin Vennie, Speaker, Health Coach, &
Author of *Strong in the Broken Places: A Memoir of
Addiction and Redemption Through Wellness*

I used to work in the finance industry, and I made a nice amount of money, more than I knew what to do with. Prior to that, I was a car salesman for about eight years, and I made a lot of money at a fairly young age. Despite earning all of that money, I was totally unhappy. I was relying on alcohol to shield me from the realities of my life. I was depending on tobacco to calm me down and relax me when things got stressful. Then, I realized that I was happier when I had less because my success was not predicated on material goods. It's a battle between happiness and success. Shouldn't happiness be the greatest success? Isn't that what we're all doing this for? We want to make a lot of money and have the nice car, the nice clothes, and the jewelry, because we think it will make us happy. But we're looking for happiness in the tangibles. We're looking for happiness in all the other places except for ourselves. I know a lot of people who go to work every day and make a lot of money, but hate their jobs. Are they successful?

▶

▶ I would rather get paid less to do what I love, than get paid more to do what I hate.

I like to wake up every morning and be glad that I'm making a difference and love what I'm doing every single day. And, if you do what you love every day, you'll eventually get to the point where you make the money that you want to make. I was in the rat race and I never believed in it. But, I understand it—why I had to go through it—because I'm doing better now than I've ever done. When I first started as a personal trainer, I trained people for free because I genuinely enjoyed doing it. It had nothing to do with money. Everything we do is to try to make ourselves happy. So, why live our lives in misery when we don't have to? In finding that happiness, we ultimately find our greatest success.

We have to be dreamers in order to be doers. If not, then we're just moving aimlessly through life. A lot of the time, we lose sight of the idea that we are in control. We have a lot more control than we think. It's so easy to point the finger at outside entities as to why we are where we are. What's difficult is to take a step back and realize that, regardless of the obstacles, we have everything that it takes to make it through and have victory. Whatever we speak out into the world, we start to

▶ believe. Subconsciously, our beliefs become our actions. At the end of the day, whether we believe that we can or we can't, we're always going to be right.

A lot of people are afraid of change. Change is a scary thing. Once we commit to changing, there's no going back. Shakespeare said, "To thine own self be true." That's the most difficulty thing for people in this world. Yet, when we accept change, we've opened up a whole world of possibility. Once we discover our truth, it's so much easier to keep that promise to ourselves. We discover our "why," we discover our purpose. It's said that possibility is endless, and that's a cliché, but it's also the truth if we accept it as such. If we know that there are no limitations to what we can accomplish, it is the believing in the possibility that opens up the door for opportunity.

If you're beginning a new journey later in life, you're not alone. When senior economics contributor at American Public Media's *Marketplace*, Chris Farrell, joined me for an interview, he discussed the topic of "un-retirement," which he explores in his book, *Unretirement: How Baby Boomers are Changing the Way We Think About Work, Community, and the Good Life*. This is the trend of people who are now hitting traditional retirement age. Rather than just stopping, they continue to find meaning in their lives, perhaps by working at entrepreneurial enterprises that fit more with their life-long or newly realized dreams that they feel benefits society in some way.

Having a dream and passionately following it, no matter our age and no matter how scary it may feel, gives our life direction and meaning. Without this sense of meaning, it's easy to feel that we're stuck in a rut, even if we have financial success from following the "safer" path. Ben Gibson, the founder of YOUvolution and co-founder of the Un.Incubator, pointed out during our interview, that by following our dreams, we can change the world and bring joy to our communities. On a personal level, it gives us a reason to get out of bed every day. Following our dreams leads to joy and excitement, even when there are disappointments along the way. And there will certainly be some disappointments. That's one fact that you can count on. "Authentic individuality is optimistic and requires courage because, unless you are deluded, you know you will experience disappointments in life," wrote Joe Hoare and the Barefoot Doctor, Stephen Russell, in their book, *Awakening the Laughing Buddha Within.*

# Chapter 2
# Women Finding Our Voices

*"I always believed that one woman's success
can only help another woman's success."*

~ GLORIA VANDERBILT

I recently attended a women's networking group. One of the issues that came up for discussion was the tendency for us, as women, to doubt ourselves and our abilities, even when we receive objective feedback that we're very competent. One advantage of being in my "middle-age" years is that I have finally come to a point in my life where I feel more confident. Many of my peers have told me that their own self-confidence has increased as well. In fact, the research has found that self-esteem is at its highest when women reach middle age. However, it was not an easy path to get to this point, and the fact that I am a woman at midlife often leads to situations in which this confidence still is shaken.

# BECOMING VISIBLE

Aralyn Hughes, Performance Artist, Storyteller,
& Author of *Kid Me Not*

As men age, they become more powerful. But, as women age, they somehow become less empowered, sometimes. It's a common concern of many women who are getting older. They don't want to be irrelevant. They don't want to be invisible.

What to do about that? I have a lot of curiosity and look at that as an opportunity to keep living, keep exploring, and keep finding out new things because there's certainly not a shortage. I can barely keep up sometimes. So, getting out there, and doing what you say you want to do is important. I find that women spend a lot of time trying to find out what their "calling" is, so to speak. Sometimes that doesn't empower them to actually go ahead and live. If you just get out there and live your life every morning, if you don't want to miss an opportunity of any kind, you will be living your "calling." Life will just take you there. Trying to determine your calling is exhausting. People spend a lot of time doing it and not living their lives.

> ▶ I know my calling every day by what I do. That's my calling. I do what I want to do. I choose what I like to do. I also spend a lot of time to be with people who inspire me and who are also living their own lives. I like to be around those kinds of people. And that helps because they inspire me, I inspire them, and we're just kind of moving and shaking all together.

On a recent visit to see my mom, who is in an assisted living community back East, I joined her in the dining room one evening. After dinner was done and we were working on dessert, one of her tablemates, Betty, told me that she was still trying to determine if she was 100 years old or 101. I commented that she must know a lot of history. Betty then began to tell us about some of the history she has witnessed. For example, she told us that she remembers when women first were given the right to vote. Her mother, as it turns out, was a suffragette.

"Did she ever go to Seneca Falls?" I asked.

"Of course," Betty responded, "that was Mecca!" She went on, "I used to be a bookkeeper during prohibition. After it ended, we had to keep track of the taxes paid on liquor. There was a man who came around to check my books. He was amazed that my books were clean. I didn't accept graft money," she told me. "He was so happy with how well I kept my books that he said to me, one day, 'You're smart like a man!' He thought he was complimenting me. Now, when

I'm upset with something that my son has done, I tell him, 'You're smart like a man!'"

Having been brought up in a time when what men had to say was taken more seriously than what a woman said, and when men were considered to be the smarter sex, it's taken a certain level of courage for many of us to stand in our truth and let our voices be heard. We frequently received the message of invisibility in subtle and not-so-subtle ways from the media, our peers, our teachers, and our bosses throughout our lives. I'm grateful to have a mom who has always been a strong role model, receiving her bachelor's degree, master's degree, and advanced certificate in education all while I was growing up, teaching me that as women we have as much to offer as men do—and to stand up and be heard.

But, the influences outside of home were also very powerful while I was growing up— and the message that what men had to say was much more important—was so strong that it was hard to avoid making agreements to believe this message and abide by it, without even knowing I was doing this.

I came across this same message during my training in graduate school. There I was in a doctoral program with few role models of successful women psychologists to model myself after and to give my voice some validity until near the end of my graduate school training. It was during my pre-doctoral internship year that I finally had strong female mentors. At that point, something shifted within me. I suddenly had women in my field to look to for answers, and began to feel that I, too, could be an expert in my field. I am grateful for having those women mentors. Yet, it's not the case that all women have this experience, especially when entering fields that are mostly dominated by men.

Today, women may have "come a long way," as the old commercial stated, but the perception that what men have to say is more valuable, versus what women have to say, still exists. Women have a much higher tendency to question our own abilities, as well as have our abilities questioned by others. Researcher Adrian Furnham, at University College London, analyzed thirty studies regarding gender differences in perceived intelligence in 2008 and found that, consistently, men and women demonstrated equal intelligence on IQ tests, but that men were more likely to overestimate their own intelligence, while women were more likely to underestimate their intelligence by an average of five points.

While middle-aged women often have the advantage of finally believing our abilities and expertise, there is a new set of obstacles that come about because of age. Many of us feel suddenly "invisible." Pulitzer Prize-winning author, Elizabeth Janeway, wrote of the aging woman in her book, *Between Myth and Morning: Women Awakening*, "We are in a double bind. We are expected to feel inferior not only as women, but because we are old." Although we've made progress in this area since she wrote this in 1974, these two obstacles still very much exist for us. Women are told much more than men that how we look is most important, and, in this youth-focused society, looking younger is seen as critical for our success in all areas of our life—especially for women. Middle-aged women are not as respected for what they have to say and what expertise they have to offer, as they are for how young and "attractive" they look "for their age." They are often demeaned for looking and being older, what author Clare Shaw calls "failed-to-be-young syndrome," in her book, *Sageism: How to be an Older Woman*.

Writes Shaw, "Women who have reached middle-age...are too often made to feel invisible and are consequently retreating into dark corners. It's about time we came out into the light and shouted about how great older women are and how much they have to contribute to this society, which is sadly still rife with ageism and sexism."

One of the most powerful ways of reclaiming our power—to step into our light—is by following our passion and "bliss."

---

# PUTTING OURSELVES ON THE TABLE

Kathy Sparrow, Leadership Expert,
Message Strategist, Author, & Founder of
*Writing at Your Edge*

Many of us have a story that can help other people. When we have the courage to tell our story, not only do we heal, we inspire others to be become brave enough to start their own path to healing and revise their stories. When we share our story, it's a way to share who we are, to share our humanity.

It's important for each of us to recognize that we all have a right to live our own lives based on what we believe is true for us. I spent a good bit of my life running around, trying to make everyone happy. And when we do that, we're people pleasers and are not taking into account our own needs. I've come to think of this as *not* "putting myself on the

▶

▶ table"—with all the other responsibilities of my life. That creates an imbalance and we experience disharmony with everybody with whom we relate. We need to take care of ourselves first. Put our own oxygen mask on and then we can help the people around us. We really need to make ourselves a priority and, when we do that, we show up better for everybody.

Sparrow shared that her daily mantra is: *Allow me to be present for everyone, including myself.*

Said Aralyn Hughes, in our interview, "Growing up in the sixties, we changed the culture like it has never been changed before. And, in our sixties, we're doing that again. We do not have the role models that we had before. We're creating those role models—we're becoming those role models. We're taking up rock-climbing, and we're starting new careers, and in my case, going on stage as a storyteller, performance artist, and speaker. We're changing the culture again."

Most of the gains I've made have come with the support of other women, both through female peers and through being mentored by other successful women. There is tremendous power in women supporting women. Surrounding ourselves with women of all ages who want to assist each other in following our paths is so powerful that it has been found to have a chemical effect in reducing stress hormones and increasing feelings of happiness. This also helps us in developing those female role models who show us that our own success is possible and that a woman's voice can be powerful. In addition, collaboration and networking between women have been found to lead to greater success for women. I have seen that every relationship that I have built along my journey has been a tremendous asset when creating the life that I want.

---

# JAZZY LADIES

*Jan Leder, New York City jazz flutist and author of, Women in Jazz: A Discography of Instrumentalists, 1913-1968*

When I was in college, the Dean of Music asked me to write a paper about women in jazz. I went to the library and I found that there was nothing ever written about this topic. I decided that I had to become a historian. For the next year and one half, I compiled the discography of women in jazz instrumentalists. I left out the vocalists because the vocalists were prolific and everyone knew them, but we didn't know the instrumentalists. I managed to finish it for my undergraduate thesis in 1979. It was published in 1985 and it was called *Women in Jazz* because there was no book ever published on the subject.

Unfortunately, it's not much better for women in jazz all these years later. Women are still only about 3 percent of the jazz players. This problem

▶

▶ is specific to jazz because, as soon as the classical orchestras started having blind auditions back in the eighties or nineties, they filled up instantly with half of them women. They recently began doing this with jazz orchestras, but not many are inspired to go into the field because it's very much a "boys club" to this day. It's remarkable how unrepresented women are in this business. Hopefully, this will change soon.

I belong to a group called, *The International Women in Jazz*. We've been around for many years. It's a great organization and it's a sisterhood, so to speak, because, again, it's not a very pretty atmosphere out there in the world of competing with the boys. We have to stay together and support each other.

Support also means standing up for each other. If we don't accept our sisters being demeaned for the way they look, for being "too old," or for being women, we can change our culture toward one that respects what women have to offer at any age and for our expertise when we have the benefit of years and experience behind us.

Let's remember that every bit of progress we have made in our own lives, as women, toward living out loud, in our power, and in the light, has been made possible not only by our own hard work and perseverance, but on the backs of the pioneering women before us, who literally put their lives on the line for us to be able to do so. It is our responsibility to our foremothers to continue their work, be good role models for the generations of women who will follow us, and to have the backs of our sisters as they share their voices in the world.

Having said that, I will add that it's important for both men and women to support each other, as we all have important gifts to share and we will all benefit from sharing with each other.

**Chapter 3**

# Discovering Our Path of Dreams and Creating Meaning

*"If your dreams do not scare you,*
*they are not big enough."*

~ Ellen Johnson Sirleaf

Our dreams and our desire for a meaningful life are often hidden behind a long list of to-dos and responsibilities. And they can't be uncovered as we're dashing from one task to another. To create a life filled with vitality and passion, we need to set aside time to consider what it is we truly want to be experiencing in our life. So here is my invitation: set aside some time to think about what it is you would really love to do that would infuse your life with more meaning and joy. Is there something you've always wanted to do, but you've shelved it because you fear you might fail or you worry what others might think? Perhaps, you've already started down the path toward a dream, then you ran into obstacles, you decided that it was too difficult to keep going, and you gave up. What if you were to consider removing your dream (or dreams) from under the clutter of life obligations, dusting them off, then taking a small, realistic, step—and then another and another—toward your passion? If not now, when?

You might not have a clear dream, but know that there's something more you want to do. How do we find our own *edge*, as Kathy Sparrow puts it, or the path to discovering our dreams? Sparrow suggests, "Each of us has to define our own edge. The first step is creating time to be with ourselves, to listen to our own inner wisdom, and ask, 'What am I being called to do?' I use mind mapping to discover the activities that make me happy and that fill me with meaning. Then I look at my life and ask, 'Am I doing that?' And if I'm not, I mind map on what's holding me back, what I'm allowing to get in the way. Then I mind map ways to take action. That's where a lot of people stop. We have to be brave enough to take those risks and say, 'This is what I need right now.' Taking action can have a ripple effect and cause discomfort with those around us—our family, friends, and our partners. But we have to be willing to take that risk if it's something that we need for ourselves. That's when we begin to 'thrive at our edge.'"

Sparrow, whose self-defined edge is primarily in writing and secondarily stretching her horizons in nature, informed me that she also believes that spending time in nature is a must—and the reason she created nature-based leadership programs that include fly fishing and hiking, among other activities such as contemplative writing. "Nature restores us and helps us reconnect with our souls, our dreams, our passions," she explains. "It's here that I can step away from the busy-ness of my life and the noise of distractions. When I do that, I do my best writing. I can hear what needs to come through me."

Taking the time to contemplate what we desire is a good first step. "I think you really have to go on a discovery process to figure out what turns you on. You've got to figure out how to fall in love with life. Remember when you had joy and you had experiences and you laughed? Let that be the navigation tool," said Tuck Kamin, owner of *Potential Being*, and author of the book, *Design Your Age*.

Not knowing what our *dream* or purpose is, in itself, not a bad thing. When I interviewed Jihan Barakah, founder of *Global Quantum Shift*, for my radio program, she described this as an exciting time of being "curious." We can use this time to embrace childlike openness and seek what feeds the soul. It may involve reading books on many different topics that appeal to us, taking classes, trying new things, talking to people who are involved in various careers, or volunteering to help people in any of a variety of ways. By jumping in and getting involved, we can find meaning and purpose to our lives and our *dream* may be revealed to us. Once we have figured out what our path is, then Barakah recommends having clear intentions of what we want to experience and what actions to take each and every day. This is essential, she says, in order to remain optimistic and to reach our full potential.

Once we know what we want to do, it's often the case that we end up becoming overwhelmed by the responsibilities of life and find that there's no time left over to follow our calling. To remedy this, Sparrow suggests following what she refers to as the "15-Minute Practice." She recommends setting aside at least fifteen minutes each day for that which sooths your soul. For her, this consists of writing and creative expression. "I use my creativity each day in guiding my clients through the writing process and while editing their work; however, I still need to allow my own voice to be heard." She recommends setting a timer on your smart phone and focusing on taking action that will move you into your desires and dreams. "Many times, I extend the time of my writing, even on the days when I have a full slate of clients and appointments," she adds. "That makes my soul very happy."

Yet, fear holds many of us back. It's scary to take a new path, especially later in life. It's comfortable to stay in the roles that we're used to—for us and for those around us. But, we must ask ourselves: is comfort what makes us feel alive? I asked some of the experts how they deal with the fear of living their own dreams.

"Change is scary for some people," Sparrow told me. "I've learned is that if we can look at our *edge*—the edge of our comfort zone—and embrace expanding it with a sense of adventure. We play with it and see what happens. Change doesn't have to be a big dramatic ordeal. It can be an adventure and fun. If we can go into any situation with the anticipation of excitement and discovery, we're *dancing at our edge*. I have a pretty incredible life, doing what I refer to as *thriving at my edge*. I wouldn't have left unfulfilling relationships, met really wonderful people from all around the world, and developed meaningful relationships with friends and family if I had settled, if I wasn't willing to dance at my own edge and make some changes."

Said Aralyn Hughes, "I certainly fall back into fear about things that I think are silly every once in awhile. But, I've been called fearless. And in some ways, I'm fearless because every time I step through that fear, it's always been such an interesting experience and it makes me feel alive. So, I force myself to do it. You know, those things like shame and fear, you just have to say, 'I'm leaving those on the back burner. I don't have to mess with that anymore.'"

# DREAMS COME TRUE THROUGH ACTIONS

don Miguel Ruiz, author of
*The Four Agreements*

Wherever I go, I see what humans create, and I assure everybody that, whatever we perceive, first

▶

▶ exists in the human mind, and, through action, we make it real. And, what I want to say is this: we have the capacity to make our dreams come true through action. We humans have a very powerful imagination. That is to say that imagination is more powerful than knowledge. And, if we take the action, we make real whatever we imagine. We have so many ideas, but most of those ideas just dissipate because we don't take the action.

We have the capacity to create all the time. We have so many ideas, and at the same time, many other people can have those same ideas that we have. The one who takes the action is the one who makes it real. Then, when we see that someone else did what we thought of, we think, "Why didn't I do that? I wanted to do it." We didn't have the courage to do it. We didn't trust ourselves in order to take the action and make it real. And, if we don't make it, somebody else will because this is how humanity is evolving all the time. And many times, we live our whole life hardly taking any action.

While reading the book, *Einstein and the Rabbi: Searching for the Soul*, by the bestselling author, Rabbi Naomi Levy, I came to the realization that what I've been describing as following our *passion* or following our *dreams* are really descriptive expressions for something much deeper—what Levy describes as listening to our *soul's calling*.

When Rabbi Levy appeared on my show, she explained, "So many so-called 'life questions' are actually *soul* questions and the answer actually lies within us. There is a voice of knowledge and a voice of reason that can help us turn work into our calling, that can help us find the soul mate we've been seeking, that can help us rekindle relationships, and that can help us parent in ways of wisdom."

There are many ways to find more meaning in our lives. Here are some questions and steps to take in order to begin this process: Do you want to find more meaning in your life by helping people or animals? Check out what volunteer opportunities there are in your community. There is a whole range of activities that can make big differences in the lives of other people and in animals, which in turn, will create a greater sense of purpose and fulfillment in your own life. Helping to feed the homeless, volunteering in nursing homes or in an animal shelter, or becoming more politically active in your community are just a few of the possibilities. Do you feel the desire to express yourself more creatively? Take a writing class or painting class, or just begin to take the risk of putting your ideas onto paper through words, drawings, or paintings. Try a dance class or a yoga class (See Chapter 25, *Time to Hit Your Mat*, for a discussion of the benefits of yoga).

"Every day is an opportunity to take a tiny step," Rabbi Levy told me. "It doesn't have to be a quantum leap, but a tiny step in the direction of what you feel internally is calling to you. There are pieces of ourselves that we need to reawaken. We're only whole when we welcome all the pieces of ourselves."

As you must see by now, I'm certainly a proponent of discovering your big dream. However, sometimes, when we give ourselves a chance to really listen and, as Rabbi Levy describes, "somehow find a way to lower the volume of those other voices and to raise the volume of our soul's voice, a voice that knows why we're put here, a voice that knows about our calling, the voice that understands that every day of life is calling to us with a mission," we discover that our meaning, mission, and our joy might be to simply give of ourselves in our daily lives (See Chapter 18, *Giving Without Expectation*), to create light in our own lives and the lives of others.

On another recent visit to my mom in New York, the residents in her community threw a farewell party for a religious leader who was retiring. When this leader got up to speak to her well-wishers, she asked the group of elderly residents, some as old as 100 years old, "How will you bring light into your life today and how will you share your light with the world?" These two questions struck me as extremely powerful ones, especially when asked of this particular group, driving home the fact that we all have light within us that we can connect to, and the capability of sharing our light with the world, no matter our age or physical capacity.

Hence, I pose these simple, yet powerful, questions for you to ask yourself now and each day forward upon rising: How will you uncover the light within you? Perhaps, you will decide to spend more time connecting to Mother Earth, as Kathy Sparrow has suggested. Rabbi Levy also tells us that, when we go into nature and practice quiet and stillness, we are better able to hear the "whispers" of our own soul and to reconnect with ourselves. The world seems to have become more chaotic most recently. We could sure use more light in the world. What will you do to become part of the solution—and to borrow the phrase from Terry Hershey, author of *The Power of the Pause*—"spill your light" into the world, your community, or your family?

Through my radio program, I've met many people who have followed their passions. I love to hear their stories about how they ended up doing what they do. Often, their story includes an accidental meeting of the soul's desire, that which really fires up their joy and zest for life. The common ingredients for most of these *dream-followers* included being *open* to whatever happened to show up along their path, to any opportunity for growth and discovery about themselves, and to listening to their heart's voice along the way. My own life transformed into a much more joyful and meaningful journey when I welcomed the growth that new and unexpected experiences opened up for me along this path as it has twisted and turned.

"There is not a day that isn't an opportunity to help someone or to learn something," said Rabbi Levy in our interview. "Every day has its purpose. Every moment of life has its purpose. And there's not an age in life when we're not continuing to grow. There isn't an hour in a day when we don't have the occasion to learn to grow and to give."

My dad used to quote the often tongue-in-cheek baseball hero, Yogi Berra, who said, "When you come to the fork in the road, take it."

And as Rabbi Naomi Levy writes in *Einstein and the Rabbi,* "All throughout your life your soul's been tugging at you…The next time you feel a tug, don't let it slip away from you. Ask yourself, *What was that?* Reach for it. Let it in…Grab on."

And, as we will see next, sometimes, we have to grab on tightly and, even, buckle our seatbelts for the wild ride.

# Chapter 4

# No Path is Straight and Narrow

*"We can try to control the uncontrollable by looking for security and predictability, always hoping to be comfortable and safe. But the truth is that we can never avoid uncertainty. This not knowing is part of the adventure."*

~ PEMA CHODRON

The nature of life is that it always ebbs and flows. The time of ebb can be the time to rest and re-energize. And sometimes there will be obstacles that bring us to a complete halt, at least for a while.

At the beginning of 2015, I began the year with unbridled enthusiasm and optimism. I published the first blog on my website, *Happy New Year! What Will You Dream into Reality This Year?* I wrote, "I have a feeling of anticipation when saying out loud, 'This is going to be a good year, the year that I realize my dream!' For me, this excitement injects new energy into any goals that I've already set and it helps me to generate new ones." Early in the year, I could see the light at the end of the tunnel with completion of this book expected by the end of that year, I was accepted as a regular contributor to Huffington Post, and my radio program was already in its third year, with many well-known expert guests lined up for the months ahead.

Even with my enthusiasm, I found my own tips in that blog to be especially helpful for dealing with the challenge of sticking to resolutions and staying on the path. "As we go about our more mundane daily responsibilities, we often lose the energy and excitement or become frustrated by obstacles," I wrote. "It's easy to get sucked back into life-as-usual and to feel too drained to devote time to new goals or to exert energy into changing habits in order to achieve a healthier lifestyle." Then as happens to many of us, the year may have started off with a lot of energy and momentum, but obstacles appear that can easily sideline us and cause us to lose our focus or, even give up—even with our best intentions. However, I was unprepared for the enormity of the challenges that were to appear in my life just a bit later in the year. In fact, to call them "challenges" does not give an accurate sense of the life-changing events that were in store. Life was happening for me in ways that were unforeseen and extremely severe.

First, I found myself on an uphill climb in early spring of that year, when I developed severe tendonitis in both wrists, making writing this book and my blogs much more difficult and physically painful. Even working to keep the bills paid, which requires a lot of report writing, was challenging because of the wrist pain when using the computer.

Midway into 2015, life hit me upside the head with the devastating blow of a sledgehammer, and things went from very irritating to outright traumatic. My path became a distant blur, as everything came to a screeching halt. My dear dad fell in late spring and spent four months fighting a losing battle until his ninety-three-year-old body gave up the good fight. I was close with my dad, and so this process, along with his death, was devastating to me. It took every bit of my focus to just keep putting one foot in front of the other to keep up with my daily responsibilities and to keep my bills paid, never mind any enthusiasm or energy to follow my dreams. At that point, I learned in a very real way that we can plan all we want, but ultimately, we aren't in control of what life hands us. As Jack Canfield, author and creator of the *Chicken Soup for the Soul* ® series says, "Our responsibility lies in our response—and only that will affect the outcome."

Pausing to take care of myself was essential and helped me to find some peace of mind during this time, in spite of the continued sadness as that year came to a close.

I learned a hard lesson to no longer expect a smooth or straight path in following my dreams. I now know, in a very deeply raw way, that we can't predict what life will bring. We can't count on having the weather cooperate or the events of the world or in our own life to always be uplifting. It's a given that we will be occasionally knocked off track and sometimes completely sidelined. These experiences have taught me that we have it within us to keep going toward our dreams, even if we have to pause for a period of time because of unpredictable events. When the journey has reached a slower, up-hill point in the road, and the atmosphere appears dark, placing our focus on our passion fans the flame of hope inside of us, making it grow stronger, so that it will warm us and light our way. This, in turn, gives us the energy and can help us to find a glimmer of joy to keep going.

During the worst time of my life, having a dream to follow and making my way back onto the path, as shaky as it felt or as blurry as it looked to me, served as my North Star. This kept me from losing hope that joy and vitality would one day return. I knew that my dad would not have wanted me to give up, and I could sense his twinkling eyes smiling at me, as I lifted myself back up from the crumbled heap in the corner that I had become. I gradually began to take small, slow steps to get back onto this twisting turning path. At this point, I know deep within that I have no choice but to follow my *soul's whisper*, as Rabbi Naomi Levy calls it. Like oxygen and water, it is what breathes life into my life. Now, I can see that the turns in the road actually lead us to new opportunities or provide us with the raw material to use for our creative expression.

And even when we may feel that things are going smoothly on our path, becoming too complacent and too comfortable will also lead us to wander far from our actual path. "Any time that you feel 'my work is done,' or 'I'm washed up,' or 'I've arrived,' then you can be sure that you've lost your way," says Rabbi Levy. "One of the reasons that most people don't have a meeting with the soul is that they mistakenly believe that meeting your soul will lead to bliss, that having a soulful experience is equivalent to Nirvana. Meeting your soul can actually keep you up at night because the soul doesn't deal in bliss. It deals in open eyes. And open eyes are eyes that notice somebody who is sleeping on the street. Open eyes are eyes that notice what is broken in this beautiful broken world."

"There is a crack, a crack in everything. That's how the light gets in," sang Leonard Cohen. We grow the most when we're awake and intensely mindful of the cracks in everything and we're open to allowing the light that flows through those cracks to guide our way. Staying on this road also requires the mindfulness about when we need to take the time to pause and to just *be*—in stillness.

## Chapter 5
# Know When to Pause

*"For fast-acting relief, try slowing down."*

~ LILY TOMLIN

I had hoped for a softer, easier, year come 2016, as I started to very gradually get back on my feet. Amid the din of my loud inner voices of grief and pain, I began to hear a soft whisper of my *soul's calling*. I knew that I really wanted to give purpose to the pain and to find a way to, once again, feel joy and passion. And, so, I willed myself to keep paying attention to those soft whispers, to keep listening to what they were saying, how they were guiding me, and to keep moving along on my path, even if, at times, it felt as though I was slogging through mud, or quicksand, with only a small dull spark lighting my way through the fog. I slowly moved along, two steps forward, one step backward, and, when I least expected it, joy leaked in.

At first, it was just a brief glimmer, I suspect to remind me of what joy felt like and how much I longed to experience it again. After awhile, though, the light began shining with increased intensity through the cracks in my heart. I noticed that joy would stay for longer periods of time, making itself more at home, comfortably sitting nestled up against the pain that I knew would remain a permanent resident of my battered heart. I now had a deeper understanding of Cohen's song. While those painful cracks will never truly heal, they can create a deeper appreciation for the joy that sits right there amidst the pain, a more abiding pure happiness, made that much brighter by a much more genuine compassion for our true selves.

Once again, my life felt like it had purpose and meaning, in spite of the sadness. However, as it turned out, the year 2016 was anything but soft and easy, although, thankfully not as devastating as 2015. The year brought continued losses and great disappointments, as well as increasing stress and anger throughout the world. I reminded myself to take those healing pauses that had helped me during the year prior. This has gone a long way toward allowing me to pursue my passion in spite of the less-than-perfect circumstances.

A pause may consist of daily moments, pausing from *doing* and allowing ourselves to *be*, focusing on our breath, noticing what's around us, and taking the time to smell and appreciate "the roses." Sometimes, a pause is time spent with family or friends, sharing heartfelt moments. I am particularly grateful for such moments that I've spent with each of my parents because, after all, there are no do-overs. A pause might consist of days filled with play. There are times when a pause is longer, taken to heal the wounds we've sustained on our journey.

We also need to take breaks even when everything appears to be going well. "When I give up [the] need for urgency and say, 'No, this can wait,'" wrote Terry Hershey in *The Power of Pause: Becoming More by Doing Less*, "I can do so because I know that I have value apart from the externals of life. I have the permission just to be, to embrace the sacred present." Hershey suggests that we pause and notice the ordinary moments as a practice. They are morsels with joy hidden deep within.

I've learned that I can't just keep hitting my "dig deep" button, as author Brenè Brown refers to this lack of pausing in her book, *The Gifts of Imperfection: Your Guide to a Wholehearted Life*. "The dig-deep button is a secret level of pushing through when we're exhausted and overwhelmed, and when there's too much to do and too little time for self-care," writes Brown.

If I've pressed that button too much, there has been little left for me to give. Brown tells us that when we take a break and refuse to automatically hit that "dig-deep" button, it doesn't mean that we don't find a way to eventually get back on track and push on toward our dreams. It means we care for ourselves enough to take some time to reflect and rejuvenate.

So, how do we deal with major obstacles—and even on-going minor ones, which can be cumulative in their stress values—so that we don't end up spiraling into addictions, including the addiction to busyness? How do we get back on track to our dreams, after being knocked off the track and may not be able to even see that track anymore?

It's, first of all, most important to pause for stillness regularly in order to cope with stress, prevent depression, and to have the energy and freshness of thought to move forward with any goals. Make time to sit still and be without judgment no matter what's happening around you.

"If we can hold to each breath in order to track this unlit pathway, we will be taken into the sanctuary of our unshakable, indivisible, brilliantly sane, undying, and loving heart. And it is this true heart that will save us," wrote the Buddhist nun, Thanisarra, in her essay, "The Descent."

When we take the time to relax and relish in the *gap*, focusing attention on those "in-between" moments, the gaps between breaths, the gaps between thoughts, the gaps between the completion of one action and the start of another, that's where we find our true selves.

In *Radical Acceptance: Embracing Your Life with the Heart of a Buddha*, Tara Brach writes, "Through the sacred art of pausing, we develop the capacity to stop hiding, to stop running away from our own experience. We begin to trust in our natural intelligence, in our naturally wise heart, in our capacity to open to what arises."

Deep within ourselves, there is a knowing that we are at peace, that we are worthy of loving ourselves fully, warts and all, that life is worthy of feeling joyful about even with all of the sad times, and that there are precious moments right in front of us, waiting to be embraced. Paying attention to these in-between moments are what will lead us to that knowing.

# CHANGING DIRECTIONS MIDLIFE

### Terry Hershey, Speaker, Blogger, Author of *The Power of Pause*

I'm sixty-one and I still call that middle life. It's interesting that we have had expectations about what life was "supposed to be" like and it's not necessarily that way. But, it is *this* life and the extraordinary thing is if we give ourselves the permission to pause and live in *this* life, in *this* present moment, we have gifts of wonder and awe. We have sadness, too, but it's still okay when we're present with that.

Wired in the way that we are in this culture, we want to climb the right ladder, and we want to

► climb it in a rapid way. We do a lot of things in this culture that are detrimental to our own well-being. I've discovered, as I've gotten older that care of any kind begins with self-care. I didn't always know that. I was going to climb the ladder, and I was doing well. But, just because you have success, doesn't mean you have health. I had not stopped, I had not listened, and there was no pausing. I had not given myself the permission to ask, "What does it mean to be a healthy?"

I found myself in Orange County, California, and I didn't know who I was. So, I decided to change that direction. I now live on an island near Seattle, Washington, which is radically different. I came here and I studied gardening. I now live on a large plot of land with a garden, and the garden brought me to sanity. Since that time, I've been writing about that.

I'm always asking, "What does it mean to be replenished and renewed?" Our DNA is wired to be replenished, renewed, and restored. I am now in the refueling business. You know, life takes it out of us, that permission to be present. In my case it got buried, it got pushed aside for something that I was *supposed to* do. So, I now write about refueling.

►

▶ I may be juggling a lot of things and I may be doing all of those things well, but that doesn't mean that it's not to the detriment of my spirit. And then, someone says to me, "You know it wouldn't hurt you just to do something for Terry." We're actually afraid sometimes to take that permission. We live in a culture where it feels selfish or we feel like we're giving up control. Isn't it really hard to receive a gift from someone? We think we have to be so strong, so together. The wonderful thing about pausing is that I get to ask, "What does it mean to accept the gift of *this* Terry?" along with whatever's going on in my life. That's an extraordinary gift.

Just so you know, if you actually do this, take a pause, there are going to be people who are not going to be happy. It's as if we have to justify it or explain it. We fear the pause because the pause is the permission to be enough, the permission that this moment is enough. One thing, perhaps, I'm afraid of is that I'm going to be loved and I don't have anything to show for it. I'm not going to earn it. But, when you have these moments, it's like a weight has been lifted off your shoulders and there's a gladness of well-being that comes over you.

Pausing is intentional permission to be in another space. It's a mental time-out. It can be a physical

► time-out, too. It's OK to start small with a five-minute or ten-minute pause. What I encourage people to do with that pause, and what I do, is to actually literally take myself away from whatever is bombarding me. It's a chance to say, "Wait a minute. Time out. I need to recalibrate here." You can set up your smart phone to alert you once an hour to pause for one minute or five minutes. Your pause consists of doing something that is replenishing, something that's renewing. I'm not going to pause to do something that causes stress. For example, right before this interview, I was out in my garden. Or, it might just be closing your eyes and going through some wonderful memory.

Some people might even say, "I paused, but I must not have done it correctly because I don't know that I had the right result." It's not easy because when you pause, you might think, "Something wonderful is supposed to be happening, but it's not happening. All I feel is worry that I should be getting back to the rest of the stuff I was doing." And I say, that's fine. When you're pausing, you're present. Notice you were present, even to things that were uncomfortable to you. But, you were present and that's good. So, try it again tomorrow, and try it again the next day, and the next day.

> ▶ Every pause makes a difference, even if you don't feel it right away.
>
> We live in a world that says that there are certain things that are OK to feel and other things that we can't feel. When I'm OK to pause and be present, then I'm not putting a moral price tag on certain feelings. Every one of my feelings is part of who I am.
>
> And if you want to change something in your life, that's fine, but you can't change anything until you can love it. You can't love anything until you can just hang out with it for a little while. I'm not telling you it's easy, I'm just telling you it's worth it.

Sometimes, we need a little help to heal when we take such a pause. After my dad's death, when that painful noise in my head kept me from hearing the whisper of my own inner knowing, I realized that I wasn't just experiencing grief, but also the after-effects of trauma, and I sought help. I went to a practitioner of EMDR (Eye Movement Desensitization and Reprocessing), a guided mindfulness meditation that helps the brain to rewire itself back to more flexibility following a trauma. Any traumatic experience can have the effect of hardwiring our brain to a constant *fight or flight response* (the stress response), making it difficult to function effectively in life.

On a daily basis, I work with veterans who are suffering from full-blown post-traumatic stress disorder (PTSD) and I would not begin to compare my trauma with theirs. I don't believe that I actually had PTSD, but I did see how I had developed enough of the symptoms to wreak havoc in my health and well-being. The EMDR really worked. It felt like a dark cloud had been lifted, at least enough to let some sunshine in. This type of therapeutic pause can make all the differnce in the world with regard to which direction our life will take, a downward negative spiral vs. a life of purpose and meaning.

I have learned that during the still moments, when I pay complete attention, the pit of despair is not bottomless while passing through a dark part of the journey, that I can feel joy even while feeling grief, and that, by taking time to just *be* and allow, rather than constantly giving in to the compulsion to make myself busy *doing*, inspiration does begin to flow again.

In spite of the obstacles, I believe that it's worth our time and effort to stay focused and to keep moving toward what we are being called to do. Most of all, I've found that taking the time to pause, regularly, even when feeling optimistic and "on a roll," is necessary for creating joyful and inspired action.

# Chapter 6

# Twelve Pauses to Get Back on Track (and Keep from Becoming Depressed)

*"My heart might be bruised, but it will recover and become capable of seeing the beauty of life once more. It's happened before, it will happen again, I'm sure."*

~ Paulo Coelho

Bruised and battered, I got myself back on track, even when it was very tempting to just give up and sit on the sidelines. "Why not just do the minimum needed to get by in life," temptation whispered in my ear. "You have a good job. There's no absolute need to muster up energy to follow any dreams." We can always take this *easier* route in life. But, having the deep desire to live a life filled with joy and purpose, I knew that this was not an acceptable choice for me. And my guess is that if you're reading a book about living "The Passionate Life," this would not be an acceptable choice for you either.

This "easy" route may not be all that easy on us. Giving up on our dreams because life became rough and the road got bumpy is tantamount to blowing out our own pilot light. We might be able to coast along, but the outcome will likely be that we're led to a place of darkness and despair. If we're lucky, at that point, we'll experience a "dark night of the soul." It is often a painful time that breaks us open in order to reawaken our search for the meaning of our life.

I've met many, including some of my clients, who have given up their dreams when things didn't go smoothly on their path. This choice has often caused them to spiral down into the anxiety and depression that has led them straight through my office door, asking for help.

The fact is, although the bumps are uncomfortable, they are inevitable in life. So, rather than asking if it's time to give up on a dream, the better question to ask is how to ride the emotional roller coaster of life, with its many ups and downs, without allowing it to cause us to become lost and spiral down into dark despair. Here is a summary of a few ways to stay on track. Most of these will be discussed more deeply in later chapters of this book.

## 1. Relax

It's important to practice relaxation regularly in order to cope with stress, prevent discouragement and depression, and to have the energy and clarity of thought to move forward with creativity and enthusiasm. When we practice stillness, we reduce the stress hormones cortisol, norepinephrine, and adrenaline. A reduction of these chemicals puts our body into "the relaxation response."

Mindfulness meditation is a powerful way to achieve relaxation, so that we can have new inspired and creative ideas about what we really want to do and how to do it. It's as simple as sitting quietly and focusing attention on our breathing or on a word, just noticing thoughts that pop into our mind and letting them drift by. There have been several recent studies that have found that meditating regularly (even just five minutes per day) has numerous health benefits and improves mood. It's through our silent mind that we discover our strength and regain peacefulness in the midst of storms. (For more ways to relax, see *Ten Tips for Manifesting the Relaxation Response* in Chapter 11, "Reducing Stress.")

There are many books and on-line videos with guidance about how to do mindfulness meditation, such as the works of Drs. Jon Kabat-Zinn and Jack Kornfield. You can download my free-guided meditation for Inner Peace, Joy, and Vitality by following this link: https://drmarakarpel.com/free-guided-meditation/.

## 2. Get moving

As we know, there are many health benefits that we can generate by moving our bodies. Indirectly, these health benefits improve our emotional well-being. If we're feeling good physically, and we're able to do more, then we feel happier and more confident. Exercise has also been shown to directly improve mood and increase energy, thereby increasing enthusiasm for the journey. (For more about Exercise, see Chapter 24: "Let's Get Moving!")

Here are some ways to get your move on:

- Walk
- Try Tai-Chi
- Take a yoga class
- Take a water aerobics class
- Dance

*   *Note: Check with your physician before starting any new exercise program.*

## 3. Socialize

While having time alone to relax, meditate, read, explore nature, follow our dreams, and/or think about what we're grateful for is extremely important, balance is essential. Isolation can lead to a decline in mood, especially if we're already feeling depressed or stressed out. Ironically, stress, anxiety, and depression all cause us to want to isolate ourselves. Forcing ourselves to be around other people—even if we don't necessarily feel like it—can help to break this cycle.

Find like-minded people who share some of your interests. They don't have to have the same dream as you do. People who are in the state of mind of enthusiastically seeking can give tremendous support to you in your unique journey. If you can find people who are doing what you dream of doing, you're likely to find that some freely give you important information, help you with ideas, and can increase valuable networking connections for you. People often love to teach and give advice.

Get together with friends or family who are positive and emotionally supportive. Enthusiasm is contagious, just like negativity. So, be mindful of the company you keep.

More ways to increase positive social interactions:

- Take a class.
- Exercise with other people.
- Join a dance group.
- Make plans to get together with friends or relatives, rather than relying on cold and distant social media connections.
- Join a MeetUp.com group that focuses on a topic or activity that's interesting to you.

## 4. Commune with Nature

I recently attended a lecture by the well-known author and speaker, Dr. Deepak Chopra, during which I learned from him that walking barefoot on the earth has an immediate effect of resetting our entire nervous system. He recommended this as a way of creating better physical health. This has been frequently echoed to me. In Chapter 3, Kathy Sparrow suggested spending time in nature in order to discover our own unique calling. Rabbi Naomi Levy spoke of going for a walk alone in nature in order to "be still enough to hear what's really going on inside of us," to hear our *soul's whisper.*

Did you ever notice that a walk on the beach or in a park will completely shift your attitude when you're feeling stressed? Getting out in nature can be one of the most powerful ways of shifting our mood, lifting it, when we're feeling down, or calming it, when we're anxious or stressed-out. Richard Louv, author of *The Nature Principle: Reconnecting with Life in a Virtual Age,* has been campaigning for our reconnection with nature, noting the physical, mental, and emotional, and spiritual benefits.

Even having a view of nature through a window has been found to have benefits, such as speeding up recovery from surgery, increasing work performance, and improving work satisfaction. In fact, if you have difficulty quieting your mind and finding that place of stillness, as discussed in Tip #1, author and speaker, Eckhart Tolle, describes an easy way to start the process, through communing with nature, in his book, *Stillness Speaks.* "Look at a tree, a flower, a plant. Let your awareness rest upon it…how still they are, how deeply rooted in Being." When you connect with nature in this way, it will help you to become still, Tolle explains, and it can then lead to a longer meditation practice.

Here are some more ways to commune with nature:

- Take a walk in a park or near a lake, river, or ocean.
- Walk barefoot in the grass.

- Sit under a tree. Hug a tree. Sit with your back up against a tree, feeling the calming energy emanating from it.
- Plant a garden or some indoor plants.
- Stroke and talk to a pet.

Over a century ago, one of our greatest American writers knew the importance of connecting with nature. "I believe that there is a subtle magnetism in Nature, which, if we unconsciously yield to it, will direct us aright," wrote Henry David Thoreau.

## 5. Laugh Regularly and Make Time for Joy

Laughter not only reduces stress and improves mood, it also strengthens the immune system. In addition, humor stops the downward spiral of energy-zapping thought-habits that interfere with our confidence. Laughter immediately decreases muscle tension, enhances creativity, increases optimism, and creates joy. (For more about the benefits of humor and laughter, see Chapter 10, "The Power of Humor.")

## 6. Have an Attitude of Gratitude

Focusing attention on what we feel thankful for changes our perspective and even our reality. "What you focus on expands," states Oprah Winfrey. Having gratitude for what we have and looking for the silver linings in the less-than-ideal situations bring us feelings of optimism, peace, and enthusiasm to keep us on this trek as a peaceful warrior. When experiencing gratitude, Dr. Deepak Chopra, in his article, "3 Essential Practices for Gratitude," wrote, "You embrace the wisdom of uncertainty and you sense yourself as a field of infinite possibilities. Gratitude is a fullness of heart that moves you from limitation and fear to expansion and love."

Dr. Robert Emmons, professor of psychology and researcher at the University of California–Davis, completed extensive research in the area of the effects of gratitude on our emotional and physical well-being. His overall finding has been that gratitude is what gives life meaning. Among his findings, was that people who kept gratitude journals felt physically healthier and had a more optimistic perspective.

We are constantly bombarded with outside messages from the world about what we "should" be, what we "ought to" look like, or what we "must" have in order to feel like we are enough or that we have enough. An attitude of gratitude for what we already have and already are is something that will counteract those scarcity beliefs. Keeping a gratitude journal is an easy way to create this habit of having an attitude of gratitude. Write down three to five things, big or small, daily that you feel grateful for. See how you feel at the end of one week of keeping this journal.

The ups and downs, the ebb and flow, the dark and light—this is the adventure we call life, and having gratitude for this adventure, and all that it consists of, allows the darkness to be that catalyst for making the light that much brighter. Gratitude for what we already have is a sure-fire way to open us up to allow more of what we want to flow to us. Be ready for the upcoming flow that will inevitably follow.

## 7. Become a "Glass Half-full" Person

Remain optimistic about following your dreams, rather than becoming sidelined by obstacles. An obstacle may just be a sign that we need to pause and be patient, before continuing on the journey. Remind yourself, daily, that by following your dreams and sharing your unique gifts with the world, you're serving humanity and inspiring others to follow their own dreams. Then, take at least one small step every day toward your dream, toward discovering what your dream might be, or to help your community and/or the world. Spend some time every day planning the small steps you'll take the following day. Kathy Sparrow says embrace the 15-minute practice and do your follow-through. (Read more about optimism in Chapter 7, "Realistic Optimism.")

## 8. Find Meaning

Finding ways to be part of the solution is an extremely powerful antidote to depression when bombarded with bad news of negative events. Taking time to discover our passion, and then taking the steps to follow it, is one way of finding meaning in our lives. There are many ways to do this, even when we feel that we have hit rock bottom. (Read more in Chapter 8, "Staying Positive in Spite of Bad News Cycles.")

Dr. Victor Frankl, psychiatrist and Holocaust survivor, wrote about what he learned from his experiences in concentrations camps in his classic book, *Man's Search for Meaning*. Dr. Frankl shared that prisoners of the camps who fared the best during these horrifying circumstances were the ones who were able to find meaning in their lives by taking care of one another. When he was freed, Frankl turned his insights into a type of psychotherapy called *Logotherapy*, used to help his patients to overcome depression by finding meaning and purpose in their lives, which consisted of focusing on helping others, in spite of whatever circumstances they were in.

Here are some suggestions for finding meaning in your life:

- Volunteer for a cause that you feel passionate about.
- Help someone in need.
- Look for the deeper meaning in an unfortunate circumstance.
- Do a good deed for a neighbor.
- Make someone who is feeling blue laugh.

- Give without expectation of anything in return. (Learn about the benefits of this practice in Chapter 18, "Giving Without Expectation.")

- Express yourself creatively, such as through dancing, drawing/ painting, playing an instrument or singing, or writing.

## 9. Challenge irrational beliefs

We humans tend to have the bad habit of talking ourselves out of things that are good for us with negative, self-sabotaging statements, such as "What's the point?" or "Who would be interested in what I have to say, anyway?" We talk to ourselves in ways we would never speak to a friend, if we want to keep our friends. This type of negative and irrational self-talk is likely to keep us from moving forward and will often keep us on the bench, if we listen to and believe this negative chatter.

Take some time to look at what thoughts and beliefs might be causing some of these negative emotions and to ask yourself if these beliefs are based in reality. The technique of mindfulness meditation, described above, has the added benefit of helping us to become more aware of our thoughts, noticing when we make those self-sabotaging statements, and giving us the ability to better discern those thoughts and beliefs worth keeping versus those that no longer serve us.

Check *Appendix A* at the end of this book for resources that are useful for building the skill of challenging your own irrational beliefs. (Also, for more about this, read Chapter 9, "Taming Your Inner Troll.")

## 10. Don't Run from the Pain

Running away from pain only gives it more power to grow, so that it becomes much larger and scarier, when it finally catches up with us (which it always does), and causes even more suffering. "Sticking with uncertainty is how we relax in the midst of chaos, how we learn to be cool when the ground beneath us suddenly disappears," wrote Pema Chodron in her book, *Comfortable with Uncertainty: 108 Teachings on Cultivating Fearlessness and Compassion*. Remember, as Rabbi Levy noted earlier, often, when we are following our soul's calling, we are actually more aware and awake to the pain of others.

Go back to Tip #1 and make time to be still, to slow down your thinking, judging, and worrying. When we do this, we can actually heal our pain and have the compassion to help to ease the suffering of our friends and neighbors, giving our own life more meaning.

Wrote Eckhart Tolle, "Whenever you deeply accept this moment as it is—no matter what form it takes—you are still, you are at peace." And, when accepting this moment, rather than numbing it, "You become aligned with the power and intelligence of Life itself. Only then can you become an agent for positive change in the world."

Unleashing our creativity, following our passions, and making the world a better place, require some level of discomfort. By putting ourselves out there, in spite of the discomfort, risking disappointment and acknowledging our own dark moments and the pain in the world, our dreams can blossom, we can experience true happiness within, and we can help construct a more peaceful world. "Without mud, you cannot have lotus flowers," wrote the world-renowned speaker, teacher and author, Thich Nhat Hanh.

## 11. Eat Well

The food that we eat has a direct effect on the health and vitality of our bodies. In addition, food affects the health, sharpness, and vitality of our brains and has a direct influence on the hormones and neurotransmitters (brain chemicals) that affect our emotions. Food can cause depression and anxiety, and it can also heal our body and our "soul," helping us to feel happy, energized, and ready to take on the world. Most recently, a direct relationship has been found between the amount of fresh fruits and vegetables one eats and their mood and level of energy. People who eat more produce tend to feel calmer, happier, and more energetic. (For more about the effects of food on our mood, see Part IV: "Food for the Soul.")

## 12. Sleep

While the first eleven recommendations given in this chapter are crucial, getting enough restful sleep is the glue that holds it all together. Sleep is essential for having a good mood and for having the energy to follow our dreams, as well as critical for concentration, memory, and disease prevention. We often feel that we can cheat sleep, but we can only get away with that for just so long. Without sleep, everything is likely to begin to crumble, including our health, our emotional wellness, our creativity, and, even, our cognitive abilities. (Chapter 27, "Getting Your ZZZs," and Chapter 28, "The Quantity and Quality of Your Sleep," give tips for increasing higher quality sleep.)

These deliberate pauses in our schedules, in our thoughts, and in our habitual patterns will help us to sail smoothly, peacefully, and even joyfully—and reconnect us with our passion. And for men and women, alike, our passion can be that North Star that we follow in the darkness, our dreams can create the magic in what could, otherwise, be a bumpy or mundane life. All it takes is the spark of an idea to bring about this dream.

"Ideas *are* alive…ideas seek the most available human collaborator…ideas *do* have a conscious will…ideas *do* move from soul to soul…ideas *will* always try to seek the swiftest and most efficient conduit to the earth (just as lightning does)," wrote Elizabeth Gilbert in her book, *Big Magic: Creative Living Beyond Fear*. Let's be sure to catch that magical idea and be its most efficient conduit for it to come to life, so that our lives can be full of light and joy.

Or as George Bernard Shaw colorfully wrote, "This is the true joy in life: being used for a purpose recognized by yourself as a mighty one, being thoroughly worn out before you are thrown on the scrap heap, being a force of nature instead of a feverish, selfish, little clod of ailments and grievances complaining that the world will not devote itself to making you happy."

# Part II
# Emotional Well-being & Self-Care

Optimism is
Planting flowers in the mud –
Expecting that at least one or two will survive and
blossom – And knowing that their beauty will give us
the strength & Conviction to keep moving
Forward.

# Part II
# Emotional Well-Being & Self-Care

*"Like the moon, come out from behind the clouds! And Shine!"*

~ Buddha

When I look at my own life, the most interesting occurrences along my path, those curves in the road that have taken me to the most amazing and fulfilling opportunities, were all unexpected and unplanned. Rather than fighting to stay on the path I had set out on, when I followed the "detours" and allowed the changes, I found myself viewing the most spectacular vistas and discovering new things about myself, including new directions to pursue. I would not be doing what I'm doing today—writing this book, broadcasting a radio program where I get to interview my favorite authors and speakers, and meeting the most interesting and amazing people whom I had only dreamed about having conversations with—if I had fought the changes, the unexpected twists and turns. And I would have felt much more stressed out because my plans didn't happen the way I had mapped them out.

Life is constantly in flux, yet, we humans often have a hard time dealing with change effectively, so that we don't become *stressed out*, feeling threatened by the very nature of life. Stress can be a major obstacle in continuing to follow our soul's calling. Having some tools to cope with stress, which is a natural part of life, is necessary to remain on the journey.

# Chapter 7

# Realistic Optimism

*"There are only two ways to live your life. One is as though nothing is a miracle. The other is as though everything is a miracle."*

~ ALBERT EINSTEIN

I haven't always been an optimist and I certainly continue to have moments when I feel defeated. I would describe myself as having an optimistic "streak," a part of me that wants to feel optimistic and happy, driving me to find hope even in the most difficult of situations. That streak has been there for as long as I can remember. It was that streak of optimism that gradually drew me back to my journey after the devastating blow of my dad's death knocked me on my butt. It was that flicker of hopefulness that kept me moving forward along my path when facing bankruptcy several years ago after opening my own business. And it was that glimmer of faith that kept me trucking down that seemingly endless road of my graduate school program many years prior, when I was ready to give up after seeing a sign outside of the classroom where most of our classes were held, stating, "This program will last for the rest of your life."

Frankly, as you read this chapter, you might notice that my current relationship with optimism can best be described best as, "It's complicated." But, I have seen the evidence in my life that there are many good reasons related to emotional and physical well-being to foster and nourish that "streak" of optimism within rather than giving into the temptation of pessimism.

When I took "Introduction to Psychology" in college, I remember learning about the research of Dr. Martin Seligman in the area of depression. He had trained dogs to become pessimists. Dogs! Dogs are born optimists! The dogs that were subjects in this study were powerless to change the annoying and uncomfortable situation (a mildly electrified floor on the bottom of the cage in which they were placed). These dogs then developed, what Seligman referred to as, "learned helplessness," so that, when the dogs were then actually capable of getting out of the uncomfortable situation (another cage in which they could escape from the electrified floor simply by jumping over a low wall to get to the other side), they had already given up and did not take the required action to receive relief from their discomfort. The dogs had become depressed. He posed that this same phenomenon is responsible for depression in humans, when we have the experience of being in situations where we feel powerless. Basically, what he was describing was learned pessimism, the acquired belief that there is nothing we can do to make our situation any better than it is. The resulting behavior is to give up trying, even in situations where we do genuinely have control.

By the time I was in graduate school, Dr. Seligman had changed his focus to that of how pessimistic humans can learn to become optimists. His book about his research in this area was titled, *Learned Optimism: A Leading Expert on Motivation Demonstrates That Optimism is Essential for a Good and Successful Life – and Shows How to Acquire It.* The findings he spelled out in his book showed that many of us have had early experiences resulting in our training to be pessimists. However, luckily, we can unlearn pessimistic thought habits and can become optimists through learning new optimistic thought habits. Neuropsychologists now know that our brains can actually be rewired, creating new neural pathways, based on accidental experiences or purposeful retraining of our thought habits, and that these changes in neural pathways can actually be viewed on an MRI of the brain. This ability of the brain to be rewired, whether intentionally or unintentionally, is referred to as "neuroplasticity."

Pessimists often argue that they're more realistic about the gloomy facts of life. And, yes, life realistically is filled with dark painful moments and the world is broken in many ways. Yet, at the same time and just as realistically, life is filled with beauty. I'm sure most of you have heard the old adage of either seeing a glass as half empty or half full depending on whether you're a pessimist or an optimist. The reality is that both perspectives are correct about a half-filled glass. Such a glass is *both*, half-empty *and* half-full. Whichever reality we choose to focus most of our attention on will affect how we feel, emotionally, will affect what actions we will then take (giving up versus forging ahead), and, over time, will impact our physical health. And there are many good reasons to be optimistic, even when it's hard to see the light at the end of the tunnel.

If you're already an optimist, congratulations! For the rest of you reading this book, you might at least have the desire and willingness to be open to more optimism and joy. Otherwise, I don't think you'd have picked up this book and read this far into it.

First and foremost, a good reason to train ourselves to be optimistic is that optimism feels good! In fact, it has been found that optimism leads to a more positive mood and defeats feelings of depression. One reason for this is that when we're optimistic, we tend to talk to ourselves in a positive way, which creates a better feeling about life. Pessimism, on the other hand, involves negative inner chatter, directly causing a downward spiral in mood and eventually leading to depression. Furthermore, optimism increases the release of endorphins in our brain. I like to refer to these endorphins as "happy" chemicals because they're natural mood elevators and pain relievers. In contrast, pessimism tends to increase the release of stress hormones, leading to anxiety, depression, and physical pain. In addition, when we're optimistic, we tend to have increased problem-solving skills, so that we can work our way out of problem situations, while pessimism clouds our thoughts and impairs our problem-solving abilities.

Having a positive perspective is also good for our physical health because this attitude has been found to be an immune system booster, helping us to fight off diseases ranging from the common cold to cancer. On top of this, believing that we can have an affect on our own health increases the likelihood that we'll stick to healthy regimens. If I feel that I have the power to improve my health by making good food choices and by exercising, for example, I'm more likely to eat a healthier diet and to be more physically active, thereby bringing about better health.

It's always been very striking to me that people who have a positive view about aging and about the world tend to look younger. In fact, the science backs this up. Having an optimistic attitude stabilizes our hormonal balance and gives us increased levels of the "youth hormone," DHEA. This actually boosts our energy level and creates a more youthful appearance, while normalizing our heart rate and stabilizing our blood sugar.

Optimism also leads to better resiliency following negative life events. For example, pessimists have been found to be more likely to die within the first six months after the death of a spouse, than are optimists. And behavioral researchers, Dr. Becca Levy and her associates, discovered that people who have positive beliefs about their own aging tend to live an average of 7.5 years longer than those who are pessimistic about growing older.

Obviously, I'm all for being optimistic and looking for silver linings. But, living life for over a half a century, working as a therapist for over a quarter of a century, and working with veterans who have PTSD for almost a decade, has shown me that life is not all rainbows and unicorns. Denis Waitley, writer, motivational speaker and author of *Seeds of Greatness* and *The Winner's Edge*, says, "Expect the best, plan for the worst, and prepare to be surprised." And that's the best advice we can follow.

Optimism is planting flowers in the mud, expecting that at least one or two will survive and blossom, knowing that their beauty will somehow give us the strength and conviction to keep moving forward. "Out of the mud, grows the lotus flower," taught the Buddha.

But, completely ignoring the mud also leads to being buried by it. There's a danger to being overly optimistic as it can lead to engaging in risky behaviors without taking proper precautions. It's also unproductive to believe that challenges will magically disappear or that our dreams will manifest into reality without taking the creative actions inspired by our vision. Even the eternal optimist, the Dalai Lama, tells us, "Change only takes place through action." And, as my radio show producer, Art Mendoza, often likes to say, "The universe rewards action." (I actually looked up the origin of this quote and it appears that it might be properly credited to Dr. Phil.)

Disregarding emotional pain and sadness is not healthy or even genuine. This is avoidance, which leads to such pain eventually catching up with us in very destructive ways, causing depression and even severe illness. There's been a recent "spiritual" movement that shames and blames us for negative events that might occur in our life and for feeling sad or angry about such occurrences, warning that these are negative manifestations of our negative thinking. The movement also suggests that we must view obstacles as a positive, having happened for "a reason," such as being a necessary catalyst for a beneficial transformation in our life.

Realistically, bad things do happen to good people for no reason other than this is how life is sometimes. Feeling sadness about such events is healthy. Glossing over them and running from them does not allow healing to occur. Emotions are emotions. There are no "good" vs. "bad" emotions. One does not make us a better person or a *stronger* person than the other. All emotions are temporary, if we allow them to be fully experienced and to move through us. By being honest about what we feel and acknowledging our feelings, we allow them to move on, rather than clutching onto them. Only then can we move forward and experience some level of healing.

Some pain never completely goes away, such as the grief over the loss of someone close to us. As grief counselor and author, Megan Devine, writes in her book, *It's OK That You're Not OK: Meeting Grief and Loss in a Culture That Doesn't Understand*, "There are losses that rearrange the world...Some things cannot be fixed. They can only be carried...We can never change the reality of pain." But, we do have a choice as to whether we hold onto despair and make that our identity, expecting more negative events to occur in our lives, essentially giving up on joy, or to focus on gradually finding a way to carry our pain and find joy once again.

We can *consciously choose* to make a negative event, and our resulting pain, into that catalyst for change for ourselves and, perhaps, our community or world. Megan Devine and Stephanie Harris, both grief counselors and authors, have spoken on my Internet radio program about how they have *allowed* their grief to be transformative, using it to help others who are also dealing with grief, thus, giving meaning and purpose to their own emotionally painful experiences of loss. "All of the work that I do now has grown out of my experience of somebody grieving an accidental, or what I would call, an out of order death. And I'm trying to make things better for those of us who experience any kind of grief, but especially that sort of grief, the kind that tears down our world and reorders our lives and our views of control and safety," Devine told me.

Grief counselor and author of, *Death Expands Us: An Honest Account of Grief and How to Rise Above It*, Stephanie Harris spoke to me about her choice to turn the sudden loss of her brother, with whom she was close, and her intense resulting grief, into, what she describes in her book as a *crucible event*. "For me, I don't think I would ever be the same again. The way I thought, the way I looked at the world, it all seems very different after that experience," Harris told me. "But, I think we need to be open to the possibility that grief could turn into anything for each of us. We're all on very different journeys. I may have chosen to make something positive and transformative out of it. However, that might not be the case for everyone. I'm just putting it out there that it doesn't have to be the end for people. There is an opportunity to make something of it and to grow from it. If we have nothing else, at least we have choice."

Realistic optimism means that we know that pain is an inevitability of life, but that this does not diminish the beauty of life and that, at some point we will find a way to give such pain meaning and purpose for our lives and for the world. Being a realistic optimist means we're aware of challenges, that we know we need to take the appropriate actions in order to achieve what we want, that we focus on looking for the best steps to take, and conversely, that we work on accepting those things that cannot be changed. Such an optimistic attitude helps us to best cope if things don't work out the way that we wish, while embracing the idea that "this too shall pass" or that we'll find a way to carry the pain along with the joy on our journey.

# Nine Steps to Becoming A Realistic Optimist

1.  **Combine a positive attitude with an honest evaluation of the challenges you may encounter on your path.**

    Along with imagining what it is you'd like the outcome to be, planning the steps to overcome any challenges that might occur will help us to be best prepared to handle them.

    Take for example, that you're planning to return to school. Imagining any possible obstacles along the way to achieving your degree, such as having to take some classes that are particularly difficult for you, and then planning the steps you would take, such as researching the tutoring resources that are available, will lead to a better chance of a positive outcome.

2.  **No matter how much you might prepare, there will always be the chance of stumbling upon unexpected obstacles.**

    Expecting the unexpected and knowing that you have the inner tools to deal with these challenges and the ability to pick yourself up if you're knocked down, will help to decrease your anxiety, will prevent you from being tripped up and then giving up, and will help you to remain resilient in spite of the inevitable bumps in the road. (See Chapter 6, "Twelve Pauses to Get Back on Track," for a reminder about how to regain your footing.)

3.  **Making it a point to keep from obsessing about any unpleasant events along the way will help to prevent you from spiraling into defeat.**

    In his book *Learned Optimism*, Seligman suggests doing something that we enjoy in order to take our mind off of unpleasant situations and to get back into a better feeling state. Then come back to the situation with a problem-solving attitude. With this approach, you'll be more likely to think of better, more creative solutions.

4. **Contribute in positive ways toward someone else's life, help your community, or help the world.**

Using their own pain and grief to help others who are experiencing similar painful experiences of loss is what transformed the lives of grief counselors, Megan Devine and Stephanie Harris. (See Chapter 18, "Giving Without Expectation" for more about finding meaning and purpose through generosity and serving others.)

When you get out of yourself enough to help other people, this begins the flow of positive energy. Remind yourself of the larger-than-just-you reason for your dream and how it will help your community, inspire others, educate, or entertain. Doing something for the greater good and keeping your focus on that aspect of your dream, will keep your determination and inspiration alive, keeping you moving forward in spite of any obstacles.

5. **Laugh daily and look for the humor in stressful situations.**

Humor immediately produces feelings of joy, amusement, hope, and confidence. It completely changes a negative, pessimistic, view into a more positive one. Finding the humor in a stressful situation and turning a problem into an absurdity takes the power from a negative belief and immediately reduces our stress about it. Have you noticed that, if you make light of a situation, that situation loses its power to make you feel threatened? (See Chapter 10, "The Power of Humor," for more about how to find humor even in the darkest of situations.)

6. **Following the basics of self-care can change your attitude when faced with a stressful event.**

Exercise and meditation, for example, help to release those wonderful endorphins, and thereby creates a more positive attitude. Eating well and sleeping well are both needed for emotional balance and effective brain functioning, which are necessary to be a more creative problem-solver rather than pessimistically giving up. (See the chapters in Parts IV and V for self-care tips.)

7. **When you have a pessimistic thought, as yourself, "Where is the evidence that this is true?"**

   Look for alternative explanations, rather than assuming the worst. Often the obstacle exists in our own imagination. Our habits of negative and illogical thinking can be that which causes us to feel that there is an insurmountable obstacle in our way. (See Chapter 9, "Taming the Inner Troll" for more about overcoming the obstacle of our inner critic.)

8. **Practice "thought-stopping."**

   This is a technique often suggested by cognitive-behavioral therapists to halt repetitive and obsessive negative thinking that cause us to get caught in a downward spiral of negativity. Wear a rubber band around your wrist and, whenever you notice a repetitive negative thought, snap the rubber band as a signal to *stop*. This slight sting from the rubber band will stop your thought momentarily and give you the opportunity to, then, replace this thought with a positive thought. You will need to do this again and again until it turns into an internal habit that no longer requires the snap of a rubber band.

9. **Keep a daily journal or scrapbook to log your successes.**

   Jack Canfield's in *The Success Principles* recommends keeping a "victory log," a daily journal where we keep track of our successes from the day and even those successes we remember from long ago. It can include photographs, certificates, or any other mementos that remind us of our successes. "When most people are about to embark on some frightening task, they have a tendency to focus on all the times they tried before and didn't succeed, which undermines their self-confidence and feeds their fear that they will fail again," he tells us. "By recalling and writing down your successes each day, you log them into your long-term memory, which enhances your self-esteem and builds your confidence. And later, if you need a boost of self-confidence, you can re-read what you have written."

Buddhist psychologist, speaker and author, Jack Kornfield, in his book, *No Time Like The Present: Finding Freedom, Love, and Joy Right Where You Are*, writes, "Human life is a tainted glory—messy, paradoxical, filled with contradictions. The cloak of the world is woven with magnificence *and* limitation, triumph and disappointment, loss and eternal re-creation....You can set your goals, direct your energy, work with vigor, and try for the best, but the results are always uncertain." The choice of whether to be optimistic or pessimistic is in our own hands.

Choosing to be optimistic is the necessary ingredient, the *spark* if you will, that propels us forward toward the outcomes we want. Having optimism, we have the confidence to put ourselves out there, to walk the edge, and to take the risks needed to achieve our dreams, to "feel the fear and do it anyway," as the Susan Jeffers classic advises. "Because our brain expects something to happen a certain way, we often achieve exactly what we anticipate...when you replace your old negative expectations with more positive ones—when you begin to believe that what you want is possible— your brain will actually take over the job of accomplishing that possibility for you."

Optimism gives us resilience, it keeps us going, even when we run into an obstacle or completely lose our footing. The most successful people, those who have realized their dreams, are those who have *failed* the most because they kept taking the risks and then picked themselves up and tried again, perhaps tweaking their approach until they finally got it right or found the one person they needed to believe in them and give the opportunity they were seeking. Most of all, optimism is what makes the journey fun and, if it isn't fun, then, really, what is the point of the journey in the first place?

"In this imperfect world...we have the ability to be perfectly ourselves," writes Kornfield.

# Chapter 8

# Staying Positive in Spite of All the Bad News

*"Be the change you want to see in the world."*

~ MAHATMA GANDHI

Just when you think things can't get any more insane in the world, just flip on the news or look at your social media and, the insanity has increased. Every day we seem to sink to a new low of absurdity. And the news seems to be happening faster and faster. It's quite dizzying and difficult to even attempt to keep up. To top it off, it feels as if we can't escape from the constant barrage of anger along with the bizarre and contorted developments. At times, to try to cope with it and keep my head on straight, I make believe that I'm watching a dark comedy, with unexpected twists that are so extreme that they appear silly and comedic. At other times, I feel that I'm involuntarily stuck inside an endless *Twilight Zone*, and I'm waiting for Rod Serling to come onto the scene, with his smart suit and puffing on his cigarette, to smoothly signal the wrap up of this episode, so we can get back to a more "normal" existence.

We're all connected, more so now than ever before, because technology has given us immediate access to late-breaking news, which is now just a routine event. In this age of twenty-four-hour news coverage and social media, we're constantly bombarded with mostly bad news. Just turn on the television, computer, or smart phone, and there's a breaking report about some horrific event. With technology at our fingertips, the information is conveyed to us immediately and in greater graphic detail than ever before.

I'm a believer in the adage that knowledge is power and that it's important to be aware of what's happening with our global neighbors. World issues, such as war, famine, water shortages, and human rights issues, won't get any better for anyone if we don't compassionately work together toward solutions. Having compassion and being part of the solution requires acquiring accurate information about what's actually occurring both locally and globally. Because of this, I'm a bit of a news-junky.

But, while having consciousness of what's happening in our community and our world is important to being a participating member of this planet, there comes a tipping point when our frequently recurring reactions of fear, sadness, and anger become part of the problem that we wish to resolve. This continuous focus on the constantly *breaking* news will lead to a relentless "fight or flight," or *stress* reaction, eventually resulting in the helpless feeling of "gloom and doom."

I become physically and emotionally exhausted when I allow myself to get too wrapped up in the obsession to turn on the news first thing in the morning, in order to see what catastrophic news might have occurred while I was sleeping, and then keep it on in the evening until I, ironically, attempt to fall into a peaceful sleep. Without such a break from the stress reaction, we are much more susceptible to illness (see Chapter 11, "Reducing Stress," for more about the damaging effects of constant stress.) When that happens, not only are we unable to help our neighbors, but we also lose focus on being present for those close to us in our lives, as well as for our own emotional and physical health. We can develop what's called *compassion fatigue*, which leaves us emotionally numb, socially isolated, and withdrawn from life. This phenomenon often leads to anxiety, chronic stress, and depression. And it can certainly get in the way of following our dreams and of creating more positivity in the world. The question that I often ask myself in order to loosen the grip of anxiety about the news is, "Will I allow this to defeat me?" The answer is always a loud and resounding "no."

# EVERYTHING HAPPENS TO OUR ADVANTAGE

The Barefoot Doctor, Stephen Russell author of, *The Barefoot Doctor's Guide to the Tao*

Firstly, it's important to remember that the perception we get of the world is coming through the lens of a very tiny filter, the media. And any time that you put a frame around something, it seems much bigger than it actually is and is blown out of proportion.

Secondly, everything cycles from yin to yang, it goes from easy to difficult, from good to bad, and the same thing that's good one day is bad the next, and so on. You can take that as being either terrifying or exciting or a combination of the two. The idea would be to cut it at least 51 percent to exciting, rather than terrifying. That would be the minimum that we want to have and then, from there, get more excited than terrified, as we go along.

The problem is that we look at life through the model of "either/or." It's either good or it's bad. But, as we know, in reality, it's never one or the other; it's always both. We need to not jump to conclusions or react from fear, but rather to trust that everything and everyone is a manifestation of the same mysterious presence that informs us and makes this entire universe. No matter the disguise of someone, no matter their hairstyle, or no matter the things they say, even, no matter the things they do, ultimately, what lies behind them is the same presence, God or the Tao, or whatever you want to call it. And we need to trust that the presence is benign and to trust that the people in power will be filled with enough decency and soul that, in the balance of things, more positive than negative will come through.

And, individually, we need to look at every occurrence and say, "Even if I don't know why, this turns to my advantage. I don't even know why, everything turns to my advantage." You keep saying that, it happens because that's what you're focusing on, so that's what grows. You start taking

▶ the advantages and they grow and they proliferate. And then expand that to humanity: "Everything that's happening right now is to the advantage of humanity. One way or the other, I don't know how that's going to work, but everything that's happening right now is to the advantage of humanity." If you keep saying that to yourself, it builds up a force of positivity in your chest and your belly that informs you and, in your own small microcosmic way, you transmit a feeling that's more powerful than anything we can say that spreads. It's a feeling of kindness and humaneness and it will affect absolutely everyone. No one is immune to that feeling of *bon ami*, that feeling of kinship—that's who we are. We are one big family, and the more we remember that, the more we stop blaming the anti-heroes. The more we realize we're all in this together, that we're all responsible, then each of us has a power from right inside our heart to really powerfully influence the collective.

The following are some tips for staying balanced in spite of the news:

1. **Feel what you feel and accept reality.**

In his book, *The Five Things We Cannot Change*, Dr. David Richo reminds us of what the spiritual masters have been telling us for centuries, "Pain is a given of life." If we avoid feeling it, rather than "embracing it," as he points out, it will cause greater suffering. In fact, as I've seen with my clients who've experienced traumatic events, if we try to numb ourselves from the pain, we will not be able to feel joy. That's because we can't pick and choose which emotions to numb and which to feel. t's all or nothing. By allowing ourselves to embrace the inevitability of pain and being present with the sadness, the intensity will eventually decrease, and then we can enjoy positive emotions and have the creativity and enthusiasm to work at solving some of the problems in the world.

"Acceptance allows us to relax and open to the facts before us," writes Jack Kornfield in his book, *The Wise Heart: A Guide to the Universal Teachings of Buddhist Psychology.* "[It] does not mean that we cannot work to improve things. But just now, this is what is so….[It] is not passivity. It is a courageous step in the process of transformation." It's important to not live in a bubble and to allow ourselves to feel sad and grieve. This compassion helps us to then be part of the solution.

## 2. Avoid social media debates.

I've learned this lesson the hard way. It usually starts off innocently, when engaged in what I believed was a very respectful disagreement and that we can, somehow, get the other to understand our point of view. Then, we will have successfully changed one mind. This actually has happened with a couple of people whom I knew outside of social media so that there was a basis for trust and even for respect. But one out of several hundred is not a good statistic and the anger and wasted time that often results when this seemingly respectful debate quickly turns into something much more venomous and downright mean no longer feels worth it.

Healthy debate is positive, but, with the frequent breaking news stories, including those that are un-vetted and often false, coupled with the feeling of safety to say whatever you feel like when speaking through a computer screen, debates frequently deteriorate into unproductive and nasty arguments. Such debates that include name-calling are not only unhelpful, but also cause more anger, anxiety and despair. Resist the often-present temptation to have to prove that you're *right* about an issue. (See the section, "Shades of Gray," in Chapter 15, "Surviving the Critics." Also, see Chapter 16, "The Power of Forgiveness," for ideas about how to let go of the anger, once someone has crossed the line to nastiness.) A good way to avoid getting pulled into an argument is to delete or hide from your view any negative comments made on social media. Take control of your social media, rather than letting it control you.

### 3. Do not *feed* Internet trolls.

Since posting blogs in public sites, such as Huffington Post and Thrive Global, I've occasionally experienced the phenomenon of being "trolled." It's somewhat surprising when it happens in response to an apolitical blog meant to give free and helpful advice, but I've come to see that a "troll" really has no interest in the actual topic of discussion. Such trolling is even more rampant and nasty when we're involved in discussions with strangers about what's happening on the news. Wikepedia defines the fairly recent slang expression, "Internet troll," as "a person who sows discord on the Internet by starting arguments or upsetting people, by posting inflammatory, extraneous, or off-topic messages in an on-line community...with the deliberate intent of provoking readers into an emotional response or otherwise disrupting normal on-topic discussion, often for their own amusement."

Recent research has found that those people who demonstrate trolling behavior tend to have similar personalities to those people whom we might consider to be *bullies*. The findings also show that, if victims of trolling react in an emotional manner, the trolling will intensify just for the amusement of the troll. The best and most common advice, when confronted by someone bullying you on social media is, "Do not feed the trolls." Don't respond to them. The main goal of a troll is to receive attention, even if the attention is negative. So, don't give it to them and they will likely give up and leave you alone.

**4. Take a bad news break by looking for good news.**

Decide on a time when you're going to turn off the news. Yep, I said it. Turn off the news. And I mean news from the television, radio, social media, Internet news outlets, or any other source from which you receive your news. We need to take breaks from the bad news and, frankly, bad news is the bread and butter of most news sources, so that's mainly what you'll hear from any of these outlets. There has always been bad news in the world and there always will be bad news. We're just more able to hear about it and see it play out through technology.

But, there is also good news that we don't tend to hear about from such typical news sources because good news doesn't sell as well. So, it's up to us to try to find the good news in order to create balance. Sources, such as the websites of spiritual teachers, like Eckhart Tolle (EckhartTolle.com) and Deepak Chopra (DeepakChopra.com), as well as magazines such as *Live Happy* magazine and, even, *AARP* magazine, are great places to find out about positive news in the world. Make it a point to look, daily, for five pieces of happy news, those stories of overcoming obstacles or people demonstrating their humanity by helping other people. Go to your local bookstore and ask for a book about any of these topics. You'll find many in the biography section. Such feel-good stories provide balance for the bad news and helps us to remember that the glass is *both* half-empty *and* half-full, that the world is both broken and beautiful at the same time—and that we have the power to turn painful events into something meaningful.

## 5. Find meaning.

Get involved, rather than sitting at home and stressing about the news. "As individuals, we have to start with the reality of our own suffering. As a society, we have to start with the reality of collective suffering, of injustice, racism, greed, and hate," wrote Kornfield in *The Wise Heart.*

Creating meaning from situations in which people are suffering by helping them will change your own life dramatically, practically in a quantum leap. There are many ways that you can do this. One powerful way is to be sure to exercise your civic duty to vote and help others to register to vote. Write letters to your representatives about how you wish for them to vote on various bills. Run for a political office on a platform that you feel strongly about. Volunteer for an important cause. Help at a soup kitchen, nursing home, or animal shelter. The benefits to our own health, as well as to the health of our society, by acting out of generosity, giving of ourselves and our time, are immeasurable. Every act of kindness, no matter how small, can have the effect of actually changing the world, especially if we have no expectation of receiving anything in return. (See Chapter 18, "Giving without Expectation," for more about the benefits of generosity.)

# REDUCING TECHNOLOGY STRESS

These days, it's hard to go anywhere without seeing people looking at their devices, even when surrounded by friends and family who are available to interact in-person. As I mentioned earlier, the bombardment of information has become constant, and often the information we're receiving is negative, causing us more stress. Ask yourself how long you can go without watching the news, texting, talking on the phone, or checking your e-mails or social media. There's something hypnotic about these forms of communication. They're a mixed blessing. Having the world at our fingertips literally opens up doors to infinite information that can change our lives and connect us with people whom we may never have been able to connect with otherwise. But, this comes with a price if we allow it to take over every minute of our waking hours.

The antidote to this type of technology stress is to take time-outs or vacations from technology. I've found that this isn't an easy task. I actually crave checking my messages and social media when I turn off my computer and smart phone

▶

for a period of time. It's an addiction. No wonder that when Blackberries first came out, they were often referred to as "Crack-berries!" In fact, these devices are addictive partially because they serve, similar to a consciousness-altering drug, as a way to escape from what is actually happening in our own lives, the "is-ness" of life, with all of its ups and downs and mundane moments, or long stretches of mundaneness that make up life. So, being present in our own life without constantly checking a device is actually a form of mindfulness. We get to experience life without distraction.

Once you get through the cravings that will at first hit strongly, there will come a sense of relief, a feeling of peacefulness, similar to what happens when we use mindfulness meditation. Plan a time-out every day for at least an hour, when technology devices are turned off. Once you get used to that, take a complete day off from your devices, including the television. You might find it so relaxing that you won't want to turn them back on. Spend those hours or that day doing some meditation, exercising, reading from an actual paper and ink book, walking in nature, socializing with flesh-and-blood people minus the smartphone interruptions, following a dream—the possibilities are endless.

For more tips on staying centered, check out the section, "Tips for Manifesting the Relaxation Response" in Chapter 11, "Reducing Stress," and, also, you can go back and read Chapter 6, "Twelve Pauses To Get Back on Track." Kornfield states so beautifully in *No Time Like the Present*, "We have the laughter of the wise, the freedom to choose our spirit no matter the circumstances. We have the freedom to love… amid the glorious, terrifying, and unshakable beauty of it all. We have the wisdom and courage to care sweetly in this fleeting, evanescent play of days."

As always, we have the choice about how we feel and whether we will focus on the empty or full of the glass. Remember that with fullness, we have the nourishment, energy, love, and creativity to create more beauty and fullness in this cracked world. The world is calling. Will you answer the call?

## Chapter 9

# Taming the Inner Troll

*"Trolls suck."*

~ Betty White

I've noticed that when I get into a negative spiral in my own thinking, it's easy to wear myself down in a matter of moments with beliefs that are factually untrue. On the other hand, I've also discovered I can quickly feel better by choosing to change my perspective. At times, I will widen my lens and take a broader view or maybe I will attend to the "half-full" part of the metaphoric half-filled glass.

In determining the source of our negative inner chatter, Louise Hay, author of the acclaimed *You Can Heal Your Life*, posed this conclusion, "We tend to live our lives based on what we believe about ourselves, our world, our capabilities, and our limits. Where do those beliefs come from? From what other people have told us. What if they're wrong?" We often allow the beliefs of others to become our own, such as the belief that we may no longer be relevant because of our age or that our dreams are no longer important or possible to fulfill.

The reality is that just because we believe it doesn't make it true. A belief is really just a thought that we think over and over again until we believe it. Some of our beliefs help us in our lives, but others only serve to make us feel bad about ourselves or to give up on our true calling. The latter beliefs can create deep pain for us. We might be more productive and happier in our lives if we're willing to let them go.

Such ways of viewing the world are essentially *programmed* into our brain through our repetitive thoughts and our behaviors based on these thoughts. Our brain picks out realities in our environment that appear to match our worldview and only pays attention to those realities, discarding all of the information that doesn't match. As I wrote about earlier, in the old adage of the half-filled glass, if you're an optimist, you're likely to see the glass as half-full, while if you're a pessimist, you're likely to see that same glass as half-empty, but, in reality, the glass is actually *both* half-empty *and* half-full. In each of these cases, your belief causes you to ignore the *other half* of the glass, supporting your pre-existing belief. With this cycle of belief-building, every time we notice something that fits with our belief, we believe it *more* and see our belief as a *fact*. Our brain then shows us more evidence to support this "fact." It's a self-perpetuating cycle.

One such programmed belief that causes us pain is the belief that we need to be perfect. This need for perfection is the enemy of most writers, artists, musicians, public speakers, performers, and, in fact, most of us trying to master our journey. My writing, my radio programs, my work, my relationships, my choices, and my interactions with the world are all far from perfection. This is the case for all of us—we aren't perfect beings, we are humans. If I were to allow myself to overthink my mistakes of the past in order to achieve perfection in the future, I'd be paralyzed and wouldn't be able to write a single word or do a radio interview.

When I was sixteen years old, I had the opportunity to watch the famous psychologist, Dr. Albert Ellis (one of the founders of Cognitive Behavioral Therapy and the founder of Rational Emotive Behavior Therapy), while he was leading one of his famous Friday night workshops in New York City. He became one of the most influential psychologists in my career as a psychologist. He often wrote and spoke about perfectionism as an extremely paralyzing obstacle that he helped his clients and the readers of his books to overcome. Ellis, himself, was a very prolific writer, having written fifty-four published books, including the best-selling *A New Guide to Rational Living*, and over 600 articles, right up until his death at age ninety-four. One reason that he was able to write so many books and articles was that he didn't allow the need to be perfect to be an obstacle in his own life.

"*Irrational idea number one* is 'I *must* do well (or perform perfectly well!) in important tasks I choose to perform and *must* win the approval or love of the people whom I choose to make important to me,'" wrote Drs. Albert Ellis and Irving Becker, in their book, *A Guide to Personal Happiness*. "This profound, absolutistic *must*…almost inevitably results in deep-seated feelings of anxiety, hypertension, and obsessive-compulsive thoughts and actions…. [as well as] profound feelings of depression, despair, shame, guilt, and self-hatred after you have presumably functioned poorly as you think you absolutely *must* not." In fact, this "*mus*turbatory" belief, as Ellis called it, is most often the reason for what we commonly refer to as writer's block. It's also the biggest and most insidious reason for giving up on our dreams and aspirations—and for ignoring our soul's calling.

"It's our own minds, so often, that defeat us. We say things to ourselves that tear ourselves down," The Human Behavior Coach, Beverly Flaxington, and author of *Self-Talk for a Calmer You: Learn How to Use Positive Self-talk to Control Anxiety and Live a Happier, More Relaxed Life*, pointed out when I had a chance to interview her. "The self-talk that we use on ourselves absolutely drains us. Lack of confidence and low self-esteem is very typically an outgrowth of too much negative self-talk too often." This negative self-talk is also the primary reason for depression.

"Depression is thought of as a disease, almost like a virus that you catch," The Barefoot Doctor told me. "But it is actually something that you do to yourself. You are de-*pressing* yourself. You're pressing down on your own human wild spirit. You press your "self" down and you don't even realize that you're doing it. That leads to a vicious spiral downward until you feel alienated, isolated, and angry at the world. If you treat it like something that you are doing and, therefore, can do something different, bit by bit, you can really help get yourself out of the depressed state." Therefore, if we gradually change our habits of thinking, we can climb up out of the abyss of depression and into the light, where we can live our life to its fullest.

## So, how do we stop the inner troll in its tracks?

I'm certainly quite familiar with this ugly little fella who has made an appearance many times during the writing of this book. If we become aware of our own negative chatter and know that this is not a reflection of the absolute *truth*, even if we aren't able to turn the noise off completely, it will lose its power over us and, perhaps, the volume will soften.

When we change our patterns of habitual thinking, we also shift the chemistry in our brains and our bodies—often as well as or better than medications, such as antidepressants (Prozac or Zoloft, for example). In fact, we can improve our health, our relationships, and our entire life by making a simple shift in our thoughts and a resulting attitude adjustment.

"As humans, we are born with…the ability to think about our thinking…We can philosophize about our philosophy, reason about our reasoning…which gives us *some* degree of self-determination or free will…The more we choose to *use* our self-awareness and to *think* about our goals and desires, the more we create…free will or self-determination. This also goes for our emotions," wrote Dr. Ellis in his book, *How to Stubbornly Refuse to Make Yourself Miserable about Anything—Yes, Anything!* "If you understand how you upset yourself by slipping into irrational shoulds, oughts, demands, and commands, unconsciously sneaking them into your thinking, you can just about always stop disturbing yourself about anything." We have the power to increase our awareness of thought habits, giving us control over this inner troll.

Eckhart Tolle told us in *Stillness Speaks*, "When you recognize that there is a voice in your head that pretends to be you and never stops speaking, you are awakening out of your unconscious identification with the stream of thinking. When you notice that voice, you realize that who you are is not the voice—the thinker—but the one who is aware of it. Knowing yourself as the awareness behind the voice is freedom."

The first step in taking back our power is to become aware of our self-critical thoughts and of our beliefs about how life has disappointed us by being different than what we think it "should" be. The next step is to remind ourselves that these thoughts and beliefs are not who we are, they are often lies generated by our inner troll.

And then, finally, we achieve freedom when we stop listening to the troll. "The keys to liberation are universal and essentially simple: disengage from all the stories you've been telling yourself about life and who you are or should be as you negotiate your way through, and all at once, you know yourself as divine, all-powerful, unstoppable, and magnificent, as any divine, all-powerful unstoppable being would," said The Barefoot Doctor in his foreword to the book, *F\*\*k It: The Ultimate Spiritual Way*, by John Parkin.

Creating emotional distance from our thoughts will help us to have increased awareness of our thinking, giving us greater ability to change what is not serving us well. According to a new research study by Dr. Ethan Kross at the University of Michigan, published in the *Journal of Personality and Social Psychology*, there's a simple technique that we can use in order to create a powerful shift in our thinking.

Dr. Kross and his associates demonstrated that referring to ourselves by our own name in our own inner talk, rather than by first person ("I" or "me"), increases distance from our thoughts, and subsequently, our ability to change them, which will result in different behaviors and emotions. More specifically, he found that when people referred to themselves by name in their self-talk, they tended to be more supportive of themselves and to give themselves more helpful advice, similar to how they might advise a close friend. In another study, Kross and his associate Moser found that the brain scan images of people addressing themselves by name during self-talk actually look similar to those of people giving advice to friends, while those using the personal pronouns of "I" or "me," do not. They concluded that using our own name in our thoughts elicits more wisdom and brings clarity into our problem solving while dealing with life events. (For another effective way to create the emotional distance from our thoughts necessary to shut down that *inner troll*, check out Chapter 12, "Finding Our Way to Happiness With Meditation.")

Life is difficult at times, but we don't need to add to that by making ourselves feel worse with how we speak about ourselves to ourselves. Just knowing that we have the capacity to change our feelings by transforming our thinking gives us great freedom. "The situation or the circumstance, the trial or the tribulation, is not the problem. The problem is our reaction and our response to it," speaker, author, and wellness coach, Quentin Vennie, told me. "If I can't change that problem, changing how I view it, will ultimately change how it affects me."

# Chapter 10

# The Power of Humor

*"A clown is like an aspirin, only he works twice as fast."*

~ Groucho Marx

I was going through a time when changes were coming quickly in my personal life. I had to suddenly and quickly find a new place to live. With that, came the big decision about whether to find something to rent (again) or to purchase. After deciding on buying, I came up against crazy bidding wars on every house that I liked within my price range in the area. Lots of people want to live in Austin, and it seemed that everyone looking to buy had the same budget as I did. At the same time, I was grieving the recent death of a dear friend, who was one of my first close friends upon moving to Austin. Added to that was the daily roller coaster of events shown on the news. I got to the point where, every time I put my head on the pillow, a loop of my own voice would play in my mind, saying, "This is all too much," causing my heart to race and leading to me gasping for air. During the day, I was drained from the stress and from the lack of sleep. Even with all of the tools I have in my toolkit to de-stress, I was in a state of extreme stress. This went on for about three exhausting weeks. Then, one day, while zoning out on social media, a video popped up. The title was, *Its Hard to Stay Angry with Squeaky Shoes.*

In the video, a little girl, about two or three years old, was standing with her arms crossed and her back to her father, who was, apparently, holding the camera. Every time her dad tried to reason with her and to move in front of her with his camera, she would quickly turn away, stomping her little feet as she turned. The off-camera father could be heard giggling. He would then run in front of her with his camera and his little daughter would stomp her little feet more quickly and, again, spin away from him. The little girl was wearing those children's sneakers that make a funny squeak whenever weight is put on them. So, as she stomped harder and more rapidly, the squeaking became louder and quicker, causing increased laughter from her off-camera dad. Soon, the little girl began giggling at her own squeaking shoes and, before long, she was purposely twirling about, stomping her little feet, and laughing with full all-out abandon at her power to create the hilarious squeaks. While watching, I soon found myself laughing along with the dad and the little girl in the video. Tears were running down my face. It felt great and, on that day, it felt like relief.

My own whole-hearted belly-laughter successfully broke the cycle of stressful thinking along with my stressed-out feelings born from these thoughts. "I think I need to buy myself a pair of squeaky shoes," I told myself, as the feeling of relaxation took over after I stopped laughing and found my composure. In fact, I believe we all need those shoes right about now. Can you imagine everyone stomping around in squeaky shoes? We would never be able to stay upset, stressed out, or angry for very long.

The ability of this video in breaking my own cycle of feeling stressed-out is not unusual. In fact, it's well established in the research that one very powerful way of diminishing the strength of our inner troll, adjusting our attitude, and increasing our optimism, is by allowing ourselves to laugh, especially full-belly guffaws to the point of tears. In his book, *Anatomy of An Illness: As Perceived by the Patient*, Norman Cousins described how he incorporated humor therapy into his own treatment of a very painful illness, spending several hours per day belly- laughing while watching Marx Brothers movies. He eventually recovered from the disease, and since then, the medical world has taken the adage, "Laughter is the best medicine," much more seriously.

Did the squeaky shoes video completely halt my stress reaction and change the realties of what was happening in my life? Well, it actually went a long way toward doing that. When I had the chance to laugh like that, I had a feeling of liberation and remembered how good it feels to laugh. And, with that freedom from intense stress, came more clarity of thought, making it easier to accept those things that I had no control of and to deal with the rest, one do-able step at a time. Since then, I have tried to remain more conscious of taking opportunities to find humor in life situations and to laugh out loud regularly. This has opened the way for using all of the other tools for coping with stress that much more effectively

Humor interferes with the downward spiral of energy-zapping thoughts, by helping us to notice the absurdity of situations that trigger anger or the feeling of being threatened. The mere act of laughing creates positive emotions, such as joy, amusement, hope, confidence, and overall well-being. In the short term, this stabilizes blood pressure, massages inner organs, stimulates circulation, helps improve digestion, increases the supply of oxygen to the muscles, and decreases muscle tension. In the longer term, it boosts the power of the immune system, by reducing damaging stress hormones.

# ADDED BONUSES OF HUMOR AND LAUGHTER

- Enhanced creativity.

- Deeper relationships: Sharing laughter with a loved one can improve communication and bring joy into the relationship.

- Freedom from the tendency to overthink.

- Detoxification of the body: The tears produced by laughter are chemically different from the tears produced by sadness. Laughter tears contain toxins released from our body. When we laugh until we cry, we're cleansing ourselves of these poisons.

- Reduction of physical pain by releasing endorphins in the brain: Norman Cousins reported that ten minutes of laughter gave him two hours of pain-free sleep during his recovery.

- Achieves some of the benefits of an aerobic workout: A belly laugh gives a workout to the diaphragm, increases the body's ability to use oxygen, and provides cardiac conditioning.

You might think it unreasonable of me to suggest finding humor in the midst of a very stressful life circumstance or when you're not feeling particularly well. But, in fact, it's at times such as these that humor is needed more than ever for its unique power to brighten even the darkest situation. You may have noticed that the funniest comedians are the ones who get us to laugh about the most stressful or saddest situations that are universal and that we can all relate to. Intuitively, we must want to feel the relief of the laughter while feeling that we are not alone in our difficult experiences.

From early in my life, I've made it a point to find friends who share my love of laughter. I have fond memories, from childhood and into adulthood, of laughing with my friends through the stresses of school and of making our way through the world. In fact, some of the happiest moments I've had with those closest to me involved that kind of belly-laughter. The fondest memories I have with my grandmother were when we would laugh until we were crying together. In her hazy fog of Alzheimer's Disease at the end of her life journey, she was still able to experience pure joy with me while we shared a heart-felt connection during mirthful moments of laughter. Even memories of sad events, such as my grandmother's funeral, are mellowed by the memory of how I began giggling uncontrollably at the service. The Rabbi told a story about how my grandmother used to do somersaults with my mom, when my mother was a little girl. I heard people gasp and I imagined that they were all picturing her the same way I was, as a tiny eighty-five-year-old woman doing gymnastics. This smacked me right in my funny bone. I knew my grandmother would also find it quite amusing, and at that moment, I felt like she was giggling along with me, as we had done so many times together.

I recently told this story during a lecture I gave at a retirement community about humor. Honestly, I didn't know how my audience would react to such a story about giggling at my grandma's funeral. But, much to my delight, before long, the audience members were all telling funny stories about the many funerals they had each attended. This seemed to unite us all. Laughter had achieved the ultimate desire of any public speaker, to bond my audience and myself together. And, we all came to a consensus that being able to laugh during such sad times, not only gives us the gift of finding a glimmer of light in the darkness, but that it had turned those funerals from grief-filled events into celebrations of the lives of our dearly departed. Since my own dad's death, my brothers, my mom, and I have found comfort in sharing humorous experiences we each had with him. I know he would appreciate it, as I can still see my dad's twinkling eyes, tears running down his face, and his nose turning red, as we spent time and time again laugh-crying together about the absurdities of life.

## MAKE IT A POINT TO LAUGH EVERY DAY

- Laugh at yourself, rather than criticizing yourself for your mistakes.
- Look for the comic absurdity of an obstacle.
- Watch a funny video.
- Read a funny book.
- Share a funny story with friends.

▶

► • In their book, *Awakening the Laughing Buddha Within,* the Barefoot Doctor and Joe Hoare related that even listening to the sound of laughter significantly reduces stress. You can find laughter apps that are available to download on your smart phone with many varieties of laughter to choose from.

Maybe the reason that the comedian George Burns lived to the ripe young age of 100 was that he saw the humor in everything, including growing older. Once, when asked how long he planned to work, he responded, "I'm gong to stay in show business until I'm the last one left."

# Chapter 11

# Reducing Stress

*"Blessed are the flexible, for they shall*
*not be bent out of shape."*

~ Unknown Author

This is one of the longer chapters in this book, I noticed. Perhaps, this is a reflection of, both, my own experience of frequently being called upon, personally and professionally, for help by those feeling stressed, as well as my own constant dance with stress and the tools to tame it. The level of stress in our society, as a whole, appears to be continuously increasing, and it has become such a constant experience that we often don't even notice how ramped up our own stress level is. Stress is the new normal, and at times, it appears to be a competitive sport, each of us fearing that we're somehow missing out in our lives if we aren't as frantic and frenzied as our friends and social media connections.

There's a price to pay for this. Whether we're running around at a frenetic pace, hitting roadblocks in our daily lives, or constantly hearing about bad news around the world, we will, at some point, feel overwhelmed and experience the stress reaction. If we keep re-experiencing the reactions of feeling overwhelmed and stressed-out, it will lead to going down the rabbit hole to anxiety and deep despair.

Any significant events in our lives, even ones that we expect to be positive, such as falling in love, usually cause many changes in our daily existence, and affect our perception about our life or plans for the future. As creatures of habit, these deviations in our routine create stress, as do more difficult situations such as the loss of a job or a loved one. If we were to have no stress at all, we wouldn't get to experience new and exciting adventures. Good stresses consist of positive events, such as commencing on an exciting new path toward our dreams. These stresses are referred to as *eustress*, and while too much of a good thing can cause us to feel overtaxed, in general, eustress is caused by those stresses we can cope with and that motivate us. It focuses our energy, and it creates excitement and a feeling of vitality and passion about life—even improving our performance. *Distress*, on the other hand, is caused by situations that we believe we can't handle and result in our feeling of being *stressed out*.

Whether we perceive that the changes caused by a life event are exciting and that we can handle them—or we believe that they're overwhelming and beyond our ability to cope with effectively— determines if we'll adapt smoothly and enjoy the excitement of a new experience or feel stressed out by it. Therefore, it's our reaction to the changes we face, as well as our ability to adapt to them, which creates the impact they will have on our lives.

The *stress response* is also called the *fight-or-flight* response. Our body prepares to fight or to run from any situation we view as dangerous or threatening. Both mind and body then make adjustments in order to deal with what we perceive to be a potential threat. These include increases in blood pressure, rate of breathing, metabolism, and muscle tension. Even brain waves rise in intensity and frequency. Blood flow to the muscles of our arms and legs actually elevates by 300 percent to 400 percent when we're in this state of mind. Adrenaline, norepinephrine, and cortisol will course through our body in order to increase our energy and alertness. Now, because of these biological adjustments, we're prepared to fight or to flee from any real dangers that we're confronted with.

# INDICATIONS OF THE STRESS REACTION

The following are some of the mind and body symptoms we experience when in *fight or flight*:

- Rapid heart beat

- Shortness of breath

- Increased blood pressure

- Muscle tension: tight muscles, tension headaches, clenched jaw and grinding teeth, tense stomach, chest pains caused by tightness in upper body muscles

- Decreased blood flow with cold extremities (hands and feet)

- Sweating

- Increased brain activity (racing thoughts, unable to focus attention and easily distractible, irritability, increased worry, difficulty sleeping)

- Gastrointestinal distress: upset stomach, "butterflies," decreased appetite

The research has shown again and again that if we chronically experience this stress reaction, it will cause damage to every system of the human body, as well as depression and anxiety disorders, consisting of frequent or constant feelings of fear that interfere with enjoying life. If we don't actually have to fight or run because the danger only exists in our imagination, which is often the case, then, according to cardiologist, stress researcher, and author of *The Relaxation Response*, Dr. Herbert Benson, we won't burn off the energy that we produced during this reaction. And this is the culprit of many of the resulting health problems. So, for example, the chronic intensification of blood flow will lead to a chronic rise in blood pressure and this can then increase our risk for cardiac problems, arthrosclerosis, strokes, and internal bleeding. The production of adrenaline and norepinephrine, if continued for an extended period of time, can cause an irregular heart rhythm and greater sensitivity to physical pain. It can also lead to anxiety, depression, lower tolerance to frustration, irritability, and quickness to anger.

But, here's the good news. The very same mechanism that turned on the stress reaction can also turn it off. Dr. Benson coined the term the "relaxation response" to describe this. When we are in a relaxed state, it's impossible to experience the stress response because these are two totally opposite biological states. You can't have the slow deep breathing of relaxation at the same time as the shallow, rapid respiration of the stress response, for example. Nor can your heart beat slowly, as in the relaxation response, at the same time as the rapid heart rate of the stress response. You get the idea.

According to Benson, "The human body is geared to react by providing this calm state—the opposite of the fight-or-flight response—whenever the mind is focused for some time and disregards intrusive, everyday thoughts. In other words, when the mind quiets down, the body follows suit. So powerful, in fact, is this process that you need not believe." So, even the skeptics will get results when taking steps to intentionally create the relaxation response.

More good news is that by inducing that relaxation response on a regular basis, we can heal health issues and psychological distress that has been caused by stress. "Just as repeated activation of the fight-or-flight response can lead to sustained problems in the body and its mechanics, so too can repeated activation of the relaxation response reverse those trends and mend the internal wear and tear brought on by stress," wrote Benson.

---

# THREE BREATHS TO DE-STRESS, A MICRO-MEDITATION

Dr. Michael Brant DeMaria, Psychologist, Poet, Speaker, Grammy-Nominated Recording Artist, & Author of *Peace Within: Clear Your Mind, Open Your Heart, Embrace Your Soul, and Heal Your Life*

One of my favorite techniques is called, "Three Breaths to De-Stress."

*Take a nice deep belly breath, closing your eyes, and accentuating the out breath. So, you blow out until you have no more air and, when you think there's no more air, blow out a little bit further. Do this three times with your eyes closed.*

Closing your eyes reduces brain activity by two thirds. It takes so much brain activity to process

▶

▶ visual information, so that simply the act of closing your eyes is a relaxation process. Also, when we do these three long breaths, we really reduce the respiration rate and kick in the parasympathetic nervous system, which is known as the "rest and digest" part of our nervous system. Immediately, with these three deep breaths and long extended out-breaths, we're able to bring ourselves into the here and now, into the present moment. Most people are respirating at fifteen breaths per minute or more, and we know that, when people get to twelve and below (with the three breaths, we actually can drop it down to six, seven, or eight breaths per minute), their overall health and wellness increases dramatically. It only takes twenty seconds to do this little practice. It's what I call a micro-meditation. Just try it and I promise you'll be in a totally different place after those three breaths.

"We can build our resilience to stress by shifting our awareness to our body and our breath," yoga instructor, Steve Kane, told me during our discussion of meditation. "Just a few minutes per day of conscious breathing can help us to build this resilience."

# Eleven More Tips for Manifesting the Relaxation Response

1. **Enjoy a time-out to just stop "doing" and "be."**

   Take an honest inventory of your activities and ask yourself these questions: How much of what you're "doing" is "necessary" for the betterment of your own life, of your family, or of the world? Which activities are you doing because you feel that you "should," because they're expected of you, or are just to keep you busy so that you don't have to be with your own thoughts? Now, see if you can eliminate some of those unnecessary activities, so that you can have some more time to "be," and try one or more of the following tips to keep you in the "being" state of mind.

2. **Try *Alternate Nostril Breathing.***

   - Place your right thumb on your right nostril, closing it, and gently and slowly breathe in through your left nostril. Hold for two or three seconds. Then, gently and slowly breathe out through your left nostril.

   - Now place your right ring finger on your left nostril, closing it, and gently and slowly breathe in through your right nostril. Hold for two or three seconds. Then, gently and slowly breathe out through your right nostril.

   - Repeat this for nine cycles. And then breathe normally.

3. **Be like a child again and color.**

   Adult coloring books are the new craze and for good reason. Coloring has been found to calm the mind, slow down thoughts, and ease anxiety and stress.

4. **Gaze at the moon.**

   Terry Hershey, in his book, *The Power of Pause*, suggests looking at the moon, if you can. "Stare at it and breathe in, breathe out. Think of this moonlight bathing your whole life—even the parts that are disorganized and unfinished."

5. **Use relaxing imagery.**

   There are endless imagery techniques you can use, many guided imageries are easily found in videos on the Internet. Here's one example of a relaxing imagery: Close your eyes and imagine that you're floating on a giant leaf and gently drifting along with the slow current of a lazy river.

6. **Meditate.**

   Meditation is essential for most of us to calm our minds and regain our balance. Read more about meditation in Chapter 12, "Finding Our Way to Happiness with Meditation."

7. **Practice yoga.**

   Yoga is a powerful way to bring our mind into the present moment, rather than obsessing about the past or future, and to be present in our body, rather than obsessing with stressful thoughts in our mind. Read Chapter 25, "Time to Hit the Mat," for the benefits of yoga and check out my interview with yoga teacher, Steve Kane in Chapter 29, "Mindfulness to Break the Pain Cycle," for more about the use of yoga for relaxation.

8. **Take a twenty-minute Epsom salt and lavender oil bath**

   Epsom salts, which isn't really a salt, but a blend of magnesium and sulfate, has been used for hundreds of years as a natural remedy for a number of ailments. According to the website, Saltworks, "Some of the countless health benefits include relaxing the nervous system, curing skin problems, soothing back pain and aching limbs, easing muscle strain, healing cuts, treating colds and congestion, and drawing toxins from the body."

And when you add lavender oil, you'll likely be blissed out, as lavender has properties that reduce stress and anxiety, and helps with insomnia, depression, and restlessness.

**9.  Get a massage.**

According to Dr. Axe's website, Food is Medicine, massage "increases circulation, relieves tension, reduces stress, relieves anxiety, improves sleep, and promotes relaxation throughout the entire body, as well as many other benefits."

Combine that with an Epsom salt and lavender oil bath and you'll be in heaven.

**10.  Listen to relaxing music in combination with any of the above techniques.**

I end each of my radio programs with a musician because of the strong healing benefits of music. "I feel that music is the perfect metaphor for life," said Dr. DeMaria, during our interview. "A line in one of my poems says, 'Each moment is a note in the song of today.' We view our life like a song when we don't get into a rush because the goal of the song is not to get to the end, but to enjoy each moment fully. This is one of the big healing aspects of music. Also, we know that music shifts us into the *right* brain, the spacial/temporal brain, which really induces a sense of unification, a sense of synthesis, and a sense of connectedness. So, music has this quality of inner connectedness, of slowing the heart rate down, of lowering the blood pressure, and of connecting us with the heart, which is the organ of what matters to us, what touches us, what speaks to us."

### 11. Be curious.

Try an attitude of curiosity and openness about changes in your life, even allowing yourself to feel excited, rather than fearing new experiences.

## Staying Grounded

I often walk around with my head in the clouds. This is great at times, but being untethered to the earth eventually results in feeling anxious. Taking time to consciously connect with the earth, or "grounding" ourselves, brings us the gift of the level-headedness and sense of security that we need in order to make clear decisions, to remain strong in the face of adversity, and to prevent anxiety. Take a moment and imagine yourself similar to a tree. Like a tree, your feet are rooted to the nourishing earth, and your trunk stands firm and unshakable, even by the gustiest winds. Meanwhile the top half of your body, including your head, your heart, and the reach of your arms, are like the branches of the tree, reaching higher and higher to your dreams, swaying easily in the winds of life. From that place, I am much more able to reach for the stars, while staying strong and focused. Try walking barefoot on the earth. Touching our bare feet to the grass and the dirt has an almost immediate effect of calming our nervous system.

# ENERGY MEDICINE AND "GROUNDING" FOR MIND/BODY WELLNESS

Integral Yoga Instructor & Occupational Therapist, Dara Steinberg, M.S., OTR/L Staying Grounded and Protected from Absorbing Others' Pain

I was an occupational therapist for about seven years. During that time, I spent a lot of time working in pediatrics in hospitals and school settings. And what I found was happening to me was that I would come home from work every day feeling emotionally and physically exhausted. I felt like my energy had been zapped, and I didn't understand why because I was eating well, doing yoga, exercising, and I was a pretty healthy person. I also found that my emotions were all over the place. I would be feeling fine at one moment, and, suddenly, I wouldn't feel well. I found it hard to stay in balance. I also felt like there was something more that I needed to be doing with my life.

Eventually, I wound up going to an *energy healer*. She helped me to learn about myself and to understand what was going on in my physical

▶

body, in my emotions, and in my energy field. It really changed my life. I started training under her and a few other energy healers to learn my own craft and to start using energy healing with other people. This is because I see that there are a lot of people out in the world who are a lot like me, walking through their lives sometimes sensing or feeling other people's emotions, as well as worrying about other people. Energy healing can help us to feel better physically, emotionally, and energetically. We can use these practices in our everyday life and they're very functional.

Energy medicine is a belief that we have the ability to alter the way that our physical body and our emotions are functioning by using our energy field to make changes. It's a way of changing things from the inside out. Science has found that we can alter the way we feel using such practices as yoga, breathing techniques, changing the way that we think about things, and meditation. With energy healing, there's a belief that we each have an energy field, and that, sometimes, there can be a block in that energy field. We want our energy to be flowing like a stream. Using energy healing techniques help us move things that are blocking that flow through our system on a regular basis and to use our energy to have an affect on our emotional state and on our physical state.

▶

▶

Frequently, those of us who are empathic or intuitive or sensitive tend to go into professions where we can help other people. But, we become overwhelmed by everything that we're taking on as we go through our day. People will frequently ask me, "What can I do to prevent myself from taking on other people's energy and then what can I do if I have taken on other people's energy?"

When you're about to go out into the world, it's a good idea to have a little bit of, what I would call, a "shield," just a little bit of protection. This is not based on an idea that the world is dangerous. It's more about the idea that you don't have to take on other people's energy in order to help them. In fact, if you do take on other people's energy, it often doesn't help them but causes you the problems that I described earlier as my experience. The beauty of energy healing is that you can be clear about who you really are and can express your true self, without anybody else's stuff blocking you.

**Creating a protective shield:**

Before any meditation, I always start with having people do what's called, "grounding." This allows us to release quite a bit and to really relax. It also allows our bodies to heal by connecting to the earth. This is a really good thing to do before going

▶

▶

to work in the morning or before doing anything in your day, to really connect with that feeling of grounding into the earth: Imagine that you're growing roots that go into the center of the earth.

Then, when I'm about to go into a situation where I know there will be a lot of other people, I like to imagine a sacred container. This can be something like a rose or a beautiful bowl, or a shield in front of you. It can look however you want it to. Imagine that you're putting that up in front of you, as you're about to go through your day, so that, anybody else's energy that you come in contact with will be collected by that container, rather than going into your body. Then, at the end of your day, you can imagine that you're throwing that container up into the center of the universe and destroying it. That transforms all of the energy that's been collected. Then that energy can go back to the other people in a way that's been transformed.

## Removing other people's energy from yourself

We often wind up taking on other people's "stuff" anyway. So, at the end of the day, I recommend a very simple meditation where you might imagine a container, very similar to the one I just described. This time, you would imagine that container pulling the energy out of your body and space. Set an intention, "Anything that is not mine and

▶

▶ that is no longer serving me can be released into this container." You might imagine the energy that is inside of your body as a color or you can imagine it as a feeling. Ask yourself, "Where is it in my body?" See and feel the sacred container pulling it out of your body. Then, as before, throw that sacred container, with all of the energy that it collected, up into the universe to be destroyed.

Whenever you release something, you always want to make sure that you're filling, very consciously, with what you want. So, at the end of the meditation, I always do this visualization:

Imagine a golden sun. You can visualize it or imagine the feeling of the sun above you. Imagine that you're filling that golden sun with anything that you feel that you would like to have more of in your life, such as love or abundance or clarity. And then imagine that you're popping that golden sun, and, either visualize or feel, golden light is filling you from the very top of your head, all the way down to the bottoms of your feet.

▶

My experience with using these meditations/visualizations is that they have been very helpful for me in maintaining my equilibrium and feeling of inner peace while in my work to help those who are going through some pretty incredible stresses and changes within their own lives. Using such grounding techniques decreases my feeling of being drained throughout my workday.

One of the greatest causes of stress is our lack of acceptance of what is. "What is" includes how things are right now, as well as the fact that everything changes and ends. Wrote Dr. Richo, "Changes and endings are inevitable for any person, relationship, enthusiasm, or thing. Nothing is perfect, permanently satisfying, or permanently anything. Everything falls apart in time. Every beginning leads to a finale. Built into all experiences, persons, places, and things is a life span." When we cling to things or to situations, we feel stress because no matter how hard we try we can't stop this reality of life.

Ironically, when we don't fight the unchangeable rules of life, we not only avoid the stress of clinging to try to control things that can't be controlled, we find a deeper happiness and appreciation for the miracles of life.

---

# MOVING TOWARD CONSCIOUSNESS AND WHOLENESS

Dr. Dave Richo, author of *The Five Things We Cannot Change: and the Happiness We Find by Embracing Them*

First of all, by the things we cannot change, I mean the givens of life that we have no control

▶

▶

over. The first one is central in Buddhism—the fact of impermanence, the given that everything will change and end. Second, pain is part of everyone's life; there's no way to avoid it, and there's nothing wrong with us just because we experience pain, psychologically or physically. Third, the people that we meet up with in life are not always going to be as loving and as loyal as we would want them to be. Fourth, the plans that we make don't always come to pass. We have certain ideas about the way things are supposed to go in our life and it doesn't necessarily happen that way. And, finally, the one that's so obvious is that life is not always fair.

By sayings "yes" to these givens, rather than complain about them, something happens inside us that gives us more depth as people, that gives us more compassion for other people who are dealing with the same givens. And it also gives us more character.

Here, I refer to the prayer/affirmation that's used in 12-step programs, that we would have "the serenity to accept the things we cannot change, the courage to change the things we can, and the wisdom to know the difference."

When we accept these givens with the realization that, if the world is like this, and since everything

▶

is evolutionary and moving toward more consciousness and more wholeness, it must be that these are the givens we need if we are going to evolve and grow. So, I'm not accepting them in resignation, I'm accepting them as if I am aligning myself to the ingredients or the components of true growth.

The "unconditional yes" to the conditions of our existence is a quote from Carl Jung. The basic idea is that when we are in the world, sitting in the saddle in the direction that the horse is going in, we're going to have a much smoother ride than when we are trying to go the opposite way. The way we would say "yes" is, first of all, by reminding ourselves that this is a given. It's not something that's my fault. I don't blame God or man. I simply say, "Oh, it's like this." I must find a place in myself that is able to say "yes" to the way it is, which would be equivalent to a loyalty to reality, rather than living in an illusion that things are different than the way they are. Secondly, is to notice that every given also gives us an opportunity. For instance, let's take the given of things not going according to our plans. That gives us the opportunity for surprising, spontaneous, synchronicities, unusual coincidences, new paths opening up, different from the standard routine that we've been trying to follow.

► So, I believe that there are wonderful possibilities in each of these givens. Some of these possibilities are not so appealing; for example, the given that "things change and end" gives us the possibility to grieve and let go. That's not much fun. But, when we do that, we notice that we become stronger, that we're living our life in keeping with the way reality is shaking out for us, rather than continually quarreling with it.

Accepting the "good" and the "bad," even embracing the stressful facts, is a form of mindfulness, according to Richo. Developing this ability can be achieved through engaging in mindfulness meditation. This is a practice of sitting with what is, without judging or trying to hide from it (see more about mindfulness meditation in Chapter 12, "Finding Our Way to Happiness with Meditation," and Chapter 29, "Mindfulness to Break the Pain Cycle.")

Feeling excitement about the unknown, how things may change in ways we could never dream of, is another way of embracing the is-ness of life and allowing ourselves to experience life to its fullest and in its most fulfilling aspects. Even painful experiences help us grow, and they prove that we're actually living life and taking risks, opening the doorway for new experiences and deeper love.

Best-selling author and speaker Dr. Deepak Chopra, writes about the sixth law of success, "The Law of Detachment," in his book, *The Seven Spiritual Laws of Success: A Practical Guide to the Fulfillment of Your Dreams.* He says, "In our willingness to step into the unknown, the field of all possibilities, we surrender ourselves to the creative mind that orchestrates the dance of the universe." If we allow ourselves to be with the "is-ness" of life, instead of wasting our energy trying to change the unchangeable, we will discover more meaning, fulfillment, joy, and vitality, with less anxiety and despair.

"I will step into the field of all possibilities and anticipate the excitement that can occur when I remain open to an infinity of choices. When I step into the field of all possibilities, I will experience all the fun, adventure, magic, and mystery of life," writes Chopra.

# Chapter 12

# Finding Our Way to Happiness with Meditation

*"Breathe and let be."*

~ Jon Kabat-Zinn, Internationally
known Meditation Expert

One very effective way to lower our stress level is through the practice of meditation. There are many different types of meditation. Meditation may include guided imagery, where we close our eyes and listen to someone leading us on a relaxing inner journey or guiding us to visualize different parts of our body relaxing. It might include focusing our attention on our breath, noticing the sound of our breath coming in and going out and/or counting our breaths or the length of our inhalations and exhalations. Meditation might include chanting a *mantra*, either aloud or silently. This might be a word or a phrase chanted in another language with a translation that we don't understand or in our own language with a peaceful meaning or an emotionally neutral connotation, just to give our mind a focus. One active mantra meditation includes chanting aloud the phrase, *Nam-myoho-renge-kyo*, which is a Buddhist chant from a Japanese sect of Buddhism, that is a combination of Sanskrit and Japanese and translates to mean, "devotion to the mystic law of cause and effect (karma) through vibration." There are many mantra meditations that are chanted aloud and/or silently from many different traditions. Just chanting silently with each breath, "peace," or the word, "one," can make a very effective practice of meditation.

Other forms of meditation might involve listening to relaxing music, nature sounds, the sound of a beating drum or a gong, or even singing. "Loving Kindness Meditation" (otherwise known as, "Metta Meditation") helps to increase a feeling of compassion and love within. This type of meditation involves feeling love, wishing happiness, and praying for the well-being of, first, yourself, then a good friend, then someone whom you don't know well, then for a person whom you have difficulty with, and then all humans on earth. In Chapter 25, "Time to Hit Your Mat," the benefits of yoga, which is, both a physical exercise and a moving meditation, will be discussed in greater detail, but yoga is a very effective form of meditation. Tai-chi and Qi-gong are also moving meditations, as is the very simple, but no less powerful, walking meditation. Then there is the practice of *Mindfulness Meditation*, which also overlaps with some of the meditations that were just mentioned.

I recommend trying a few different types of meditation and then deciding which you like the best. No matter which you choose, the bottom line is that meditating daily, even for just a few minutes, will lead to multiple benefits, including preventing and easing depression and anxiety, decreasing physical pain, and increasing emotional well-being, physical health, and cognitive sharpness (such as focus, concentration, memory, and attention).

"The brain science is very clear that meditation can also lower our blood pressure, lower our heart rate, and that it can allow us to manage chronic pain," Cathy Bonner of Austin's *Meditation Bar*, told me. "Meditation makes space in our brain for creativity and innovation." Brain imaging studies have found that meditation can actually change the structure of the brain. A study conducted by Britta Holzell and her fellow researchers, "Mindfulness Practice Leads to Increases in Regional Brain Gray Matter Density," was published in 2010 in the journal, *Psychiatry Research: Neuroimaging*. In this experiment, it was found that brain images of people who participated in a mindfulness-based stress reduction program showed changes in the gray matter density in those areas of the brain that are needed for new learning, memory, problem-solving, and emotional stability. Some of the research has found that mindfulness meditation can actually decrease the experience of physical pain so much so that some hospitals are now prescribing it for a variety of painful physical conditions and illnesses. In Chapter 29, "Mindfulness to Break the Pain Cycle," I discuss the use of mindfulness meditation specifically for decreasing physical pain and increasing the ability to cope with pain.

I can already hear the grumbling. "I tried to meditate, but I'm just no good at it," "I just can't sit still or clear my mind," "I have no time." But, before you skip this chapter, let's talk more realistically about the practice of meditation. I get it. Our lives are busy and most of us don't have hours at a time to sit in quiet contemplation, like Buddhist monks. And, when we do have time, it's difficult to get our thoughts to be quiet on demand. As soon as we sit down to be still, our thoughts are off to the races, with worries about what's on our to-do list or "should-haves" and "could-haves" from our day. Sometimes, we just completely conk out when we sit still because of our exhaustion from lack of sleep (if so, please be sure to read Chapter 27, "Getting Your ZZZs"). All of the above is actually fine. Just showing up for a few minutes on a regular basis is all that's needed for the benefits to occur. You don't have to be a "master" meditator (if you have this need, please re-read Chapter 9, "Taming the Inner Troll," for the link between the need for perfection and increased stress). The two "c's," *consistency* and *commitment* are the most important elements in order to see the benefits of any type of meditation you choose.

Mindfulness meditation, although born in the practice of Buddhism, is not a religious practice. It "has nothing to do with Buddhism per se or with becoming a Buddhist," writes psychologist, mindfulness meditation teacher, speaker, and author, Jon Kabat-Zinn, in his book, *Wherever You Go, There You Are: Mindfulness Meditation in Everyday Life.* "So, mindfulness will not conflict with any beliefs or traditions—religious or for that matter scientific—nor is it trying to sell you anything, especially not a new belief system or ideology.... Mindfulness means paying attention in a particular way: on purpose, in the present moment, and nonjudgmentally. This kind of attention nurtures greater awareness, clarity, and acceptance of present-moment reality." Mindfulness *meditation* "is about stopping and being present, that is all."

Yoga and Zen Buddhism teacher Frank Jude Boccio, in his article, "Calm Within," in the April 2018 issue of *Yoga Journal*, writes, "Mindfulness is like a floodlight, shining awareness on the whole field of experience – including sensations, emotions, and thoughts – as they arise and pass away in the dynamic, ever-changing flux that characterizes the human mind-body experience." Boccio, who also wrote the book, *Mindfulness Yoga*, adds, "Mindfulness allows you to see the nature of the unfolding process without getting caught in reactivity, without identifying with your sensations, emotions, and thoughts...The waves will keep coming, but you won't get swept away by them."

I was told that, when I was born, my parents were looking for a girl's name that began with the letter "M" in order to honor my dad's mother, Marie, who had died prior to my birth. My mom said she had wanted to find a name that was unique. She saw the name "Mara," had never heard it before, liked it, and so that was that. Since I was a child, people have frequently asked me the origin of my name upon introducing myself. Out of my own curiosity, as well as in order to be able to answer this question, I've done a little research about my name. I've discovered several stories about the name, Mara. For example, it's the original form of the name Mary. It's also the name of a river in Africa. But, the most surprising and, for me, the most ironic story of my name was the one I discovered when I had become interested in learning more about Buddhist meditation practices.

In Buddhist stories, Mara is the name of a god. He is a god who tempts us to lose our focus, creates self-doubt, and whom, if we pay too much attention to, will cause us to give up on our own calling and passions in life. On the positive side, Mara loses the power to tempt us off of our path when we accept him as a natural part of life and of ourselves and when we welcome him to, as the Buddha described it, "have tea" with us.

In her book, *Radical Acceptance: Embracing Your Life With the Heart of a Buddha,* therapist and meditation teacher, Tara Brach, describes the practice of Radical Acceptance as making "ourselves available to whatever life is offering us in each moment." It is "having tea with Mara," which is "pausing and then meeting whatever is happening inside us with…unconditional friendliness. Instead of turning our jealous thoughts or angry feelings into the enemy, we pay attention in a way that enables us to recognize and touch any experience with care. Nothing is wrong—whatever is happening is just 'real life.' Such unconditional friendliness is the spirit of Radical Acceptance" and it is the basis of mindfulness and *mindfulness meditation.*

# A SIMPLE WAY TO MEDITATE

*Sit comfortably, close your eyes, and focus on your breathing. There's nothing to change, nothing to control. Just notice the feeling of your breath as it comes in and as it goes back out. You might choose a simple word to say, silently, to yourself, as you breathe in and as you breathe out. For example, you can use the word "peace." Continue for about five minutes the first time. Your mind will want to jump to other thoughts. That's normal. Simply, notice your thoughts and label them, such as, "Oh, that's a thought about work. Oh, there's a thought about what I'm going to cook for dinner." Whatever it is, label it and tell yourself that you'll have plenty of time to think about that later. Every time a thought comes into your mind, notice it, let it go, and bring your attention back to breath or that word. If, at the end of five minutes, you have only had thirty seconds where you were fully focused on nothing but your breath and that word, then you were successful. The other four minutes and thirty seconds were the most important part of this meditation. That was the training time.*

Think about it like a paper-training a puppy. Your mind is like the puppy. Every time the puppy goes

▶

▶ off the paper, you don't yell at the puppy. You gently bring the puppy back onto the paper. In the same way, every time your mind goes off focus, you don't berate yourself or stop the meditation, you gently bring yourself back to focus. This is all part of the meditation. You may not feel relaxed the first time that you do it. But, after a while, you will start to notice the difference. It will get easier if you continue to show up the next day and the next day. You will start to notice that you're more resilient to the changes in your own life and in the world. You will feel less reactive, more focused, and more peaceful, no matter what's happening around you.

*To download my free Guided Meditation for Inner Peace, Joy, and Vitality, go to: DrMaraKarpel.com/ free-guided-meditation/.*

"Meditation is the simplest thing in the world to do," Jan Bidwell, MSW, LCSW, author of *Sitting Still: Meditation as the Secret Weapon of Activism*, told me in our interview. "There isn't anything simpler. But, that doesn't mean it's easy." Bidwell recommends finding a teacher to help with this practice and to practice once a week in a group when first learning to meditate.

Over and over again, the meditation teachers I've interviewed have all told me that there really is no "right way" to meditate and that the harder we try to get it "correct," the more we defeat the purpose of meditation, which is to feel calm. Several years ago, while I was living in New York, I heard about a Chinese Buddhist meditation center that was open to the public and had free meditation groups on Wednesday evenings. I decided one Wednesday that I could use some meditation with a group and that I would go check it out. Just before I left to find this place somewhere in Queens, a friend called to see what I was doing. When I told him that I was going to meditate, he asked to come with me. That was great for me because I had no idea where I was going and I figured that it's better to have company when getting lost in Queens at night.

When we arrived at the house, converted into a meditation center, we were told to take off our shoes and go upstairs. Then, the Chinese Buddhist monk met us at the meditation room and he said very few words. We were the only two meditators there besides the monk. "I'm going to ring the bell when it's time to start meditating," he said. "After an hour, I'll ring the bell again for you to stop meditating." "Wow! A whole hour," I thought to myself. "This is going to be challenging."

The monk handed each of us a pillow. "You sit on this pillow and face that wall," he directed my friend. "You sit on this pillow and face that other wall," he instructed me. Just before we sat on our respective pillows, each facing in opposite directions to have this "magical" experience of a full hour of relaxing meditation (or, so, I had hoped), the monk turned to my friend and said, in a cynical-sounding tone, "Do you know *how* to meditate?"

My macho friend from the Bronx puffed up his chest, as he replied, "Of course I know how to meditate!" The monk walked away, leaving us to our pillows and our walls, he sat down on a pillow facing the front wall, and then he rang the bell. As soon as I sat down, I thought about my friend, "I don't think he really knows how to meditate!" Soon my mind began to race and I could feel the anxiety rising, my chest pounding, my breath growing more rapid and shallow, "Do I know how to meditate? What if the monk can tell we're frauds who really don't know how to meditate correctly?" What an incredibly long and stressful hour that was! I was so stressed out that, after the bell rang, I quickly put on my shoes, ran outside, and burst into uncontrollable laughter, a reflexive release of tension. My friend looked at me in dismay. "You dragged me to this meditation hour and now you're laughing?" he asked, incredulously.

The stress that I created for myself during an hour of what was supposed to relax me was so absurd that it still makes me laugh, whenever I think about it. Said Terry Hershey, when he returned to my radio show for another interview, "We need to be able to laugh at our obsession of having to be perfect, like someone is going to win an award for finding sanctuary" —or for meditating perfectly well.

Although I've stated that there is no "right" or "wrong" way to meditate, spending the whole time of our meditation, however long it might be, wondering if we're doing it correctly or feeling that somehow we are a "fraud" in the way that we meditate, is so silly that it would probably be the definition of the "wrong" way to meditate.

## Part III

# Love & Relationships

Don't allow someone else's small-minded view of you
To take such a large space in
Your own mind.

# Part III
# Love & Relationships

*"Every morning, when we wake up, we have twenty-four brand new hours to live. What a precious gift! We have the capacity to live in a way that these twenty-four hours will bring peace, joy, and happiness to ourselves and others...Peace and happiness are available in every moment. Peace is every step."*

~ Thich Nhat Hanh, author of Peace is
Every Step: The Path of Mindfulness
in Everyday Life

We, humans, are social creatures by nature. We crave deep connections with others. However, when the lines of our connections are misfiring, relationships can cause us more pain than just about anything else. When we are disconnected from our inner knowing, our inner voice, and our soul's calling, our relationships with those closest to us will likely suffer the most.

Having a solid relationship with our self, knowing who we are and what we want, as well as finding that place of peace and love that always exists within, are the most important factors to fostering thriving relationships with others. This may be as simple as focusing on being peaceful within ourselves and peacefully accepting our partner with unconditional love. We could view this as a win-win situation, and one worth taking steps toward, even if this expedition sometimes consists of moving two steps forward and one step back. Most importantly, nurturing our own inner peace will not only create peace in the world and in our relationships, but will cultivate our own emotional and physical well-being—no matter what's happening outside of us.

# Chapter 13

# Phases of Relationships

*"Love gives naught but itself and takes naught but from itself. Love possesses not, nor would it be possessed, for love is sufficient unto love."*

~ Kahlil Gibran

We all know couples that have suddenly split up after being together for almost their whole lives, even when they had what appeared to us as the "best relationships." Dr. Dave Richo addressed this in his book, *The Five Things You Cannot Change*. "The first given of life is that changes and endings are inevitable for any person, relationship, enthusiasm, or thing...Our relationships pass through phases, from romance through struggle to commitment. Then they end with death or separation," he explains.

I'm sad for those couples. But such surprising break-ups serve as a reminder to us that it makes no sense to compare our own relationship to someone else's, nor do we need to have a "perfect" relationship because there is no such thing as perfection. Perhaps, just the willingness to grow and change in order to create *better and better* relationships is what's most important. Sometimes it works and sometimes it doesn't. There are never guarantees in life. And, even when we create what seems perfect, everything changes, as Dr. Richo wrote, and sometimes those changes bring us closer while, at other times, they cause us to drift apart.

Life has been turbulent for many of us lately. On top of feeling the collective angst occurring in the world right now (perhaps, just a magnified version of the angst that always exists), many of us are caring for aging parents, working hard to keep up with bills that seem to just keep piling up, and are experiencing the grief of many losses. Finding ourselves closer to realizing our dreams and experiencing other positive life changes can be sources of increased tension.

During times like these, it's too easy to take out such tension on those closest to us or to set unrealistic expectations on friends, family, and/or our partner to take away our discomfort. But, this only creates increased strain in our relationships, leading the way to more pain and separation. As the saying goes, "What you resist, persists"— and possibly grows stronger, so I decided, instead, to stop struggling in my own relationships—which ultimately means, first, that I would have to stop struggling with myself.

On the fifteenth anniversary of 9/11, I had a discussion on my radio program with Austin yoga teacher, Jonathan Troen, about the anxiety and anger all around us that was palpable that day, as well as throughout 2016, with the very contentious presidential election. "Peacefulness starts from inside of us and then spreads. It's contagious, just like anxiety," he said. The solution, Troen told us, is to find a way to create tranquility within ourselves, such as through practices like meditation, yoga, or Tai-chi, in order to create peacefulness in the world. Coming from a place of stillness within helps us to make better decisions about how to overcome any obstacles in our environment and our interactions.

Despite wanting instant relief, we may not be able to change the world or completely heal our relationships all at once. As the ancient Chinese philosopher, Lao Tzu once said, "A journey of a thousand miles begins with a single step."

And, so, I set out, at that point, on such a journey of a thousand miles to increase joyfulness in my own relationships. While looking for tools to take along, I came across a mantra put forth by Dr. Chopra, "Today, I will oppose nothing that occurs. I will resist nothing." I began experimenting with this mantra, using it, if I remembered in time, whenever having the desire to react. This worked best in my close relationships because the price of ruining those relationships was too high. Using this mantra led me to take a breath, rather than immediately reacting when I didn't like something. If further action appeared warranted, pausing gave me the time, the calmness, and the clarity to ask myself, "What can I do that will bring the most value to this situation?" The experiment went well, even when I didn't always remember the mantra immediately and used it, instead, after I'd already started to react. It worked to short-circuit my first reaction and kept me from causing further damage. This has now become a regular practice. Some days, it works like a charm. Other days, well, there's always tomorrow to start again.

I, like many, often feel the pressure to discuss what seems like important issues as soon as they come to my awareness. However, this is the time when we usually feel our worst, and the result of acting immediately is often disastrous. When we're angry or upset, we tend to blame others and are defensive when they point out our part in the problem. In addition, if we're angry when we speak, our partner (this also applies to our friends and our family members, by the way) is likely to react with anger and defensiveness. This will likely escalate to an argument that resolves no issues and, again, leads to more pain and isolation.

Dr. George Pransky, professor and marriage counselor, wrote in his book, *The Relationship Handbook*, "When your spirits are low is when you are most compelled to 'talk about things' and least advised to do so. Many of the statements you make then will seem false or damaging from the perspective of a higher mood…. Notice your inner feeling, your state of mind, before you deliver a sensitive message. If you have a chip on your shoulder, get your heart in the right place…When your heart is back in the right place, you will bring out the best in others."

In addition to our distorted perceptions caused by our own mood changes, it's also often the case that those things that we found exciting about our partner when it was a new relationship, now turn out to be the very things that we find most annoying," wrote Dr. Pransky. "Those differences represent opportunities to learn from each other. If you take the role of the student, the respect you show your mate will raise the level of the relationship." Remembering the excitement we felt about our partner's unique qualities, as well as being accepting of their other characteristics that seem like eccentricities to us, can create a more loving partnership, while demanding that they change will often create a wedge between us.

## Compromise-Compromise-Compromise

A few years ago, on the eve of my parents' sixty-first wedding anniversary, I videotaped an interview with both parents about how they met. I asked each of them how they made their marriage last for so many years. My dad's answer was quick and concise: "Compromise," he said.

Although we were taught the virtue of compromising when we were children, as adults we often tend to want everything to be exactly as we think it should be, especially in relationships. Reality is often quite different from that. When there are two people choosing to spend time together, sharing the ups and downs of life, there are going to be contrasting styles, at least in some areas. If we're lucky, we have some of those values that are most important to us in common with each other. However, it's the smaller, less important, dissimilarities that can be the most annoying. Our differences often complement each other and are what makes life interesting. But, they can also cause relationships to end, if we don't find a way to meet each other halfway. Let's take some advice from my dad and from the Nobel Peace Prize winner, Aung San Suu Kyi, who said, "If you want to bring an end to long-standing conflict, you have to be prepared to compromise."

Perhaps the biggest cause of dissension in relationships is that many of us have come to believe that if we can change those annoying habits of our partner, it will "cure" our relationship woes. On the other hand, it's a tremendous relief to realize that, since we can't change another person's behavior, we don't have to work at trying to perform this frustrating and impossible feat. Instead, we can focus on our only responsibility, that of controlling our own behaviors. "In every relationship there are two halves of that relationship...Of those halves, you are only responsible for your half; you are not responsible for the other half," wrote don Miguel Ruiz, author of *The Four Agreements*. "It doesn't matter how close you think you are, or how strongly you think you love, there is no way you can be responsible for what is inside another's head."

Dr. Albert Ellis, wrote in his book, *Dating, Mating, and Relating*, "There is no such thing as a mystical couple merged into one being. Therefore, you have to make efforts at changing a relationship first within yourself...Know that you can only directly change yourself... If you think you can change [your partner] or that s/he automatically *should* change, trouble will likely ensue!" Ironically, when we change our own behaviors, our partner, family members, friends, or co-workers, often respond by making behavioral changes, as well.

## Ebb and Flow

Finally, when we're with someone for a long time, we're bound to go through cycles. Sometimes we feel closer to each other than at other times. Jumping to the conclusion that things are "bad" when in the *ebb* of a relationship is a mistake. Perhaps it's a sign that the relationship needs more attention, more loving care, less of taking things for granted, or more trying new things together as a couple. But, it can also be a sign that each partner is having their own issues that need to be addressed in order to make themselves happy or to follow their own dreams. Given patience, compassion, and time, the relationship will likely begin to flow again.

# Chapter 14

# Love and the
# Independent Woman

*"I have yet to hear a man ask for advice on
how to combine marriage and a career."*

~ Gloria Steinem

Watching the extremely intelligent and compassionate Michelle Obama speak with so much dignity and self-assuredness, unfazed by some of the most hateful comments made about her, has been, frankly, very empowering for me as a woman. She has remained true to her message, "When they go low, we go high," in response to personal attacks. Watching her behave with class by letting negative comments roll off of her, as she continues to express her positive messages, has made it easier for me to not allow even lesser encounters with nastiness cause me to falter along my own path. Listening to her speak inspires me and seeing her popularity, in spite of those who have tried to bring her down, as well as the popularity of such powerful and influential women as Malala Yousifazi, Oprah, Christiane Amanpour, Cheryl Sandburg, Ellen DeGeneres, and Amal Alamuddin Clooney, to name just a few, bring me hope.

As I wrote about in Chapter 2, "Women Finding Our Voices," middle-aged and older women are often demeaned for looking and being older. We certainly see that play out in the entertainment world, where women continue to be "shamed" for how they look. But, women are beginning to push back, and my observation of this has forced me take a closer look at myself and at my own beliefs about my strength as a woman—and how that affects my relationships.

One way of empowering ourselves, whether man or woman, is to follow our dreams and our passion, rather than doing with our lives what we think we're *supposed* to do or what other people want us to, and by taking responsibility for our lives, making the choices that lead us to more happiness. For women, relationships with other women through networking, collaborating, mentoring, and developing friendships, are especially important for increasing the likelihood of attaining our dreams. There is tremendous power in women supporting women. In fact, collaboration and networking between women have been found to lead to greater success for women. It also helps us to develop those female role models who show us that our own success is possible and that a woman's voice can be powerful.

---

# TAKING YOUR TURN

### Carol Polcovar, Poet, Author, Playwright, Producer, and Teacher

I came from a family where girls, especially this girl, was treated equally or maybe with a little more respect than the boys. So, I didn't get that I was supposed to behave like a girl, whatever

▶

▶

that meant. But, I knew as I entered the world that something was *off*. We went to the theater a lot when I was a child, and one time, we saw a play where the opening scene had this teacher, a very attractive middle-aged woman, and she was in Italy. (That was one of my dreams, to teach, write, and travel.) There was a great opening to the play and I was very enthralled. Then I found out that everybody on the stage was coupled and everyone felt very sorry for this beautiful accomplished woman because she wasn't with a man, part of a couple. As the play progressed, we learned that she was also miserable for that reason and became involved in having an affair with an Italian man who was married. The play became a tragedy. So, it dawned on me at that moment that no matter what a woman did at that time, she could hold any job of esteem and it didn't matter; what mattered was if she had a husband. That was the be-all and end-all of any respect that a woman would get.

What has become evident, recently, something that has reared its ugly head, is the re-emergence of misogyny, not only among men, but also among women. We never got to fight the misogyny on our terms as women. There has been, over the past several decades, a return to gender*ization*. Little girls now have nail polish parties, where boys

▶

► are not invited, and little boys are having game parties, where girls are not invited. Once again, the games have become more genderized. The old ideas are getting replanted at a time when we would imagine that this was long gone.

Women have to begin to tell who they are without regard to the misogynist narrative that is very old and very entrenched. That I see as the biggest challenge, and it's not easy to do that, to raise consciousness. I find that older women have bigger and more complicated problems that come crashing down on their egos. This is because the plight of women, the acceptance of misogyny against them by many women, comes because women do get big rewards for conforming to these demands. A woman who is married is more admired than a woman who is single. Women who don't want children are always writing about how they get a lot of flack for not wanting children. Women with children are regarded in a different way. Women who are sexy and beautiful are far more admired than, say, a brilliant woman. So, there are a whole group of women, even feminists, who unconsciously have been living off of a status that begins to ebb in middle age. Then, we have all the narrative about older people. When that happens, it's an enormous crush to the ego. After devoting your

►

▶ life to being a "good girl," there's no payback, no gold watch, and no pension.

One piece of advice is that you have to go into yourself and be willing to trust who you are at your core. Everyone has a core made up of who they really are, with all of their dreams. If you haven't found your core and the things that you love, then you will have a problem, as you grow older. It doesn't matter how old you are when you do this; it matters that you do it. Your life becomes real and exciting when you do so. For some women, particularly those raised to be, "girls" —deferential, polite, neat, and willing to "wait their turn"— this is dangerous.

You have to *take* your turn. So a lot of us have to unlearn what we've been taught and what we've been praised for in our childhoods and perhaps throughout much of our lives.

▶

Sheryl Sandburg, COO of Facebook and author of *Lean In: Women, Work and the Will to Lead*, says, "But while compliant, raise-your-hand-and-speak–when-called-on behaviors might be rewarded in school, they are less valued in the workplace. Career progression often depends upon taking risks and advocating for oneself—traits that girls are discouraged from exhibiting."

We *must* step up—whether in a career or in a relationship. *Our voices, our wisdom, and our desires matter.*

It's also still true in this time that a woman is often praised more for marrying *well* and then having children than any of the other achievements in her life. Yes, it's wonderful for men and women to find someone to share life with. But, I find it amazing that in the twenty-first century, we continue to see a marriage proposal as a high achievement for a woman. This mindset causes us as women—and our family and friends—to diminish our own *true* achievements. After all, marriage is not really an "achievement" as much as it is a choice of lifestyle. If we choose a partner out of fear of being alone, rather than for love and compatibility, it will cause us to put off our own dreams in order to live out the dreams of others.

## Dating and Mating for the Independent Woman

I received my doctorate in 1992, when I was just turning thirty. It was then that I began the quest to understand myself better, to understand the world better, and to have a clearer picture of my place in the world. It was my "spiritual quest for enlightenment," so to speak. I soon discovered that, the more educated I had become and the more focused on following my own calling, the smaller the pool of choices for a partner there were for me. This is true for both men and women, but much more so for women.

There was a research study that was published in the journal, *Personality and Social Psychology Bulletin*, as recently as 2015, which confirmed this. In this study, it was found that the men who participated in the experiment voiced a greater attraction to women whom they were *told* were smart and who had outperformed the men on intelligence tests, when those women were not present in the room with them. However, when they were face-to-face with women in the same room, these men tended to rate the smarter women as less attractive and with less romantic interest. In the latter situation, when the smarter women were in close proximity to them, the men rated their own feelings of masculinity as being lower.

When I first came to the conclusion that there would be fewer men to choose from as potential romantic partners, it scared me. "Would I be alone forever?" I wondered. A *Newsweek* article with the findings of a study about single women and our chances for finding a marriage partner came out in the eighties. Everyone was still talking about it in the nineties. More accurately, many single women my age were *freaking out* about it. This study, supposedly, found that a college-educated single woman over the age of forty, who had never been married before, had a better chance of being killed by a terrorist than of ever getting married. This study caused many women my age to settle for someone who was not ideal for them, just so they wouldn't be one of those women destined for a lonely life of single-dom. Or, perhaps, it wasn't the fear of loneliness, but of not having "achieved" marriage. In any case, much of this particular study has since been debunked. For example, it did not include women who had chosen not to get married, but to cohabitate with a life-partner, which has become much more common in the last few decades.

Although it's more challenging (but far from impossible), to meet the right partner when one is an independent woman who is following her passion or calling, finding a high quality partner instead of settling for someone who is not the right match is certainly worth the extra effort. In fact, the research supports the fact that women who remain single are significantly happier than women who are in an unhappy marriage. Furthermore, as opposed to what is commonly believed, studies have found that men benefit more from marriage, with regard to life-satisfaction and health, than women do, in general.

## Finding the "Right" Partner

In spite of all the above, the fact remains that humans are social creatures, and most of us (even us independent women) do want to have someone to share our life with, no matter how educated, enlightened, and independent we are.

One of the most important characteristics that I've looked for in a partner, after having experienced the opposite of this in the past, is one who is secure enough with himself that he's not threatened by my independence and doesn't feel the need to control me in order to make himself feel good about his own masculinity. I'm sure there are many of you who've experienced that controlling partner, who has become more and more angry when you've made bigger and bigger strides toward following your dreams and may have even tried to sabotage your success. It's much more satisfying to be with a partner who's secure enough with him or herself that they aren't threatened by our success and, in fact, encourages us. It's exciting to have a partner who's inspired by our passionate living of life and will likely be following his/her own passion, as well. An independent woman is inspired by her partner's passion in following his or her own dreams and loves that her partner is her cheerleader when she takes big leaps of faith along her path. These are important ingredients for a strong and satisfying relationship with an independent woman.

# ON DATING

Crista Beck, Love Coach

By looking at your past relationships, in order to let go of those relationships, you have to jump into the past and observe at your self in the process— what you attracted and take responsibility for your behavior. Then you can see what didn't work. You can also see what *did* work because when a lot of people have a break up, they make the other person wrong and they really dwell on the negative.

When people can get to a clearer space, they can look at what they really loved and appreciated about that partner too, what they gained, and what were the positive things. Those positives are the gifts of being in a relationship. Then, when they begin dating again, the ideal is to focus on those positive things.

A lot of people put themselves in the negative when they get onto the dating scene. They say, "Well, I don't want this and I don't want that." It's important to look at what you do want because, when your attention is on the negative, then you'll attract the negative. And if you're focusing on what you don't want, you're closed. You're

▶ kind of saying "no" to life. But, if you switch it around and say, "I really want someone who is spiritual" or "I really want someone who is a good communicator," you're starting to look at what you really need and want. Focused on that, and then when you're on the dating scene, you can tell right away if someone is that or not.

As I coach people, I have them spend time brainstorming all of the things that they can potentially want in a partner. By writing all of these things down on a piece of paper and allowing yourself to explore everything you desire, then you can decide what are the "must-haves," what are the "nice to haves," what are the "bonuses." Then I have them narrow it down to the top ten must-haves, the top ten nice-to-haves, and the top ten bonuses. Then we narrow it down again, this time to just the top five things. I like to focus on these positives because it creates a filtration system.

Dating is really hard, no matter what age you are. It's scary. It can be terrifying just because you're putting yourself out there, and you might not know what you're doing. So, when people are armed with their five things that they know they really want in their heart, that's really true for them, that gives a lot of peace. Then, they're not just throwing themselves out there, hoping that chemistry or love is going to show up for them.

In addition to wanting a self-confident man, some of the other characteristics that I have looked for in a relationship have included someone with whom I could have an interesting discussion and someone with a great sense of humor. Another characteristic that has been in the "must have" category, meaning those things that are a necessity to me, is that of sharing similar values and views of the world. We don't have to agree on everything, but we must be in agreement about core values.

It's just as important to know what we don't want. I suggest thinking about what you're "deal breakers" are, those traits or behaviors of a potential partner that are not negotiable. It would be a waste of precious energy to spend time with someone whom you know has behaviors that go against your values or traits that just don't fit with who you are. For example, when I was in graduate school, I dated someone who was extremely controlling and was threatened by the idea that I might become successful. This is a trait that I learned that I could not tolerate in a relationship, it was a non-negotiable, and it was an automatic "no" to going any further in that relationship. Another non-negotiable would be someone who did not support me in following my dreams or who would want me to give up my own voice to make *them* my one and only priority.

If you're in the dating world, it will save you a lot of time and energy to spend some time thinking about what you want and to determine your "non-negotiables."

## Interdependence

The challenges for an independent woman include, not only, how to find the "right" partner, but also how to make the relationship work. As independent women, we're used to doing everything for ourselves and to not relying on someone to take care of us. The question is how to move from that way of thinking to one of *interdependence* when we're in a relationship, which is a necessity for any intimate relationship to flourish and grow.

---

# ALL IN

### Gigi Sage, Communication Expert, Founder of Happy, Health, Wealthy & Free

Any time that we're thinking "50/50," in our relationships, in the back of our minds, we're thinking, "Ok, is he or she putting in his or her 50 percent? Well, if he's not, then I'm not going to."

Unfortunately, this mindset causes relationships break down. First of all, the relationship becomes a blame-game. So, if you feel that you're partner isn't doing his/her "part," then you're always blaming. Secondly, it causes you to have one foot "in" and one foot "out." So, you're never fully committed to the relationship. Thirdly, you create a story, "Oh, he's not doing his part, so I don't have to do my part." And then you start talking about this story to your friends, creating drama that causes the relationship to break down.

Basically, the whole 50/50 game is about not being 100 percent committed. When it comes

▶

▶

down to anything in life, if you put 50 percent in, the results you receive in return will only be 50 percent. Think about it. If we go to our work and we put 50 percent in, what's going to happen? We'd probably lose our job.

The shift from 50/50 to 100/100 is what is needed for relationships to flourish. Now, you can't make your partner put in 100 percent, just like you couldn't make them put in 50 percent. All you can do is change yourself. That's true in most situations when it comes to communication. If you're invested in a relationship, look at how much of your time and energy you have already put into the relationship.

When you make this shift to putting in 100 percent, you don't have to do everything for everyone, you just have to put in your 100 hundred percent. One hundred percent is being fully committed to taking care of your own personal responsibility in the relationship. One of your responsibilities is to ask for what you want.

Write on a piece of paper exactly what you want in the relationship. Then describe what action it would take to have what you want. The next step is to ask for it in a positive way, rather than accusing your partner of not giving you what you want.

▶

> ► Give it six months of completely investing 100 percent commitment to the relationship. If it doesn't change and you don't feel that you're getting what you want after that time, then you might need to reevaluate if you're in the right relationship.

For me, independence does *not* mean that I have to do everything for myself and by myself. I know that I *can* do many things for myself and I know how to ask for assistance from others (or to hire someone) to help me with those things that I can't manage alone. I can be self-sufficient, if necessary, so that having a partner is not to fulfill a need to be taken care of. I know that the reason for my relationship is not because I would, otherwise, be helpless on my own.

Creating interdependence once we're in a relationship means that we know that we don't need to do everything and, in fact, that we allow our partner to help us with those things that he or she might be better at doing than we are or those things that he or she enjoys doing for us. In turn, we want to do what we can for our partner. Interdependence is a partnership, working together to be more than just the sum of the separate parts, adding to the quality of each other's lives, and taking care of each other out of love and affection. As independent as we are, we often desire and appreciate having a soft place to land in our relationships.

Many of us have been trained to believe in male and female roles in relationships. But fitting neatly into these prescribed roles is not what creates a loving partnership. Neither is losing our identities and forgetting who we are or what our dreams are in order to meld "into one." Respecting and honoring each other's authentic selves, adding to each other's lives, supporting each other in fulfilling each others' dreams, and loving unselfishly are what make a happy and strong partnership.

"Let there be spaces in your togetherness and let the winds of the heavens dance between you," wrote the poet Kahlil Gibran. And this makes a healthy, happy relationship.

## Other Factors of Modern Dating for the Independent Woman

In the twenty-first century, many people are meeting potential partners on the Internet and beginning relationships from across the country. While long-distance relationships certainly increase the pool of potential partners, they bring with them a new set of complications. For example, getting to know someone in person is critical in deciding if they're compatible. So, making time to spend together and getting to see how someone acts after a day or two of romantic vacation mode is important. After time, if the relationship progresses, the question becomes who will make the move so that the couple can be together in the same geographic location

I made such a move for a long-distance relationship. I had already decided that I wanted to leave New York because of the high cost of living and the stress of living in the New York Metropolitan area before I even met my partner, so that made the decision a little easier. However, the other factor in my decision was that I visited Austin, Texas, several times and decided that I really liked the city. I came to the conclusion, before I moved, that, no matter what happened in the relationship, I would like to give living in Austin a chance either way.

But, the stress of this type of move to a completely new place for a relationship doesn't end with the decision of who will move. The reality is that, when one person moves to a completely new place, they are likely to be dependent on their partner for everything until they have created their own networks. This can be a shock to the relationship, when the person who moved might, temporarily, be more dependent and feeling a bit more "needy."

Having a job in place as soon as I moved helped enormously, as I began to make my own friends at work. I also attended a workshop in Austin before moving, so that I had some people to connect with from that workshop when I moved to town. I would recommend getting involved in taking classes or doing something of interest to you, where you will network, prior to your move, so that your dependence on your partner for all social connections will be short-lived.

## When the Relationship Ends

Many of the women I know who are in their fifties and sixties, and suddenly single again, have made the decision to stay single for awhile in order to work on following their own dreams and passions before looking for another partner. Finding a compatible partner is time consuming and energy consuming, and most women, at this point of their lives, have already devoted much of their time to a partner and/ or a family, putting their own dreams on hold. These women often see this new aloneness as a chance to devote time to themselves and their own desires.

On the other hand, I've observed that most men in this age group, who are newly single, will tend to immediately look for another partner to fill that void. Perhaps, this is because they haven't had to give up quite so much of their own dreams while in prior relationships and while raising a family. This gender difference, of course, is a generalization and doesn't necessarily apply to every woman or every man. It is a good idea, however, whether a man or woman, to spend some time alone after a break-up to engage in some introspective work about what worked, as well as what didn't work and why. Without this reflection, you will run the risk of carrying baggage from one relationship right into the next.

The bottom line is that it's often more challenging for a strong, independent woman to find a partner who is the right fit for her. But, taking that time to find a compatible partner, rather than jumping into a relationship just to be in a relationship, is worth it and can save a lot of pain and lost time. And there's nothing wrong with being alone to get to know yourself and learning to enjoy your own company in the meantime.

# Chapter 15

# Surviving and Forgiving the Critics

*"Don't worry if you're making waves simply by being yourself. The moon does it all the time."*

~ Scott Stabile, screenwriter and author of *Just Love*

We all want to be loved and accepted, and being in a tribe or relationship is healthy. Problems occur when we go too far, squelching our own dreams and desires so that we don't make others upset with us. There will always be those who say that we're wrong, whether it's about taking our desired path or regarding our beliefs about what's happening in the world.

"If everyone loves you, you're probably playing *waaay* too safe. If you're real, at least a few people might be annoyed. A little criticism sometimes can be an awfully good sign," wrote Tosha Silver in her book, *Outrageous Openness: Letting the Divine Take the Lead*.

However, while "a little criticism" might be a "good sign," sometimes people go way too far. Lately, I've been noticing people on social media, even "friends," resorting to verbally assaulting each other to a degree that I've never seen before. Perhaps, this trend reflects our way-too-extreme comfort with social media so that we feel brave enough from behind the shield of the computer screen to make rather insulting personal comments toward people whom we consider to be our friends.

Worry about what others say or think about us can certainly keep us from staying on the path toward our calling, our true purpose in life, and our higher, "bigger," mind. Recently, someone whom I barely know wrote a long negative tirade about me on social media. One of the many unkind comments stuck with me. He stated that I was "small-minded." I've put a lot of thought into those particular words. I want to have an expansive mind that keeps my eye on the larger picture of my life, the gifts that I can bring into the world, and how to truly live in the light while spreading light.

There will always be garbage to take out, laundry to do, bills to pay, traffic jams, and car troubles. Sometimes, there will even be larger stresses, losses that cause us to feel like the rug has been pulled out from under us. But, in spite of all of these, I know it's possible to get back on track and connect to our higher mind, keeping our focus on our North Star—our purpose on this earth. Doing this takes having an open and expanded heart as the "mind" does not all exist in our head, but also in our hearts. Compassion is a key element of this mind-expansion. It's also what grounds us in reality and keeps us from completely floating away into a fictional dream.

One major stumbling block that keeps our mind small and prevents us from this blissful expansion is our obsessional thinking about the mud that is more than likely slung at us, at least once, along our path. It's an inevitability that there will be people who are filled with pain and feel that attacking others is a way to release their own pain.

## One Absolute Truth

So, how do we deal with these criticisms and even verbal assaults, especially when they come from our friends, family, or partners? Even people who care about us may become frightened when we take bold steps toward following our dreams and might react with intense criticism that isn't always helpful. Richo writes in *The Five Things We Cannot Change* that one of the absolute truths that we cannot change is that "people are not loving and loyal all the time." That applies to even our closest relationships. He points out that once we accept this as an absolute truth, we won't be disappointed when it happens that those people who are dear to us say or do something that is the opposite of what we might consider loving. Letting ourselves get caught up in the slings and arrows directed at us will more likely than not lead us to stop the expansion of our own mind and cause us to end up living the words written about me, having a "small mind."

Richo's recommendation for preventing hurt feelings is to keep the focus of the disagreement on the topic discussed, rather than personally attacking each other. "The choice in communication is between two approaches: adult problem solving with focus on the issue or an ego-competitive or defensive style with focus on winning, self-assertion, and not losing face." The latter approach is most likely to lead to bitterness.

No matter how much we try to prevent it, though, there will be times that hurtful criticisms are made.

## Some Observations

While many of my mentors and teachers along my journey have been those who have touched my soul with their light and helped me to find my own light, sometimes the most impactful teachers have been those I've come across on the path who, like a venomous snake, spew their toxins at me from their own place of pain. Often, it takes a bit of digging to unearth the real lesson mixed in with the venom.

We're living in a time when anger and meanness appear to be spreading like epidemics, including friends fighting friends about differences of opinion, making it personal and becoming mean. There are also bullies who make it their goal to hurt. Remember when we were kids and we used to recite the rhyme, "Sticks and stones will break my bones, but words will never harm me?" That was a lie. Words hurt. We hear almost daily about suicides of teens that have been bullied with words.

There appears to be an increase in a general lack of compassion. Some people are losing touch with the art of really listening to one another in order to fully understand what the other person might feel or to learn about their experiences.

## Some Lessons I've Learned for Surviving the Critics and Detoxing from Venom (and for Expanding My Mind)

1. Very often people strike out when they, themselves, are experiencing deep emotional pain. Sometimes, they put people down in order to feel superior. This does not make their behavior O.K. But, having that understanding helps us to have compassion and to not take what is said personally. In *The Four Agreements*, don Miguel Ruiz tells us, "Don't take anything personally....Nothing others do is because of you. What others say and do is a projection of their own reality, their own dream. When you are immune to the opinions and actions of others, you won't be the victim of needless suffering."

2. When we practice mindfulness (see Chapter 12, "Finding Our Way to Happiness with Meditation"), we can take a step back, away from the venom, and see it more clearly as being more about the other person than it is about us. Mindfulness also gives us the ability to calm down and to better think through our response, rather than reacting in a more harmful way. "With mindfulness we

can see clearly, free ourselves from reactivity, and respond wisely," writes Jack Kornfield, in his book, *A Lamp in the Darkness*.

3. Every morning, I silently recite a self-affirmation that I created, using Kornfield's meditation, "The Earth is My Witness" as a guide. *"Let my body be solid like a mountain and my mind open like the sky. May I rest on the Earth like a Buddha and become acquainted with my capacity to witness all that arises and to remain centered and stable and steady in the midst of it all."* Imagery and affirmations can be quite potent in helping us to pull the lens back and expand the picture in front of us, rather than getting caught up in the *small mind* of feeling victimized.

4. Cry, if you feel like it. Tears are cleansing and can be a detoxing release. Also, telling a close trusted friend about our difficulties, someone who can help to put things into a better perspective, may help you view the bigger picture. Holding it all inside creates more intense energy. However, there needs to be a balance. Talking about it over and over again actually intensifies energy. So, don't keep talking about it, once you've released it. Also, choose your confidantes wisely. Not everyone has your best interest at heart and others may offer well-meaning advice that might create more problems. Sometimes, speaking to an objective mental health professional is your wisest option.

5. Surround yourself with positive people who treat you with respect and love. When we do this, it helps us to see that we are worthy of love, and it reminds us of how we want to be treated by others. It also increases our own self-love when we are around people who model genuine, not narcissistic, self-love (see Chapter 17, "Increasing Self-Love"). In addition, showing kindness and compassion to others, rather than taking out our sadness or anger on others, is extremely powerful in transforming negative

energy into healing energy (for more about the healing benefits of kindness and compassion, check out Chapter 18, "Giving without Expectation"). This also serves our greater purpose by increasing the kindness in our communities and by opening our hearts to increase our compassion. Writes Kornfield, "Your experience of being human in this way—opening to the ten thousand sorrows and joys of yourself and others—becomes a kind of salvation."

## Shades of Gray

Finally, we need to ask ourselves if we also have become so caught up in being *right*, that we find ourselves making personal attacks toward others, as well. The ego thrives on proving our rightness. But, the momentary thrill of winning an argument, if that actually happens, is just that: momentary. It doesn't bring joyfulness within, nor does it bring peace to the world. It serves, instead, to increase our grief and separation from each other. Even more importantly, it serves to increase our separation from ourselves. It eats at our time and takes away from our energy to follow our passions, to find out what our passion is, or to help our neighbors. Many arguments are based on a false belief that things are black and white, while the world, in actuality, rarely functions in a state of black and white. Most of what we encounter is filled with various nuances and shades of gray. But, gray doesn't feel secure; it's the unknown, and that makes us uncomfortable, so we grasp for black and white, making ourselves right and the other wrong, causing more distance and pain.

If we're willing to accept the many shades of gray we encounter throughout the moments of our lives, the happenings in the world, and in our discussions with others, we are more likely find to ourselves feeling a deeper connection to others and with life. By embracing the grays of the journey, past the "rightness" and "wrongness," through the ups and downs, the flavorful sips of what life gives us, even the losses—we find the effervescent colors that are hiding in our connection to a universal peace. We need only to allow life to be as it is, moment-by-moment, breath-by-breath—letting the drama just be.

As Sufi poet Rumi, wrote, "Out beyond the ideas of wrong-doing and right-doing, there is a field, I'll meet you there."

Remember, when we let the mud slinging of others become our reality, we rob ourselves of the expansiveness of our lives and who we really are. Freedom comes from knowing that our true self is the open-hearted observer of all that is and that we don't need to be pulled into the mud all around us in order to be fully alive.

# Chapter 16

# The Power of Forgiveness

*"Forgiveness is the fragrance that the violet*
*sheds on the heel that has crushed it."*

~ Mark Twain

Extremely important in the equation of healing relationships and creating more satisfying ones is the act of forgiving, both forgiving others and forgiving ourselves. The most that we can ask of people in our life and of ourselves is that we all do the best that we're able to at this moment.

In her book, *You Can Heal Your Life*, Louise Hay wrote, "Forgiveness opens our hearts to self-love…That person who is the hardest to forgive is the one who can teach you the greatest lessons. When you love yourself enough to rise above the old situation, then understanding and forgiveness will be easy. And you'll be free."

Forgiveness is necessary for our own well-being. Anger and resentment burns up our energy and keeps us stuck. Forgiveness releases this anger and increases our ability to feel joyful and peaceful. It can even improve our health, because holding onto anger has been linked to many health issues, including cardiac dysfunction and chronic back pain.

Leadership expert Kathy Sparrow says, "Miracles happen when we are courageous enough to heal for our own benefit. Then forgiveness is possible, and we become free of any hooks and resentments that ⱻep us from truly living our own lives." Sparrow related a personal story to demonstrate the power of forgiveness. Her first marriage to the father of her two children was extremely volatile, she told me, and yet eighteen years after their divorce, they were able to break bread over Thanksgiving and have since celebrated many family occasions together with their children, including the birth of four grandchildren. "We've all done our work to forgive and move on. What a beautiful legacy to leave to our children and grandchildren," said Sparrow.

## Forgiveness is for You

We often hold grudges toward people who may no longer be in our lives, as well as people who may continue to play important roles in our lives. In order to create positive relationships with those who are still in our lives, we must forgive them. If not, these relationships will continue to bring us pain, and we will in turn bring pain to those people. What would be the point, then, of remaining in a relationship, if we were just going to create more pain and hurt?

Less urgent, but equally important, however, is to forgive those who are no longer in our lives. Without doing this, we hold onto the burden of anger and resentment and weigh ourselves down—essentially punishing ourselves. Oprah Winfrey wrote, "[Forgiveness] is letting go so that the past does not hold you prisoner." Furthermore, without forgiveness, we are likely to find it difficult to create positive, satisfying new relationships. As an anonymous author wrote, "If you carry the bricks from your past relationship to the new one, you will only build the same house."

You may feel that you don't want to forgive someone who you perceive to have wronged you. Perhaps you believe that, if you were to let go of the resentment and actually forgive that person, you would be condoning the behavior and making yourself vulnerable for someone else to hurt you. Congratulations for making the decision to not stick around when someone treats you poorly. However, there's a big difference between forgiveness and approval of poor treatment. Just because you decide to forgive someone doesn't mean that you need to ever see that person again. On the other hand, you might have decided to stay in a relationship with that person. Perhaps, the hurtful event happened long ago and that person has changed their ways. Or, maybe, you realize that the hurt was mutual, and the two of you have repaired those unhealthy dynamics in your relationship. Even if you have decided to stay, forgiveness doesn't mean that you will not set limits about how you are to be treated.

Forgiveness is all about you. It's about making the decision to release the anger and bitterness that burn up your energy and keep you stuck. It's about increasing your ability to feel joyful and peaceful. In *The Relationship Handbook*, Pransky tells us, "People think of forgiveness as a generous act, but it is actually very self-serving. If you have painful memories, you suffer. They're like burrs that rub your skin every time the memories are stimulated. Getting rid of the burrs so your wounds can heal is really being nice to yourself." I've found that as soon as I can forgive, I feel as if a weight has been lifted off of my shoulders, and I'm free to move forward in my life. I realize that when I have held onto old anger, it has kept me living in the past, re-living old hurts. Weighed down by old baggage leads to pain and is a big distraction from following my dreams, which is quite antithetical to how I want to live my life.

## How to Forgive

Having the intention to forgive is the single most powerful and important step in making progress toward releasing the pain of old anger and moving toward greater joy and emotional freedom. It might help to find someone you trust, such as a trusted friend or a mental health practitioner, to speak with about the issue. Writing about it in a journal can also be helpful.

Additionally, be willing to make an effort to see where the other person was coming from in their own life when they did whatever they did. This is not about making excuses for their hurtful behavior, but, instead, as I wrote about in the last chapter, realizing that people hurt others when they've been hurt themselves or when they don't know better. Oprah Winfrey has frequently stated, "When you know better, you do better." It's likely that the person was doing the best they could with what knowledge or internal resources they had at the time, even if their best was not very good.

"Understanding lets us see the humanity of other," writes Pransky. When we understand that "every misguided action is accompanied by an insecure state of mind...the more misguided the action, the greater the insecurity and fear," then we move closer to forgiveness and to "peace with ourselves and the painful thoughts that have been sitting in our minds tormenting us." If my feelings have been hurt and I'm having trouble seeing the other person's perspective, I will often speak to one of my trusted friends, one whom I know will strive to be objective and honest with me. This will usually lead to gaining a different perspective, one that I could not see because I was too close to the situation. And, often this new perspective gives me a better understanding of why the person I'm angry at might have done what they did. That, alone, feels like it lifts a weight off of my shoulders, especially if the person I've been angry at is one who is close to me.

Some people find it helpful to have a ceremony for releasing and letting go of their resentments. Try writing a letter to the person who you perceive as having hurt you. But, do not actually send that letter. (Seriously, don't send it. This is for you to do to release your feelings.

Sending it will only stir up more angry interactions and increase the resentment.) Then, bury or burn the letter as a symbol of letting it go.

## Learn from the Pain

Learning from your pain is an important part of forgiveness. It's important to ask what lessons you learned about yourself and about relationships from the hurtful event? Perhaps, there were things you could have done differently at the time to bring about a different outcome, even if that was to let that person know that their behavior was unacceptable. Then, forgive yourself for your part. Forgiving yourself is a critical piece of the forgiveness puzzle. In order to love yourself, you need to forgive yourself for choices you've made. Make the decision to try to do better every day.

And, maybe, what you learned was that you are strong enough to survive being hurt and are capable of continuing to create a joyful life in spite of it. "What didn't you do to bury me, but you forgot that I was a seed," wrote the Greek poet, Dinos Christianopoulos.

Not long ago, an experience triggered an old resentment. I was very surprised by this because the event was something that I believed I had long ago let go of and had forgiven, happily moving forward with my life. But, on that day, I noticed my thoughts and emotions began to spiral down on a negative course. The result was that I felt low in energy and irritable. I didn't understand my reaction. This lasted for a couple of hours until I realized what was happening. At that point, I interrupted the downward spiral by looking at it with curiosity. What I discovered was that, although I thought I had already forgiven all involved in the incident, I had not forgiven myself. I still felt angry at myself for the part that I had played in the particular situation and, mainly, for not having better protected myself from being hurt. This was an "ah-ha" moment. I hadn't been aware that I had even felt that way in the first place. When I shed light on it, I was able to rationally understand that we can't always protect ourselves from hurt. Sometimes hurt happens, and we can heal, if we allow ourselves to.

## Ho'oponopono

There is an ancient Hawaiian ritual for forgiveness, which is especially effective for self-forgiveness. It's called, Ho'oponopono. This ritual consists of four steps. The first step is "repentance," saying, "I'm sorry." This, as well as the statements that are part of the other three steps, do not have to be said out loud, in order to be effective, or to anyone in particular. The next step is to say, "Please forgive me." The third step is gratitude. Repeat, "Thank you" over and over again. And the last step is to say, "I love you." Then this series of steps is repeated over again several times in succession. Although simple, this four-step practice has been found to be extremely healing.

The more we practice forgiveness, the easier it becomes to forgive in the future. Practice forgiveness with other people and with yourself daily. When you decide to let go of grudges, notice how joyful you feel and how much freer you are to live the life you love.

I know that everything that has happened in my life, good or bad, is my story and has led me to all of the good things that are in my life now. I have grown from my experiences, and they have brought me the confidence that I can grow from all future experiences. These events have added to my compassion. Dr. Wayne Dyer wrote, "With everything that has happened to you, you can either feel sorry for yourself or treat what has happened as a gift. Everything is either an opportunity to grow or an obstacle to keep you from growing. You get to choose." I choose growth.

# Chapter 17

# Increasing Self-Love

*"If we really love ourselves,*
*everything in our life works."*

~ LOUISE HAY

As I wrote in the previous chapter, forgiving ourselves in a necessary first step toward self-love. And self-love is necessary if we are to be free to enjoy life, following our dreams and forming loving and satisfying relationships. "Before you can love others, you must love yourself first." This is a platitude that we hear time and again. But, when it comes down to it, the idea of loving oneself is a foreign concept to most.

"Love is the very core of who we are, but unaware of this essential aspect of ourselves we run around searching for it, assuming it is missing from our lives," wrote Shubhraji, in her book, *In the Lotus of the Heart: The Essence of Relationships*. "If we want to experience genuine love, we must overcome this tendency to look to the external world for it." When we can genuinely love ourselves, then we are better equipped to create more loving and fulfilling partnerships.

One of my favorite parables, painting a picture of how self-love, or its absence, affects our relationships, is the story of the "Magical Kitchen," in *The Mastery of Love: A Practical Guide to the Art of Relationship*, by don Miguel Ruiz. In this tale, Ruiz asks us to imagine that we have a magical kitchen in our home and that, we can create any food we want to eat at any time. One day, someone knocks at our door, offering us a pizza. They offer to bring us pizza every day on the one condition that we do whatever they want us to do, that we let them control our life. In such a situation, as Ruiz points out, we're likely to turn down the pizza, knowing that we can have pizza, or anything else we want to eat, whenever we want to eat it, from our own magical kitchen. "No one will manipulate me with food," Ruiz predicts we would say, while laughing at such a silly offer.

In this story, don Miguel Ruiz goes on to then have us imagine an alternative situation. In this scenario, we are starving, we haven't eaten for weeks, and we have no money to buy food with. That same pizza deliveryman comes knocking at our door once again holding a pizza. (I like to embellish this story when I tell it, saying that the pizza has anchovies on it, because I have a particular dislike for anchovies, but I know that if I were starving, I would eat the pizza anyway.) He offers to keep supplying us with pizza to fill our empty belly, but he has the same condition as before. That is, we must do whatever he wants. In this situation, we're likely to accept such a ridiculous condition of being controlled by another because we're starving, and we're promised food to fill our empty belly if we go along with such an agreement.

"Now imagine we are talking about love," writes Ruiz. "If you are starving for love and you taste that love, you are going to do whatever you can for that love. You can even be so needy that you give your whole soul just for a little attention." Just like the magical kitchen, our heart "already [has] all the love you need…You have to focus on the most wonderful relationship you can have: the relationship with yourself." Developing this self-love is necessary in order to create healthy loving relationships, in which we aren't overly needy, we aren't being controlled by another, and nor are we trying to control anyone.

Often, we go through life receiving messages from people who are important to us, as well as from the media, telling us that we're not whole unless we buy what they're selling—whether it's a belief about the way life should be lived or a product or service. When we accept these messages, we become focused on our own imperfections, rather than seeing ourselves for who we really are, beings who are "perfect" even in our imperfection.

## Tips for Increasing Self-Love

Now that we've discussed the why of increasing self-love, let's talk about how to do it. Here are some tips for increasing the magical kitchen in our own hearts:

1. **Treat yourself like you're worthy right now, even if you don't believe it.**

   This includes taking care of your body by eating a healthy diet (see the chapters in Part IV, "Food for the Soul") and exercising (see the chapters in Part V, "Vitality of Mind and Body"). And begin to take action toward achieving your dreams. By following our dreams, we contribute to creating a beautiful world (see the chapters in Part I, "Follow Your Dreams"), we create joy in our own lives, and we begin to feel worthy of experiencing joy.

2. **Do things throughout the day, everyday, that cheer you or inspire you.**

   Here are some examples of what works for me: listening to music that I enjoy, reading something inspiring, taking a nap, walking in nature, exercising, sitting still and breathing slowly, drinking a delicious cup of coffee or a cup of tea while reading an inspiring book, or doing some yoga. Do what makes you feel more vital and alive. It doesn't have to be something big. When you make this a daily priority, you are giving yourself the message that you deserve to be treated well.

3. **Surround yourself with positive people who love themselves and who treat you with love and respect.**

   Humans best learn by observation. If we observe people who love themselves and who love and respect the people around them, we learn how to do the same. Reduce or eliminate the amount of toxins you ingest and the amount of time you spend with toxic people. By being around positive, loving people, we come to realize that we're worthy of love and respect.

4. **Turn off the negative, derogatory self-talk.**

   The voice in our head might come as the voices of our parents or other important people in our lives, or as our own voice, questioning our value or telling us that we are "victims." When author of the book, *Self-Talk for a Calmer You: Learn How to Use Positive Self-Talk to Control Anxiety and Live a Happier, More Relaxed Life*, Beverly Flaxington, was interviewed on my show, she pointed out, "It's our own minds, so often, that defeat us. We say things to ourselves and tear ourselves down. The self-talk that we use on ourselves absolutely drains us. Lack of confidence and low self-esteem is very typically an outgrowth of too much negative self talk too often." In order to be able to really love ourselves, it's important that we become aware of this negative chatter and to understand that this chatter is not the "truth." Then, even if we can't turn it off completely, it will lose its power over us and, perhaps, the volume will soften (re-read Chapter 9, "Taming the Inner Troll").

5. **Stop listening to negativity of others.**

   Remember, a person's tendency to put another down is caused by his or her own lack of self-love (review Chapter 15, "Surviving the Critics").

6. **Forgive others and forgive yourself.**

In Chapter 16, "The Power of Forgiveness," I wrote that forgiveness doesn't mean that you condone other people's bad behavior. Rather, it frees you from perpetually being caught in the web of victimhood. Forgiveness of self is also important. We can't move forward to realize our dreams if we're continually beating ourselves up for our past mistakes. If we reframe these experiences as lessons, we learn, we grow, and then we can move on.

7. **Make a list of your positive traits.**

You may notice that you're very good at finding things about yourself that you don't particularly like. Now, sit down and make a list of those qualities about yourself that you actually like. Spend some time every day expanding this list.

8. **Treat yourself like you would your own best friend.**

Would you be so hard on your best friend about the same things that you so quickly and easily criticize yourself about? Try this: Sit down across from an empty chair. Visualize yourself sitting in that chair. Envision that the *you* in that chair is your BFF (Best Friend Forever), who is sharing with you all of his or her perceived weaknesses. How would you respond to your BFF? Make it a regular practice to talk to yourself with the same compassion you show to your BFF whenever you start to put yourself down.

9. **Have a sense of humor, even about your own mistakes.**

If we can laugh at ourselves, then we can foster a more realistic perspective, one that recognizes that we're only human and that mistakes are events to learn from, rather than signs that we're inept or that our character is severely flawed (see Chapter 10, "The Power of Humor").

Once we learn to love ourselves, then that feeling that there is a hole inside that we need to fill with food, drugs, unhealthy relationships, and other addictive behaviors closes up. By engaging in self-loving behaviors, we're more able to live a life of happiness and fulfillment and filled with joyful, loving relationships.

# Chapter 18

# Kindness and Giving without Expectations

*"We make a living by what we get,*
*but we make a life by what we give."*

~ WINSTON CHURCHILL

I took my mom shopping one day on one of my recent visits to see her in New York. We found ourselves crossing the street at a busy outdoor shopping mall. There were cars stopped and waiting for us in both directions at the crosswalk, as we ambled across, my mom with her walker, watching her every step to make sure that she didn't lose her footing on the uneven ground. I was concerned that the drivers might become impatient and start to move before we had safely made it across. When I looked over at each of the drivers waiting for us, one waved to signal he was waiting patiently and the other opened his window. "Take your time," he called out. "You've earned it." Smiling, he pointed to my mom, "She has earned it!"

"Yes, she has," I thought and smiled back. When we arrived at the store that we were looking for, a passing shopper came over and opened the door for us, as I helped my mom navigate the steps at the threshold. I had thought that the woman was heading into the same store we were, but when we got inside, she did not come in with us and kept walking. I realized that she had just walked over with the purpose of helping us.

These might seem like very minor good deeds, but the results of these acts of kindness were significant for us. The research shows that the minor hassles in our daily lives are responsible for greater feelings of being stressed out than even those events we consider to be significant stresses because stress is cumulative. Encountering people throughout the day who show kindness toward us, even in small ways, has the powerful effect of counteracting some of that stress. If those drivers had honked their horns for us to hurry or if no one had helped to open the door of the store for my mom and me, I would have felt frazzled and exhausted by the end of our shopping excursion. Even worse, my mom, feeling anxious about the challenging situation, might have taken a disastrous misstep.

Instead, we both felt more at ease and enjoyed our stressful shopping excursion. And, having been on the receiving end of kindness and generosity of spirit, we both felt inspired to be kind and generous toward people whom we met. In fact, the positive effects have continued long since that day. Not only that, but I bet those kind people, experiencing all of the health and emotional benefits of their generosity of spirit, have continued to feel inspired to be kind in their own daily lives, further effecting the lives of others. And so, with this ripple effect, they have begun a cycle that will create a kinder world.

The above acts of kindness are in stark contrast to my experience on the airplane on my way to New York for that same visit. On the last leg of my trip, the man next to me sat sprawled in his seat, as well as across half of the space in front of my seat and the armrest between us. And he never once acknowledged the presence of a person sitting next to him; he never once looked at me. While he wasn't outright rude, his lack of consideration was far from kind. Although I'm a relatively small person and he was tall, the assumption that he was entitled to half of my leg and arm space, without the slightest recognition of my right to have some room or that I was even sitting there, was disrespectful. I arrived at my destination feeling stressed out, irritable, and angry with myself for not having asserted myself to ask for a little consideration and space.

What I've noticed is that such boorish behavior has become more of the norm, while the acts of kindness that I mentioned have seemed to become less common. It appears that, in many ways, we have become a more selfish, self-centered, and, even, meaner society. Many rarely go out of their way to help others without wondering, "What will I get out of this interaction…behavior…gift?" Companies—that we believed were there to help us—have placed more emphasis on the bottom line than on serving the greater good. Our social media interactions have become cold and often threatening. As a society we just might be at a breaking point. We will, either, come together in the spirit of kindness or we will completely disappear down the rabbit hole of an "each person for them selves" mentality.

Yet, all is not lost. There are many who have been awakened and who have made a conscious effort to choose the former, rather than be fated to the latter. I tend to be an optimist about this and there is recent evidence that my optimism is not unfounded. I have witnessed more and more people asking, "What can I do to make a difference in the world? How can I be of service?"

Many retirees are choosing to go back to work or to volunteer in ways that will have an impact on the world, helping those who are most in need. Furthermore, many young people are now choosing careers, motivated by the goal of being impactful global citizens and making a "difference," rather than filling their own bank accounts. There is a unifying realization among us that we don't want to live in an angry world and that the antidote to meanness is, as Ghandi said, to "be the change you want to see in the world," and intentionally engage in acts of kindness and generosity.

## Benefits of Kindness and Generosity

Acting with such benevolence isn't all about self-sacrifice. The acts of kindness and generosity (I will use generosity and kindness interchangeably, as *kindness* can be called *generosity of spirit*) actually have many benefits to the giver. Several recent studies have found that being kind and generous increases our ability to cope with physical pain and symptoms of chronic diseases. Volunteering has been associated with significant decreases in blood pressure, stomach acid, and cholesterol levels, and increased Immunoglobin-A, which boosts our immune system. In fact, volunteering has been correlated with a lowered risk of mortality in older adults, decreased symptoms of stress, and better sleep. This is due to the phenomenon called "the helper's high," which is a release of endorphins (those natural mood-elevating and pain-reducing chemicals produced by the brain) when we engage in an act of generosity.

At the University of California, a study conducted by Dr. Sonja Lyubomirsky found that acting in a kind manner actually increases the serotonin in our brain, which is a key neurotransmitter responsible for our mood, energy, sleep, sharpness of thought, digestion, and health. Therefore, generosity of spirit can be more effective than taking an antidepressant for increasing our feeling of well-being, eliciting a more positive mood, and increasing our feeling of self-worth, as well as improving our ability to learn, our memory, our sleep, and our health. The students who participated in her study were asked to commit five random acts of kindness per week over a six-week period. At the end of the study, these students were found to have an increase of 41.66 percent in their level of happiness. In another study conducted by Harvard University researchers, those people who volunteered time or money to help others were found to be 42 percent more likely to rate themselves as being happy.

## Finding Meaning

One of the most powerful things we can do to find meaning in our own lives is to help others. "Since depression, anxiety, and stress involve a high degree of focus on the self, focusing on the needs of others literally helps to shift our thinking," says Lyubomirsky. "Having a positive effect on someone else can increase our self-esteem and give our life a greater sense of purpose." There has been an ongoing study at the University of Notre Dame, led by researchers Christian Smith and Hillary Davidson, called the "Science of Generosity Initiative." Their discoveries have shown that those people who demonstrate more generosity tend to have a greater feeling of purpose and meaning in their lives and to feel emotionally happier, and physically healthier. And finding meaning and purpose in our daily lives brings greater enthusiasm to pursue our own dreams.

Psychiatrist, Dr. Viktor Frankl, learned from his experience as a prisoner of two concentration camps during the Holocaust that those people who were the most resilient in this intensely horrific situation were those who found meaning by helping their fellow prisoners, giving of themselves, even if all they had to offer was a crumb. He said, "We must never forget that we may also find meaning in life even when confronted with a hopeless situation, when facing a fate that cannot be changed…when we are no longer able to change a situation…we are challenged to change ourselves." As Dr. Frankl taught, if we find a way to give meaning to our own circumstances, by helping others, we can prevent deep despair in ourselves, and we can be part of the solution when faced with even the hardest of challenges.

## The Benefits to the Observer

On a winter's evening, I was enjoying some Italian food at a local pizza joint in the Bronx, down the street from my mom. While it was a staple growing up in New York, I don't get to eat much authentic Italian food in Austin, so this was a treat and a walk down memory lane. It had begun to snow, which was another treat that I don't get to experience much in Austin. It had been a beautiful walk through the snow to get there, but as the snow came down more heavily, the sidewalks became quite slippery in this hilly neighborhood. And older man had come into the restaurant for a bite to eat after shopping along the avenue. He was carrying many packages. I overheard him ask the owner of the restaurant for the phone number of a taxi company to get a ride home, which, apparently, consisted of navigating down a steep slippery hill with his packages.

"Forget the taxi," I heard the owner say. "They'll charge you at least ten dollars. My brother will drive you home."

Out walked his brother from the kitchen, keys in hand. "C'mon," he said to the appreciative man. "I'll drive you home."

The restaurant was full and everyone there had witnessed this interaction. We were all smiling at each other, sharing in a mutual glow and feeling of warmth from the inside. I couldn't eat for a few minutes, feeling too choked up from joy. My chest felt open and my body was tingling. "That was really nice," I said to the owner.

"That could be me some day," he replied. A glow appeared to be about his face, as well.

Dr. Jonathan Haidt, at the University of Virginia, coined the term "elevation," to describe the emotions that all of us at that Italian restaurant shared with each other, upon observing an act of kindness. "Elevation is elicited by acts of virtue or moral beauty," wrote Haidt in *Flourishing: Positive Psychology and the Life Well-Lived.* "It causes warm, open feelings in the chest and it motivates people to behave more virtuously themselves." He describes the hallmarks of elevation to be "warm or tingly feelings, positive [mood], and a motivation to help others," upon "witnessing a good deed." Haidt quotes Thomas Jefferson in his writing, "When any...act of charity or gratitude, for instance, is presented either to our sight or imagination, we are deeply impressed with its beauty and feel a strong desire in ourselves of doing charitable and grateful acts also."

Another study found, what researchers referred to as, the "Mother Teresa effect." In this particular study, it was found that participants had an increase of Immunoglobin-A when viewing videos of Mother Teresa helping people. The researchers concluded that, just by witnessing acts of kindness, our immune system becomes strengthened, having a significant beneficial impact on our own health.

## As a Spiritual Path

As you can see, the benefits of simple acts of kindness are plentiful and powerful. When someone acts kind to us, we are more likely to feel inspired to act kindly. This effects the recipients of our kindness in the same manner. And so the kindness spreads further and further. Not only that, but it inspires those who witness such acts to act more kindly, themselves. According to the Oxford Dictionary, *kindness* is defined as "the quality of being friendly, generous, and considerate or a kind act." Wikipedia defines kindness as "a behavior marked by ethical characteristics, a pleasant disposition, and concern and consideration for others. It is known as a virtue and is recognized as a value in many cultures and religions...Aristotle defines it as being 'helpfulness towards someone in need, not in return for anything, nor for the advantage of the helper himself, but for that of the person helped.'"

This discussion of kindness dovetails really well with my earlier discussion of meditation and mindfulness (see Chapter 12, "Finding Our Way to Happiness with Meditation") because, as we become more mindful, we are more likely to act with more kindness. Furthermore, as we act with more kindness and generosity, this leads to an increase of compassion and an understanding that we are all connected. We then *become* the change in the world…creating a kinder, more peaceful, world. "Compassion is our deepest nature," writes Jack Kornfield in *The Wise Heart*. But, we sometimes lose sight of this understanding and compassionate nature within us, getting caught up in our fast-paced, "me first" society. Consciously performing acts of kindness and generosity can be a powerful way of uncovering our own compassion and remembering our connection to each other.

I want to point out a very important piece that I didn't mention earlier. This is that, in each of the stories of kindness and generosity that I told above that I was either the recipient of or the observer of, every single one of the individuals involved—the drivers at the mall, the woman opening the door, the Italian restaurant owner, the recipient of his kindness, and the witnesses, and myself—were all of different races and/or ethnicities, all with different accents, skin-complexions, and cultural backgrounds. This is key because it drives home, even more so, that we really are all connected and that acts of kindness remind us of this interconnectedness. In each of these instances, it felt as if we were all "in it" together, even though we were all strangers. Everyone in the Italian restaurant looked at each other and smiled, aglow and tingling, and it was as if, for that moment, we all knew each other. And we really do all know each other, don't we? Deep down, we all have the same desire for wholeness and connection. And compassion is our true nature for all of us.

"In a world menaced by all kinds of destructiveness, loving-kindness in deed, word and thought is the only constructive means to bring concord, peace and mutual understanding," Parami: The Buddhist Home writes in their article, "Compassion and Loving Kindness."

Kindness and generosity are seen as core virtues in most religions and spiritual paths, and may be key to saving our world. In Christianity, St. Francis of Assisi is known for saying, "For it is in giving that we receive." The Buddha taught that when we give to others, we give without expectation of reward, we give without attaching to either the gift or the recipient, and that we practice giving to release greed and self-clinging. Persian Poet Hafiz of Shiraz said, "Even after all this time the sun never says to the earth, 'you owe me.' Look what happens with a love like that. It lights the whole sky."

English essayist, Samuel Johnson, reminds us that, "The true measure of a man is how he treats someone who can do him absolutely no good."

And so it is with this attitude that we embark on a path of giving.

## Ways to Give

The catch is that these benefits are only available to us when we have no expectations of receiving anything in return for our generosity or act of kindness. "Whatever the gift," Peiro Ferrucci writes in his book, *The Power of Kindness: The Unexpected Benefits of Leading a Compassionate Life*, "one precondition is essential: To offer, in the moment of giving, all of ourselves. Generosity that is unwilling or cold or distracted is a contradiction. When you are generous, you do not spare yourself." The research shows that the expectation of something in return, including the recipient's gratitude, that they do something in return for us, or that our gift be used in a way that we think it *should*—even following them to make sure that they are actually in dire need of our gift of money—all diminish the benefits to us when we give.

In their book, *The New Health Rules,* Dr. Frank Lipman and Danielle Claro recommend, "Forget pay-it-forward or anything about karma. This is just about being nice and good with no expectations of reciprocity or personal gain. Let someone cut ahead of you in line, listen to someone who needs an ear, give a compliment you really mean. Make your default mode one of generosity. It's a nice way to live and it's contagious."

"We can contribute a bit of our time, a small donation, a book we have already read," writes Ferruci. "Or we can donate blood or bone marrow, or a huge effort, or a large part of our savings." Try volunteering at soup kitchen or a non-profit. Give money or objects to someone in need or to a charity that you feel strongly about. Give practical help or advice to a friend, neighbor, or stranger in need. Make someone who is feeling blue laugh. Whatever you give, whether it's time, money, or help, doing it without expectation or judgment will create benefit, not only to the receivers of your generosity and to the community, but the biggest benefit might be to you. As Ferrucci writes, "After it, we will be poorer, but we will feel richer. Perhaps we will feel less equipped and secure, but we will be freer. We will have made the world we live in a little kinder."

In 1988, The World Kindness Movement, a Non-Governmental Organization of the United Nations, introduced World Kindness Day. This is celebrated around the world on November 13th every year. On that day, we're invited to commit at least one random act of kindness. However, since it turns out that performing random acts of kindness and generosity is good for our health and can make a positive impact on the world, imagine the power of making such acts a daily habit.

Together, we can heal ourselves, and the world, one generous act of kindness at a time. And living in a kinder world, increases our own creativity, as well as greater progress as a society, greater development, and improved well-being throughout society. Finally, as the late great folk singer, Pete Seeger, said, "Being generous of spirit is a wonderful way to live." That's surely enough of a reason on it's own.

We are certainly living in unsettling and uncertain times. But, I strongly believe that love prevails, even when things appear bleak. Our relationships with our friends, families, partners, and, especially with ourselves, are fortified by our kindness and generosity, our willingness to give up the need to be *right*, and by our abiding acceptance of others and of ourselves—warts and all. These strong bonds are what provide us the strength and ability to create joyfulness in our lives and to remain rooted, even when on the shaky, changing, shifting ground of what we call *life*.

# Part IV
# Food for the Soul

Balance is everything. We can't ignore what we put into our bodies and then expect to have emotional physical, cognitive, and emotional fuel for the journey ahead.

## Part IV

# Food for the Soul

*"Food is really and truly the most effective medicine."*

~ Dr. Joel Fuhrman, internationally
recognized expert on nutrition
and natural healing

It was toward the end of my freshman year of college that I began to have frequent and intense stomach pain. During summer vacation, my mom took me to a highly recommended gastroenterologist at a large New York hospital. After running some tests, he concluded that there was nothing wrong with me and prescribed some medication to ease the pain. In spite of taking the drug as prescribed, my stomach pain persisted. I tried to alter my diet to find relief, but I was lost as far as figuring out what changes to make. And there was no one to guide me, certainly not the good doctor. I eliminated spicy foods and anything else that appeared to be obviously irritating, but had no noticeable relief as a result of these modifications.

The pain worsened when I entered graduate school in Syracuse, New York. I tried to ignore it as much as possible. I became so immersed in the all-encompassing work of the graduate program that I had no time for attending to physical pain. However, the pain again became so severe that I could not longer ignore it, as it began to interfere with my ability to focus. So, I found another gastroenterologist in Syracuse. This doctor put me through more tests, and it was, once again, determined that there was nothing wrong with me. Frustrated, I asked the doctor for any dietary recommendations he might have. Instead, he gave me samples of a new medication on the market and told me that I could eat whatever I wanted, just as long as I took the pills. This seemed to completely defy logic, but given that I still had no dietary guidance to prevent the pain in my gut, I reluctantly took this second drug. When the sample pills ran out, I didn't fill the prescription because I still felt no relief.

This pattern continued for several more years. I would find a new physician who would run me through some more tests, find nothing notable, and then prescribe another new drug on the market, telling me that I could eat anything I chose as long as I took their pills. Each time, I would stop the medication after a trial period because it would, predictably, bring no relief.

With one such drug, I had a very interesting experience. One day, while driving back to Syracuse, about 300 miles from a visit home, I began to feel sleepy. Without noticing it, I started speeding. Just my luck, I was pulled over by a state trooper. The odd part of this story is that, although I had never received a traffic ticket before, I felt absolutely no anxiety when I saw the flashing lights in my rearview mirror. Instead, I said to myself, "Wow, this is a new experience." I realized, when I finally arrived home, that this reaction was completely abnormal, especially for me. I researched the medication I had been taking that day in the *Physician's Desk Reference*, as I suspected it was the cause of such a strange reaction. What I discovered was that the drug contained Librium, a very powerful narcotic. Librium is not only addictive, but it should not be taken while driving an automobile because it causes drowsiness and lack of judgment. The doctor never warned me about driving while under the influence of this medication, and not surprisingly, it didn't bring any pain relief. It just made me not care about the pain—or anything else, such as speeding tickets, for that matter.

Another doctor sent me for biofeedback training to learn to relax. This was wonderful, and I write about the many benefits of relaxation and meditation at various points throughout this book. However, my pain was not actually caused by stress. Rather, it had become one of the sources of stress for me. Therefore, while learning to relax was helpful to ease some of my tension and to increase my tolerance of the pain, it did nothing to actually ease the *cause* of the pain, which was the food I was putting into my gut. To add insult to injury, by the time I graduated, I began to have dizzy spells, in addition to the stomach pain. This was not what I needed while beginning a new job. I always had a tendency for hypoglycemia (low blood sugar) if I missed a meal, but I began having episodes of low blood sugar right after eating lunch. I went back to my doctor, who strangely advised me that hypoglycemia was a "myth" and that my stomachaches and dizziness were all definitive signs of anxiety. "I'm going to give you some samples of an anti-anxiety medication," he said. "I bet that once you start taking them, all of your symptoms will go away." Upon walking out of his office, I threw the sample pills into the garbage and never went back to see that doctor again.

The journey to find relief continued when I moved back to the New York City area two years later. I saw yet another specialist and, similar to my previous experiences, I was prescribed another new medication. And, as usual, I discontinued it quickly when I found no relief. One year later, *that* particular medication was recalled for causing cardiac arrest.

It was only when I saw a holistic internist, who tested me for food allergies and gave me the dietary guidelines I had been requesting from medical doctors for several years, that I finally began to feel actual relief from my pain. In addition, the dizzy spells disappeared, and I had more energy after making the recommended changes to my diet. Several years later, after reading two books written by the nutritional expert, Dr. Joel Fuhrman, I made even more significant changes to my eating habits, and they brought about even more positive results to my overall health. The dietary modifications, such as eating more fresh fruits and vegetables and almost no animal products, have literally been more effective than any pill that a doctor could give me.

Perhaps, you have shared a similarly frustrating course of events with your own health issue. For me, my almost fifteen-year journey to find relief from my stomach pain is convincing proof that we really are what we eat. Dr. Scott Stoll, speaker, author, and Department Chair of Physical Medicine and Rehabilitation at Coordinated Health, told me that proper nutrition has the power to solve "about three quarters of health problems that most people are facing. And, not only do their diseases get better, but they feel better. They're happier, more joyful, and they have more energy." What I've also discovered in my quest for gut pain relief was that many medical doctors have no idea how our dietary choices affect our health and emotional well-being. They've been taught to treat most symptoms with drugs. Meanwhile, as Dr. Stoll stated, "The third leading cause of death in America today consists of complications from medical treatments. You won't find that with a bowl of blueberries or strawberries."

Food is very powerful. It can make us physically and emotionally ill, causing painful symptoms as I've described in my own life, and even life-threatening illnesses such as heart disease and diabetes, as well as mood disorders, such as depression and anxiety. On the other hand, food can also heal us, making us feel happy, energized, and ready to follow our dreams and passions.

## Food and Mental Health

Even before I attended graduate school, I had read several articles about new research findings linking serious mental illness, such as schizophrenia, to nutritional deficiencies. It was over forty years ago, in 1974, that Dr. Carl Pfeiffer began publishing research articles about nutritional treatments for severe mental illness, such as schizophrenia. He published twenty-two research articles on this topic prior to his death in 1988. "If there's a drug that can alter the brain's biochemistry, there's usually a combination of nutrients that can achieve the same thing without side-effects," said Dr. Pfeiffer, founder of the Brain Bio Center in Princeton, New Jersey. This has been coined "Pfeiffer's Law."

We were not taught about this at all during my graduate training in psychology. In fact, while working in psychiatric hospitals during my clinical practica as a graduate student, I witnessed patients with serious mental illnesses being given very strong medications, such as Thorazine and Haldol, which severely deplete nutrition from the body. The foods that I witnessed being fed to patients had been prepared to the point where any nutritional value had been virtually cooked out. I don't ever remember seeing any fresh fruits and vegetables, the crown jewels of nutrition, on their food trays. This lack of nutrient-dense foods on the menu was also the case when I worked in nursing homes for over fifteen years, counseling residents with depression and anxiety who were also frequently being treated with nutrition-depleting psychotropic medication. "Modern" medicine has dismissed the research findings of Pfieffer and other nutritional experts, favoring pharmaceuticals instead.

And so in this section, we will explore how our food is the basis for our vitality and passion for life.

# Chapter 19

# Benefits of Increasing Plants in Our Diet "Shall I not have intelligence with the earth?

*Am I not partly leaves and vegetable mould myself."*

~ HENRY DAVID THOREAU

A few years ago, I was having a conversation with a new medical doctor at the clinic where I was working. We were discussing my radio program, and I had mentioned that some of my interviews were with nutritional experts, who discussed the health benefits of a mostly plant-based diet when they were on my program.

"That's very irresponsible," he quickly quipped. His comment stunned me, and for a moment I didn't know what to say. I had been planning to invite him for an interview about his non-profit health agency, yet his reaction made me second-guess my decision.

"It's wrong to advise people not to eat meat. It's very unhealthy," he scowled, as he sipped soda from a cup with the name of a fried chicken fast food chain printed on it. I was baffled by such an extreme negative response and remained speechless, choosing to refrain from commenting on the nutritional "virtues" of his recent fried chicken lunch…or from making the interview invitation.

The doctor's comments have stayed with me since then. And I have often wondered how he could maintain such an adamant position given his own poor nutritional choices. I had the opportunity to vent during my radio interview with Dr. Michael Greger, one of the top nutritional researchers, founder of NutritionFacts.org, and author of the bestselling book, *How Not to Die: Discover the Foods Scientifically Proven to Prevent and Reverse Disease*. When asked about what he thought of such comments as the one described above, Dr. Greger stated, "That doctor must not have cracked open a medical journal in at least ten years."

Recent research in nutrition shows, over and over again, that a diet high in plant-based foods (fresh fruits and vegetables, beans, seeds, nuts, and whole grains), rather than the Standard American Diet (ironically, the acronym for which is SAD), reduces the risk of the most deadly and disabling illnesses, including cancer, heart disease, and diabetes, to name just a few—as well as mood disorders.

"The real super heroes of our health are found inside fruits and vegetables," Dr. Stoll told me. "Some of the amazing benefits of eating a plant-based diet are that plants are instrumental in: reducing inflammation in the body; fighting DNA damage; lengthening a part of the gene called the telomere, which has been shown to shorten as we age and, when eating a plant-based diet, it actually gets longer, extending our life-span; reversing heart disease; shutting down some of the hormones that may allow breast cancer to manifest itself; and cutting off the blood supply to cancer cells that are growing in the body."

On the other hand, diets high in animal protein (meat, fowl, fish, eggs, and dairy), as well as refined carbohydrates (sugar, white flour, and white rice), have been linked to an increase of deadly diseases, such as cancer and diabetes, as well as more rapid aging. In fact, a recent study in Korea found that people with Type 2 diabetes who followed a vegan diet, enjoyed significantly greater weight loss, significantly larger reduction of their HbA1C (a measure of blood sugar level over an extended period of time), and better control of daily blood sugar levels than those who followed a conventional diet typically recommended for diabetics. In another recent study, participants who ate seven or more servings of fruits and vegetables per day had a 42 percent decreased risk of death due to *any* cause, when compared to those who ate the lowest amount of plant-based foods.

Additionally, the research has found a direct relationship between the amount of fresh fruits and veggies eaten and one's mood. Those people who eat more of these nutrient-dense morsels are significantly more likely to feel calmer, happier, and more energetic than those who eat less produce. The reason for this, according to Dr. Greger, who has reviewed several of the studies, is that fresh fruits and vegetables stimulate higher levels of our body's production of the neurotransmitters, dopamine and serotonin, as well as the hormone melatonin, which increase happiness, relaxation, restful sleep, and memory. These chemicals also slow down the effects of aging on the brain and the body. In addition, plant-based foods have been found to decrease the risk for depression because they're very high in antioxidants, which protect the brain from oxidative stress, one of the causes of depression. Eating plants is "more powerful than any supplement you can buy in the store because all of the nutrients work synergistically. As you eat them, they all work together to magnify the effects in your body," said Dr. Stoll.

# NUTRITION AND STRESS

Scott Stoll, MD, Speaker and Author of *Alive!:*
*A Physician's Biblical and Scientific Guide to Nutrition*

Unmitigated stress for a prolonged period of time is a wild card in your health. It can cause disabling disease even if you're doing some of the right things. Stress raises the body's levels of cortisol and norepinephrine, the stress hormones, and this is the cause of many significant health problems.

Prolonged cortisol exposure can actually withdraw calcium from your bones, and this contributes to osteoporosis over time. Chronic stress can also suppress important hormones in your body, like testosterone, which is important for the maintenance of muscle, muscle mass, and bone density.

Long-term cortisol exposure affects our brain, causing atrophy of our neurons and can suppress serotonin, which is the hormone that maintains our mood. Lower levels of serotonin contributes to depression. In addition, high levels of cortisol causes inflammation in the small arteries of our body and that inflammation can lead to

▶

▶

arteriosclerosis or hardening of the arteries. It weakens our immune system, which makes us much more susceptible to cancer. It changes the bacteria in our gut, which contributes to 85 percent of the health of our immune system. So, as that changes, it's called a dysbiosis, you get an overgrowth of the bad bacteria. That, too, contributes to your susceptibility for cancer. It can also make the gut more "leaky," which can contribute to susceptibility for autoimmune diseases. The list goes on and on. Stress affects every system of our body over time.

The first researchers who wrote about stress, considered stress to be anything that causes our system to respond in an alarmed state. So that could be exposure to toxins and chemicals, such as what we have in our environment today, and it can also be certain foods.

The foods that cause the most stress in our body are the processed foods because of the toxins and chemicals contained in those foods. Foods like sugars are very stressful to the body. They cause the rise in production of free radicals, which damage our cells. Additionally, excessive meat intake is a stressor on the body because, over time, it can create inflammation. Also, alcohol is stressful for the body, as is nicotine. All of these

▶

▶ things we consume can cause a stress response and can damage our cells, leading to disease.

By consuming the right foods, your body is relieved from dealing with the stress of processing unhealthy food. Plus, healthy foods are full of antioxidants, which can spread throughout the body and help to repair the damage that is caused by living in a busy world and dealing with the life stressors that we are faced with. A healthy diet helps your body manage stress much more effectively than you could if you were eating a poor diet and facing the same life stressors.

As I mentioned earlier, since I've changed my diet from the *sad* Standard American Diet to one that is much higher in plant-based foods, my own feeling of well-being has improved, with decreased symptoms of gastrointestinal discomfort, blood sugar instability, and drained energy. In addition, I've also noticed reduced frequency and severity of flare-ups of an autoimmune disorder that affects my skin. I'm able to detect the difference when I've gotten off track with my dietary choices, and I definitely don't like how I feel when that happens.

►

# DEADLY DIETS

Michael Greger, MD, Speaker and Author of
*How Not To Die* Founder of *NutritionFacts.org*

The number one cause of death, as well as the number one cause of disability, in the United States is our diet. This bumps cigarette and tobacco smoking to number two, killing about a half million Americans every year, while our diet kills hundreds of thousands more. All you have to do is look down the list of our leading killers to see why that's the case.

Our number one killer of both men and women is heart disease. Heart disease can be prevented, arrested, and reversed with a healthy enough diet. That's a diet centered around whole plant foods. You can open up arteries without drugs and without surgery. This was demonstrated in a randomized controlled study back in July 1990 and published in the most prestigious medical journal in the world by Dr. Dean Ornish and his colleagues, proving that heart disease can be reversed. Yet, since then, hundreds of thousands of people have continued to die from this reversible, preventable killer, unnecessarily.

►

If the cure to our number one killer could get lost down some rabbit hole and ignored, then what else might be buried in the medical literature that could help my patients. I made it my life's mission to find out. That's what led me to start NutritionFacts.org and to write my new book.

"That chicken wing you're eating could be as deadly as a cigarette." That was a quote from a press release about a pivotal article published in the journal called, *Cell Metabolism*. This was based on research, following thousands of people for eighteen years, showing that eating lots of animal protein—meat, egg white, and dairy protein—during middle age, quadruples one's risk of dying from cancer. The research found about a 75 percent increase of premature mortality, across the board, but, specifically, a four-fold risk of dying from cancer, which is comparable to what one gets from smoking cigarettes. Chicken wings were just used as an example, but they were talking about all animal proteins, any type of meat, egg white, and dairy protein. They think it's because of the IGF-1, insulin-like growth factor 1, which increases the acquisition and progression of malignant tumors. The more animal protein one eats, the higher one's level of IGF-1 goes.

Insulin resistance is the underlying cause of both pre-diabetes and Type II diabetes. It manifests

▶

as increased sugar. It's not caused by increased sugar. By eliminating animal fat and sodium from the diet, one can reverse hypertension and Type II diabetes. There have been studies done where Type II diabetics were randomly split into two groups. One group was told to minimize their fruit intake and the other group told to eat more fruit than they currently were. They found better improvement in blood sugar control in those who were adding more fruit to their diet. This is because they were eating healthier diets. Within a matter of weeks, one can improve one's insulin sensitivity, drop blood sugar medications, sometimes get off insulin completely, just by switching one's diet to a whole foods, plant-based diet. So, that's a diet that's centered around fruits, vegetables, legumes, whole grains, mushrooms, herbs, and spices, basically real food that grows out of the ground, while minimizing the intake of meat, eggs, dairy, and processed *junk.*

There's a lot of good information from experts in the field of nutrition presented here. And again, it's up to you, as the reader, to discern what's right for you and your body. It's often best advised to seek some guidance in an individual consultation from a nutritional expert whom you trust, when first embarking on a path of changing your eating habits. There are also many excellent up-to-date books on this topic, as the nutritional science has made some very significant changes in the past few years. I've added some of those sources to the list of helpful resources in the back of the book.

# Chapter 20

# Moving Toward
# "Nutritional Excellence"

*"We are what we repeatedly do. Excellence,
then, is not an act, but a habit."*

~ ARISTOTLE

As with any changes, small steady steps are the way to succeed,
especially when we're modifying the way we eat from a diet that is
highly processed to a include more plant-based foods.

"Americans are eating a diet with 90 percent of our calories
coming from foods that do not contain the phytochemicals and
antioxidants that the human body is designed to function on," said
Dr. Joel Fuhrman. "The 5-10 percent that we're eating is not enough
for us to be healthy. Instead of eating 90 percent processed food and
animal products and only 10 percent vegetation, we have to eat 90
percent vegetation and maybe 10 percent of other things." Therefore,
the goal is not necessarily to make a sudden extreme change in diet.
Rather, making gradual changes toward a diet that is high in plant-
based foods (fruits, veggies, beans, nuts, seeds, and whole grains) will
have the effect of decreasing the amount of animal proteins (meat,
fowl, fish, dairy, and eggs) and refined carbohydrates you consume.
The more you can move your diet in that direction, the better. These
changes will have a powerful effect on our overall health. "When you

apply nutritional excellence, you not only can prevent disease, but you can reverse disease."

Realistically, getting started with creating new, healthier, eating habits can be quite difficult when we've been in the habit of consuming less healthy foods. There's a good reason for that. In his article, "The Simple Psychology of Habits," founder of the Institute for the Psychology of Eating, Marc David, explains, "The distinguishing feature of negative habits is that they come naturally, take little effort to develop, and quickly gain a momentum of their own that is difficult to offset." In fact, it has been found that foods rich in fats and sugars, especially that combination, have an affect on our brains that is similar to that of heroin and cocaine, making these foods extremely addictive.

According to Dr. Fuhrman, "The more unhealthy your diet is, the more addictive it becomes and the more difficulty you will have in even considering a different way."

# NUTRITIONAL EXCELLENCE

Joel Fuhrman, MD Speaker and Author of
*Eat to Live: The Amazing Nutrient-Rich Program for Fast and Sustained Weight Loss*

Nutritional excellence is significantly more powerful than medical interventions, like drugs and surgery. We literally eat ourselves to a point of

▶ obesity because we've become addicted to food. It's ruining families, marriages, as well as people's intellectual achievement and development. Our nation's addiction to food is keeping people in poverty, preventing our nation from providing a health care system that we can afford, degrading our economy, the ecology, and the well-being of our world.

The bottom line is: You don't have to be sick. You can be slim and healthy for the rest of your life. Heart attacks don't have to happen. We don't have to have people in nursing homes after strokes that prevent them from moving their body. We don't have to be diabetic. And we can get rid of 90 percent of cancers that affect Americans. These are radical statements and there's sufficient evidence to support these statements.

## Small Steps to Life-Saving Changes

Let's talk about how to make some simple changes with powerful results.

First of all, eat mindfully—that is, have a greater awareness of what you're ingesting. Keeping a food diary can be quite eye opening because many of us often pop food into our mouths without even thinking about it. Mindfulness also includes doing a little bit of detective work. Check out what's in the foods you're consuming. Stay away from those with lists of ingredients that are long and with hard-to-pronounce names, as well as those that are high in sugar, refined carbohydrates, and hydrogenated oils, which contain trans-fatty acids found to be directly connected to cardiovascular disease, cancer, and diabetes, among other health problems.

Eating more mindfully also consists of focusing your attention on the food that you're ingesting rather than being distracted while eating—and eating slowly to enjoy each bite of food. When we enjoy what we eat, we are less likely to overeat. Yoga instructor, Steve Kane, said in our interview, delicious food "eaten mindfully is much more satisfying. It's tastier because our attention is tethered to enjoying the deliciousness. This is a better experience than this business of eating popcorn in a movie theater, when our mind is not even on the act of eating, as it is on the movie. That's kind of crazy, since 1200 calories just went into our body, and we weren't even paying attention."

Related to the idea of eating mindfully is how you feel when you sit down to a meal. This is critical to our use of the nutrition in the food we eat. "We have noticed the relationship between anxiety and digestive problems for a long time," wrote behavioral health researcher, Dr. Leslie Korn, in her article, "Nutrition Essentials for Mental Health." "While we long believed that the anxiety was the *cause* of digestive problems, we now understand that emotional difficulties, such as anxiety, can also be caused by poor digestion because of those neurotransmitters produced by the digestive system." Dr. Korn recommends eating in environments that are relaxing rather than high-stress/high activity surroundings, turning off distractions (such as the television, computer, or smart phone), as well as breathing slowly before eating and between bites, in order to improve digestion and therefore, improve mood.

When choosing what to eat, make choices that include more whole foods, those foods that are closer to the source, with little or no processing, such as whole grains, rather than refined flour, or nuts and seeds as a source of fat, rather thank hydrogenated oils.

Increase your consumption of plant-based foods. For example, eat a large salad every day that includes vegetables that are a variety of colors. You might add some beans and seeds, as well as a healthy dressing. Seeds also have the added benefit of helping us to absorb the phytonutrients from green vegetables. This one small dietary addition may result in very big health benefits, while tasting good and filling us up.

Fuhrman recommends eating GBOMBS, daily. This consists of Greens, Beans, Onions, Mushrooms, Berries, and Seeds. "Include all of these in our diet every day and we can wipe out most major cancers in America."

Another small change with significant returns would be to eliminate soft drinks and replace them with clean water (see Chapter 23, "The Magic of Water).

Decreasing sweets, such as cakes and cookies, and dairy foods, such as cheese and ice cream will also boost your health. "The same thing that promotes fat cells to swell, also promotes cancer cells to replicate," said Fuhrman in our interview. "This most overweight population in the history of the human race in this country is going to have the highest rate of cancer, as well. You can't separate the fat growth from the cancer cell growth."

You can also reduce meat consumption by eating smaller portions of it and trying to have some meals throughout the week that don't include any meat or animal proteins. Bean burritos might be a great option for dinner one night. Or commit to a full day without meat. A trend that helps with decreasing meat intake is "Meatless Monday." You might notice that you feel better and will want to extend being "meatless" to several days per week.

## Keeping the Naysayers at Bay

The negative comment made to me, described in the previous chapter, was certainly not an isolated incident. I have frequently met with negativity from people witnessing my dietary choices. You wouldn't think that ordering the types of foods that we were told to eat as children, such as green vegetables, would cause so much angst in people around us. Maybe some people feel that our healthier choices are a silent critique of the steak and fries on their plate, or they fear our choices because of all of the years of learning the wrong information.

Just know that if you decide to make a change in your diet to a healthier one, there may be people in your life who will not be supportive of your choices and will let you know of their disagreement. There will always be naysayers when beginning on a new path. In order to be successful, we need to become a little more thick-skinned, to let those comments roll off, and, as they say, "Keep calm and truck on." At some point, those same naysayers may actually come around and ask what you've been doing to become so healthy and they may want to follow in your footsteps.

If your friends are not willing to try out your new healthier foods with you while you're just getting your own footing on this journey, and if this creates discomfort when eating with them, stick to non-food-related activities with those friends and find a like-minded group of friends with whom to enjoy "breaking bread." Check out MeetUp.com or other websites that connect people with similar interests and attend some plant-based potluck dinners in order to create a support group to help with your new lifestyle. It also helps to have guidance with any new endeavor. Some excellent books to guide you in this journey include, *How to Be Vegan: Tips, Tricks, and Strategies for Cruelty-Free Eating, Living, Dating, Traveling, Decorating and More* by Elizabeth Castoria, as well as any of the books by Dr. Joel Fuhrman and Dr. Michael Greger. There are great books coming out onto the shelves daily. For some fun recipes, check out *Crazy Sexy Kitchen: 150 Plant-Empowered Recipes to Ignite a Mouthwatering Revolution* by Kris Carr and Chef Chad Sarno, or the new gourmet cookbook, *The Wicked Healthy Cookbook: Free. From. Animals*, by Chad Sarno, Derek Sarno, and David Joachim.

Remember, in order to be successful with any new habit, it's important to refrain from berating yourself and from feeling guilty when you take a detour off-track. Every day is a chance to start over again. Reward yourself for successes and be kind to yourself when you run into obstacles and challenges, knowing that just making the effort is a sign of courage.

Finally, allow yourself to feel excited about your new healthy lifestyle and about how great you feel by taking such good care of yourself, rather than approaching it from a place of feeling fearful about eating unhealthy foods. Creating a positive emotional connection to any lifestyle change is one of the most powerful secrets to success. Then, the rewards you'll receive, including those of more vibrant health, energy, and mood, will surely keep you moving along this path with even greater enthusiasm and ease.

As my friend, Venus DeMarco, breast cancer survivor, speaker, and author of *Fearless: My Journey That Healed Breast Cancer—and My Life, Through Faith, Food, & Fun*, said to me on my radio program, "Personally, I love feeling great! Once you do, it's hard to go back to an unhealthy diet."

# Chapter 21

# I Love Coffee

*"I was taken by the power that savoring a simple cup of coffee can have to connect people and create community."*

~ Howard Schultz, Chairman and
CEO of Starbucks

I love coffee! I love how it tastes. I love the aroma. I love how it feels as it's going down. I love the whole ritual around drinking coffee, whether brewing it myself, or sitting in a coffee house with a nice hot cup of Joe and a book or a friend to chat with. And I love how it feels after I drink it—until I don't. I enjoy coffee when taken in small amounts, but I can usually tell when I've gone over the threshold from just the right amount to too much. Too much coffee will make me feel jittery and more easily stressed by small hassles.

## Less Guilt and More Pleasure

Every time a new study emerges that shows the benefits of drinking coffee, I'm thrilled to have this one guilty pleasure carry with it less guilt and more enjoyment. Some research findings are quite positive about caffeine in general, and coffee, in particular. There have been some recent studies finding that caffeinated drinks could be one factor in decreasing the risk of Alzheimer's disease and other dementias. These findings show that moderate coffee intake, 3-5 cups of caffeinated coffee per day (one "regular" size coffee actually equals two cups), may decrease the risk of Alzheimer's disease, Parkinson's disease, and decrease the risk of strokes. In addition, caffeine has been found to improve cognitive functioning in older adults, and when consumed in moderate amounts, it has been found to improve mood in adults of all ages.

## Walking that Line Between a Good Mood and Depression

In *How Not to Die*, Dr. Greger points out that moderate consumption of coffee significantly reduces the risk for severe depression and suicidal behavior. In fact, researchers at Harvard University discovered that people who drank two or more cups of coffee per day had about half the suicide risk when compared to those who did not drink any coffee. It was further affirmed that those who drank more than six cups of coffee per day had an 80 percent reduced likelihood of committing suicide.

An important note made by Greger is that adding sugar to the coffee counteracts the positive effects of coffee on mood and that adding artificial sweeteners, such as aspartame or saccharine, increases the incidence of depression.

## There's a Fine Line

However, be aware that there's a fine line between feeling good from coffee and feeling bad from it. Too much caffeine can increase the stress hormone, cortisol. Cortisol is the chemical we produce when we believe that we're in danger. Prolonged production of cortisol causes us to feel anxious, agitated, and irritable, and to have trouble sleeping. Additionally, while many people find that a little bit of caffeine helps to boost sharper thinking, the overproduction of cortisol can interfere with our ability to think clearly. Cortisol will also raise blood pressure, lower immune functioning, cause imbalances in blood sugar, and increase abdominal fat, which can lead to greater risk of heart attack and stroke. In the same Harvard study above, while a reduced suicide risk with drinking coffee was found, it was also discovered that, paradoxically, there was an *increased* risk of suicidal behavior for those people who drank eight or more cups of coffee per day.

## Not Everyone is the Same

Health expert, Dr. Andrew Weil, advises in his nutrition blog at DrWeil. com, "The way coffee affects you is your surest guide to whether or not you should be drinking it at all, and if so, how much." It's up to you to determine if drinking coffee in moderation feels good or if you feel more irritable and anxious even with a small amount. Keep in mind that a large amount of caffeine is not good for anyone and can cause adrenal fatigue. Our adrenal glands become worn out from the overproduction of the stress-hormone, adrenaline, which leads to a general feeling of malaise. Drinking a full pot of coffee, even if you don't notice the effects because you've built up a tolerance, will have a negative effect on your adrenal glands. Basically, too much caffeine can stimulate that *fight-or-flight* reaction, better known as the stress response, and having this stimulated over and over again will wear out our adrenal glands, as if we had been having frequent panic attacks.

## Coffee May Be the Cause of Your Anxiety

Some people are especially sensitive to the agitating effects of caffeine and, even a little bit of coffee can cause the stress reaction for them. If you have an anxiety disorder of any sort, I recommend that you don't drink *any* coffee, caffeinated tea, or any other caffeinated drink, such as cola. I've seen many of my clients with complaints of frequent anxiety, agitation, and/or panic attacks who, when asked, reveal that they drink at least one pot of coffee, plus iced-tea or cola throughout the day. The large amounts of caffeine they're consuming may actually be the root *cause* of their anxiety and panic, or at the very least, it's likely a large contributing factor.

## It's All in the Timing

If you have difficulty sleeping, then look at how much caffeine you're drinking and when. Caffeine tends to stay in the body for several hours after consuming it. It's, therefore, advised not to drink anything with caffeine after 2:00 p.m. if you have a sleep disturbance.

The timing of when we ingest caffeine is an important factor for a variety of reasons. Are you one of those people who will drink a cup of coffee as soon as you wake up? Is it the first thing that you put into your stomach? Probably, the worst time to drink coffee is on an empty stomach. The tendency to produce cortisol and to feel irritable from coffee will be much more extreme if you've had nothing to eat either before or with your coffee.

Additionally, when we drink coffee or anything with caffeine, it stimulates the production of hydrochloric acid (HCl) in the stomach. This production of HCl is much greater when the coffee is consumed on an empty stomach, causing irritation to the lining of the stomach and intestines over a period of time. Caffeine is a well-known irritant for those who have irritable bowel syndrome, gastritis, Crohn's disease, colitis, and ulcers. Drinking coffee on an empty stomach can also increase the chance of heartburn or acid reflux. In fact, for those who have digestive problems, it's actually a good idea for you to completely eliminate caffeinated drinks.

To prevent some of the negative results of starting your day with coffee, make it a point to eat a nourishing breakfast prior to, or with, your coffee. Notice how you feel after a week. If you do fine with the caffeine, enjoy your cup of Joe. However, if drinking coffee doesn't agree with you, you can always switch to a lower-caffeine content tea, such as green or white tea, or one of the many varieties of caffeine-free herbal teas, without missing out on the "experience." I sometimes like to decrease the caffeine by mixing regular coffee with decaffeinated.

Of interest: I recently started adding organic virgin coconut oil to my coffee. This has the benefit of creating a longer-lasting increase of energy from the caffeine, rather than a sudden jolt of energy with a later energy crash. And I enjoy the flavor it adds to the coffee.

As with all things, balance is important when we drink our morning java. Deprivation can be just another way to beat ourselves up. So go ahead and enjoy your favorite coffee bean. It's a simple way to taste the flavors of the world in our own backyard.

# Chapter 22

# Alcohol: The Good, Bad, and Ugly

*"I cook with wine, sometimes
I even add it to the food."*

~ W. C. Fields

I occasionally enjoy a glass of wine with my dinner, along with good conversation. I sometimes drink red wine, sometimes white, depending on what I'm eating and what I'm in the mood for. On a hot summer's evening, I usually prefer a chilled glass of white, while I enjoy red when it's cool outside. I'm pretty simple that way. Perhaps, you enjoy your wine this way, as well.

Whether or not imbibing alcohol is something to be concerned about, with regard to our health, really depends on a few things, including how much you drink, when you drink, as well as if you have health issues, alcohol dependence issues, and if you're taking medications that don't mix well with alcohol.

## Benefits of Moderate Drinking

The U.S. dietary guidelines have recently given "official permission" for moderate drinking because of the benefits of keeping our brains sharp as we age and decreasing the risk of diabetes or heart disease. Some studies have found that moderate drinking can raise the levels of "good cholesterol" in the blood as much as 20 percent, when this is done *along with* eating a healthy diet and exercising regularly, which can lower the risk of heart attack. Drinking in moderation has also been found to increase insulin sensitivity, which, in turn, can reduce the risk of diabetes. However, don't get too excited about this because alcohol also contains a lot of non-nutritional calories, which can lead to weight gain, linked to the onset of type-2 diabetes.

Interestingly, there was a study that was published in *The New England Journal of Medicine* in 2005 finding that women who regularly drank moderate amounts of alcohol showed a 23 percent lower risk of cognitive decline when they were compared with non-drinkers. Yet, all of the experts agree that, for those people who don't drink, the benefits of moderate drinking are not enough to make it advisable to start drinking. There are many other ways to receive these benefits that don't have the health risks of alcohol, such as eating a healthy diet, exercising regularly, maintaining a healthy weight, and by not smoking.

Moderate drinking is best defined as the optimal amount to drink in order to derive possible benefits. Both, the American Heart Association and the U.S. Dietary Guidelines specify that moderate drinking is one drink for women and two for men per day. This is for a *single* day and not the average for the week. "One drink" is 5 oz. of wine, 12 oz. of beer, or 1.5 oz. of 80-proof distilled liquor.

## Once Again, Timing is Everything

Drinking alcohol on an empty stomach can increase the chance of developing high blood pressure. On the other hand, when consumed with a meal, alcohol can slow down how long it takes to empty the stomach and, therefore, decrease the amount of food that we may eat at the meal, helping with maintaining a healthy weight.

## More is Not Better

Drinking more than the recommended amount doesn't bring more benefit and, in fact, will cause multiple problems. For example, as I mentioned, alcohol is very high in calories and very low in nutrients; therefore, over-consumption of alcohol can lead to weight gain. The risks of obesity far outweigh any benefits of alcohol, because obesity is linked to type-2 diabetes, heart disease, cancer, and many other chronic and/or severe health problems. Those people who substitute eating with the calories of alcohol, in order to keep from gaining weight, end up malnourished, leading to a high risk of developing serious and chronic illnesses, cognitive impairment, depression, and destruction to just about every organ of the body.

Some of the additional health risks of consuming excessive alcohol include: several different types of cancer, pancreatitis, cardiovascular disease, stroke, brain shrinkage, cirrhosis of the liver, miscarriage, and fetal alcohol syndrome of an unborn child. And, we know that alcohol is addictive or can lead to, at least, a psychological dependency when consumed excessively and frequently. Even a small amount of alcohol is dangerous for people with certain health conditions, such any type of liver disease, pancreatic disease, or any evidence of precancerous changes in the esophagus, larynx, pharynx, or mouth. Also, certain medications, including prescription *and* over-the- counter medications, do not mix well with alcohol. The combination can be extremely dangerous and even life threatening. Please be sure to read all warnings regarding mixing your medications with alcohol and take them seriously. Tylenol, for example, might seem like a benign over-the-counter pain medication, but, when mixed with even small amounts of alcohol, can cause liver damage.

## Alcohol as Mood "Medication"

What I've seen in my practice with my clients, as well as when evaluating veterans for post-traumatic stress disorder, is that many times, when people are experiencing emotional distress, as well as sleep disturbance, they reach for alcohol to try to find relief from their symptoms. However, using alcohol as a way of dealing with emotional issues can lead to dependence on it. In a study conducted by the National Institute of Alcohol Abuse and Alcoholism, 13 percent of study participants with anxiety disorders, who reported using alcohol to find relief from their symptoms, developed an alcohol use problem over the course of the three-year study, compared to only 5 percent of those participants who did not use alcohol in this way.

While an occasional glass of wine to ease the tension of a stressful day does not appear to put a person at risk for becoming dependent on alcohol, habitually relying on alcohol or other drugs to ease anxiety, rather than using healthier coping skills, will. And, although alcohol feels like it relaxes us in the short run, it actually causes a stress reaction in our bodies when we drink it in excess because alcohol is not metabolized like other foods and drinks. It takes a lot more energy by the body to metabolize a large amount of alcohol, which is very stressful to the body. Therefore, the feeling of stress is actually increased once the alcohol wears off.

Furthermore, alcohol is a nervous system *depressant*. That's the reason that it often makes us feel drowsy. In depressing our nervous system, alcohol actually contributes to *or causes* depression when the intoxication wears off. Also, while intoxicated, the risks are numerous if we're depressed, anxious, or angry because alcohol causes very poor judgment and impulsive behaviors. Those things that we wouldn't do if we were to take the time to think them through with a clear mind are behaviors that we might impulsively do while intoxicated, such as risk-taking behaviors, violent behaviors, or suicide, some of which have obvious irrevocable consequences. I strongly advise that if you're feeling "out of sorts," avoid alcohol completely. Also, if you notice, or the people around you inform you, that you're more irritable when you drink or the day after you drink, even if you've just had one, reconsider having even that one drink.

## Alcohol and Sleep

As for sleep, alcohol makes for a poor sleep medication. In a nutshell, in order for all of the good stuff to happen while we sleep, the regeneration of cells, the strengthening of our immune system, the feeling of being rested, the sharpening of our brains, the boosting of our mood, and so on, we need to have several complete cycles of sleep during the night (see Chapter 28, "The Quality and Quantity of Our Sleep"). Alcohol may knock us out, but it interferes with allowing the brain to go through all of those important stages of sleep. Therefore, drinking alcohol close to bedtime will keep us from waking up feeling refreshed and from strengthening our immune system. What's more, alcohol has a rebound effect and will frequently knock us out and then wake us up. There have been numerous studies showing that this wakefulness or restlessness occurs during the second half of our sleep, if we've consumed alcohol right before sleep. This is because the alcohol affects the chemicals that control our sleep, causing greater sleepiness while the alcohol is still in our bloodstream, but the effects of these chemicals reverse after the alcohol has metabolized. If you want to sleep well, stay away from alcohol close to bedtime and don't use it as a sleep medication. The more alcohol consumed, the worse it will be.

## Some More Effective Coping Strategies

The bottom-line is that, while there are times when alcohol can have some health benefits when consumed in moderation, it's best to avoid alcohol at those times when dealing with emotional issues. Instead, utilize some healthier coping techniques. For example, try meditation (Chapter 12, "Finding Our Way to Happiness With Meditation"), yoga (Chapter 25, "Time to Hit Your Mat!"), and work on eliminating negative thought habits that create our emotional distress (techniques for this can be found in all of the chapters in Part II, "Emotional Well-being and Self-Care").

# Chapter 23

# The Magic of Water

*"If there is magic on this planet,*
*it is contained in water."*

~ LORAN EISLEY,
AMERICAN ANTHROPOLOGIST, EDUCATOR,
PHILOSOPHER, AND NATURAL SCIENCE WRITER

Without water, we wouldn't survive for more than a few days. The human body is made up of approximately 60 percent water. More specifically, our brains are actually 95 percent water, our blood 82 percent water, and our lungs 90 percent. As little as a 2 percent drop in our body's water content will cause symptoms of mild dehydration, which includes difficulties with short-term memory, with solving basic mathematical problems, and with visual focus. Mild dehydration can also cause decreased coordination, fatigue, dry skin, dry nose and mouth, changes in blood pressure, and even impairment in judgment. Chronic, on-going, dehydration can lead to increased stress, depression, back pain, headaches, allergies, asthma, hypertension, and several degenerative disorders. Every cell and organ in our body relies on water in order to be able to perform their functions correctly. Without the proper amount of water, our organs gradually shut down.

# 10 BENEFITS OF DRINKING ENOUGH WATER

1. Helps with weight loss. Adequate hydration is necessary for the process of burning calories. When even mildly dehydrated, the burning of calories is much slower. Additionally, drinking water prior to a meal will help create a feeling of fullness more quickly so that we don't eat as much.

2. Gives us energy while dehydration causes muscle fatigue.

3. Clears the skin. A buildup of toxins in the body will cause inflammation in the skin, clogging the pores and creating acne. Water flushes out these toxins.

4. Decreases midday fatigue.

5. Increases concentration.

6. Relieves muscle cramps.

7. Reduces constipation and bloating.

8. Alleviates congestion from a cold. In addition, while it's necessary to be properly hydrated for our body to fight off bacteria and viruses, having

▶ an infection causes dehydration. (Mom was right about drinking plenty of fluid when we're sick!)

9. Boosts our immune system, helping to prevent colds and flu.

10. Prevents headaches because headaches are frequently the result of dehydration.

## For Older Adults, Even Mild Dehydration Can Be Dangerous

Surprisingly, over 75 percent of Americans suffer from chronic mild dehydration. This is the biggest culprit for fatigue during the course of the day. A dry mouth is a sign of dehydration, and if you're feeling thirsty, then you're already, at least, mildly dehydrated. Older adults are at a greater risk for becoming dehydrated because thirst sensation tends to decrease as we age. In addition, many of the medications that are more likely to be taken by seniors cause dehydration. Dehydration causes fatigue and weakness, which leads to an increased risk for falling. The biggest culprit of a urinary tract infection in an older person is dehydration, putting them at risk for kidney infection and sepsis (a potentially life-threatening infection). Dehydration in an older adult is likely to cause more pronounced impairments in cognitive functioning, as well.

## Other Beverages May Not Replace Water

It's a common belief that if we drink plenty of other beverages, we don't need to be concerned about drinking water. However, many of these drinks can actually cause *increased* dehydration. For example, a nice cool Margarita while sitting by the pool might taste great and feel good going down, but alcohol is a diuretic, causing cells to shrink and squeeze out the water. That's why, when you drink any alcohol-containing drink, you have a frequent need to urinate. Many doctors and nutritionists recommend drinking a glass of plain water with every alcoholic drink consumed. In addition, the sugar in sweet drinks is also a diuretic. The body reacts to the increase of sugar in the blood stream by attempting to flush it out. That's also the reason that soft drinks, even fruit juice, can cause dehydration. Apple juice has approximately 39 grams of sugar, which is equivalent to 10 teaspoons of sugar. Good-ol' orange juice has about 33 grams of sugar, equivalent to 8 teaspoons of sugar.

I live in Texas, where everyone drinks iced-tea by the gallon, believing they are staying hydrated. However, it turns out that caffeine is also a natural diuretic. While tea and coffee can be consumed in small amounts without running the risk of dehydration because their water content balances out the diuretic affect of the caffeine, overdoing caffeinated drinks will cause the dehydrating effects of the caffeine to outweigh the benefits of the water contained in them. And sodas? Don't drink them at all. Even if they're caffeine free, soda is one of the worst things you can ingest for a variety of reasons, including, but not limited to, the dehydrating effects. Diet sodas have a gamut of other risks associated with artificial sweeteners.

## How Much is Enough?

The Institutes of Medicine recommend thirteen cups of water per day for men and about nine for women. One way of increasing hydration, according to Dr. Joel Fuhrman, is by adding more raw fruits and vegetables to your meals and throughout the day, as these foods have high contents of water. This is another good reason to eat those fruits and veggies. It's still a good idea to drink water, even when plenty of fresh fruits and veggies are part of our diet, but you may not need to drink quite as much.

## Creating Water Rituals

> *"When you drink the water,*
> *remember the spring."*
>
> ~ CHINESE PROVERB

One of the reasons that we might enjoy a glass of wine, a cup of coffee, or a cup of tea is the ritual that surrounds them, including the emotional and social aspects. Perhaps you appreciate sharing a vintage bottle of wine with good friends. I often look forward to meeting a good friend to enjoy catching up over a cup of coffee at a favorite coffee house. Can you imagine similarly enjoying water? Given that water is essential to life, it would seem that we would have a basic instinctual emotional attachment to it, and because of that, we might also want to create rituals around it.

During his two interviews on my radio show, Dr. Michael Mascha, who holds a Ph.D. in Food and Visual Anthropology from the University of Vienna, spoke about turning drinking water into a passion, a hobby, or a just plain more enjoyable event. He explained that, about twelve years ago, he was advised by his doctor not to drink alcohol anymore. His time of enjoying wine and the fun that goes with tasting all types of wine from around the world was over. At that point, he took his "epicurean" curiosity, which he had toward wine, and he applied it to water, discovering a whole new world. According to

Mascha, appreciating water from different sources around the world can replace wine drinking, especially for people who may not be able to drink alcohol for a variety of reasons. His website, FineWaters.com, provides tips about incorporating water into meals, pairing the variety of tastes of different waters from different sources with foods as one might do with wine, the correct temperatures at which to best serve each of the waters, and the diverse characteristics of the water from various sources.

---

# HONORING THE SOURCE

Michael Mascha, Author of
*Fine Waters: A Connoisseur's Guide to the
World's Most Distinctive Bottled Waters*

Water is like so many things in life. If you start paying attention to these things, a beautiful world opens up. For most people, water is just water. It's a commodity. But, you will notice how different waters can be when they come from different sources, different places in the world. You can begin to get a lot of enjoyment out of water. I do a lot of water tastings around the world. I introduce people to water from a glacier or water from an iceberg. Then contrast that with water that has

▶

▶

high mineral content. Suddenly, people discover how different waters taste. You can match them with food and have them for different occasions. You can engage with water in the same way that you can engage with wine. The only thing you need to do is pay attention.

I really enjoy drinking water with a very high mineral content. And then I like to contrast this by, the next day, by drinking water from an iceberg. If you can imagine, this was snow that fell 15,000 years ago, it froze, then it became an iceberg, and it's melting now. I'm drinking water that is, basically, rain that fell 15,000 years ago. Does the 15,000 years make the water better? No. But it's a great story. You know, just the feeling about opening that bottle makes it very special.

Start enjoying drinking water. Don't consider it a chore that you have to do. Engage with the water. Appreciate that this water is from an iceberg while that other water is from a remote spring in a high altitude mountain. Emotionally engage with it, and you will enjoy it much more, and by default, you will drink more of the water.

▶

In order to create more emotional engagement and enjoyment with water, Dr. Mascha suggests reading the label of a bottle of water to see if it tells you where the water has come from, such as an iceberg, a particular natural spring, and so on. He further suggests identifying the source of the water to learn more about the region and the history of the water. Look up the mineral and trace element content of the water from that particular source. Try water from different sources to start comparing the flavor profiles. Keep in mind, Mascha warns, if it has "purified" on the label, then the water is not straight from an original clean water source.

## Emotionally Engaging with the Water Source to Increase Enjoyment

I have a joyful memory about drinking water. I was five years old when my family began spending a week every August at a lodge in the White Mountains of New Hampshire. As a child, I looked forward to those days all year long, when we left the heat of New York City to spend time in this magical place.

One of my favorite activities was to hike through the forest, filled with sweet-smelling pines and trees whose leaves were already changing to bright gold, orange, and red, to the lake, where we would swim and row in boats. It was extremely quiet and peaceful by the lake. The only sounds were those of the wind in the trees, the lapping of the water on the boats, and the calling of the loons. When swimming in this lake, the water felt like velvet.

And the water that we drank at the lodge was actually pumped from that lake. It was the sweetest water I had ever tasted. At our meals, I never wanted anything else to drink. I loved everything about that water. That water really did, objectively, have a good taste. It probably had many minerals and trace elements that contributed to its sweet flavor. But, I know that my enjoyment of the water went deeper. I was emotionally engaged with that water. I knew the source of that drinking water, and I had happy experiences around that source of water.

## Other Benefits of Enjoying Water

The benefits of enjoying water, aside from the benefits of hydration, include drinking less alcohol, soda, and other drinks that may not be good for our health. "There's a huge health benefit just alone from out-crowding other drinks that are not good for you," said Mascha, "Water can be a very good vector for minerals and trace elements. Europeans have known this for a long time. They like mineral water because it's healthy for you."

## Bad-tasting Tap Water

Many of my clients have told me that they don't drink much water because they don't like the taste of water. I, myself, have often felt that drinking water was just something that I have to do, not necessarily something that I like to do, because I don't always enjoy the taste. In many places, the tap water may have a bad taste, and in these cases, Mascha recommended a reverse-osmosis water filter for the tap, which will greatly improve the taste of the tap water.

# Part V

# Vitality for Mind & Body

I've learned that, when I pay complete attention,
The pit of despair is not bottomless
When I'm trudging through a particularly dark part of
the Journey, that I can feel joy even while feeling pain,
And that, by pausing and allowing, sitting still and
breathing,
Inspiration will begin to flow again.

# Part V

# Vitality for Mind and Body

*"To keep our body in good health is a duty. Otherwise, we shall not be able to keep our mind strong and clear."*

~ Buddha

Some of the obvious rewards of exercise include weight loss and building muscle mass. But there are also many other health benefits that are less obvious, but just as, or even more important. In this section, I will explore these benefits, including the slowing down of the aging process, improving mood, and decreasing stress-related disease. In addition, I will discuss the benefits of yoga as a form of exercise (in addition to being a form of meditation) and how much exercise it will take before we can expect to see any results.

We'll also touch on sleep. Insufficient sleep has been declared by the Center for Disease Control (CDC) as a public health epidemic in the United States. I'll discuss in this section the dangers of chronically insufficient sleep, including the effects on mood and health, as well as how to get more of the quality of sleep that leads us to feel better rested and energized.

# Chapter 24

# Let's Get Moving!

*"My grandmother started walking five miles a day when she was sixty. She's ninety-seven now, and we don't know where the heck she is."*

~ ELLEN DEGENERES

At this point, we all have a pretty good idea that how we treat our body and the state of our physical health has a tremendous affect on how we feel, emotionally. While growing up, my parents often told me that the most important thing we have in life is our health. My dad lived that message and he was one of the first "joggers" in our neighborhood, before jogging came into style. When I was five years old, my parents moved our family to Rockaway Beach, essentially a sandbar stuck out in the Atlantic Ocean and considered to be a part of the borough of Queens in New York City. The primary reason for our move was so that my dad could jog on the boardwalk by the beach. During our first years there, I remember him coming home from a jog, joking that the neighbors were wondering where he was running to or what he was running from. It didn't take long, though, before the craze hit and everyone was out on the boardwalk, "jogging" and later "running" (same action, different label).

My dad remained fit throughout his life and lived to the ripe young age of ninety-three. I took up running with him on vacations from college. Those were special times we spent together. One of our runs together is most memorable to me. I was twenty years old and my dad, forty years my senior, was sixty. We went for a run on the boardwalk and had gone about a mile and a half from home when it started to pour. We sprinted the whole way back home, arriving soaked to the bone, out of breath, and laughing. We often reminisced about that rainy run over the years afterward. It didn't strike me until much later that he was in such great shape at sixty years old.

When he was close to seventy, my dad gave up running because of back pain and he took up brisk walking. At that time, my parents were living by another boardwalk, in Brighton Beach, Brooklyn. Again, whenever I returned for a visit we would walk together on the boardwalk, my dad walking at a rapid pace while asking me questions about my life and me trying to keep up with him, too out of breath to answer his questions. In addition, my dad and mom were devoted folk-dancers, dancing almost every weekend and sometimes taking week-long folk-dance trips. This resulted in remaining much younger in mind and body than their more sedentary peers. With his eyes sparkling, he would often playfully ask strangers he would meet, "How old do you think I am?" Most people were rarely able to guess his true age. Usually, they would guess at least ten years younger than his actual age. Beaming with pride and a huge smile on his face, he would respond with his real age, waiting for the shocked look or the exclamation of "No way!" He obviously loved that game.

Weight loss and building muscle mass, as well as staying more youthful are some of the rewards of exercise. And there are also many other health benefits that are less obvious, but just as, or even more important, including decreased risks of heart disease, high blood pressure, constipation, and diabetes, as well as increased stamina, blood circulation, co-ordination and balance, and lung functioning. In addition, exercise can improve flexibility, which decreases joint pain, decreases stiffness, improves posture, and relieves muscle tension. Indirectly, these health benefits improve our emotional well-being because, if we're feeling good and looking healthier, and if we're able to do more of the things that we enjoy because of our increased strength and stamina, then we're more likely to feel happier and more confident in our lives.

There are also many ways that exercise and moving our bodies actually can have direct effects on the brain, influencing our mood, relieving anxiety and depression. For example, exercise has a direct impact on improving sleep, which is essential for decreasing or preventing anxiety and depression (see Chapter 27, "Getting Our ZZZs," for more about the importance of good quality sleep). In addition, exercise decreases our feeling of being *stressed out*, which as I wrote about in Chapter 11, "Reducing Stress," can lead to an overall feeling of anxiety and even a depressed mood.

"If you're angry or frustrated about something and you take it out in the gym, on the treadmill or the elliptical, or you take it out on the jump rope or some dumbbells, you're doing something that's benefiting you in so many ways and you feel so amazing at the end, that you're left wondering what you were so upset about in the first place," said Health Coach Quentin Vennie, when I had a chance to interview him about the topic of exercise and mood. "Anger, frustration, anxiety, and depression are all energies, and if we can find something constructive to do with these energies, like exercising, then we will fight the fight and win the battle."

Vennie also pointed out in our discussion that exercise is a form of moving meditation that keeps us in the present, while depression is related to regretting the past and anxiety is due to worrying about the future. "During these moments of physical activity, generally, we're not focused on our problems, we're not focused on those things that make us feel uncomfortable or give us pain, mentally or physically. Whether we're going for a bike ride, doing yoga or martial arts, whatever it is, it gives us something to focus our attention on and it gives us a reason to remain present in the moment. This helps to strengthen our mind."

Additionally, exercising triggers the production of *endorphins* in our brains, those "feel-good" chemicals produced by the brain that are natural pain-relievers and mood elevators. Most pain relief medications are synthesized to mimic these endorphins. Our own production of these natural chemicals by our brain is much more effective than medication and has none of the side effects.

Furthermore, studies on animals have shown that exercise increases the levels of the neurotransmitters, serotonin, dopamine, and norepinephrine, in our brain. As I mentioned in the "Food for the Soul" section, these are also essential brain chemicals that are important for good mood and good sleep, and in fact, antidepressant medications, such as Zoloft and Prozac, work by increasing the production of these brain chemicals. A study of depressed women and men over the age of fifty, conducted at Duke University in 2007, found that adding in a routine of regular exercise was as effective at reducing depressed mood as was Zoloft. So, again, if we can increase the production of these chemicals, naturally, we will have outcomes that are better than medication. When we naturally create these neurotransmitters, they are more efficiently utilized by our brain and body and without the side effects.

Another brain chemical responsible for improving mood is brain-derived neurotropic factor (BDNF). And, guess what! Exercise has also been found to elevate the levels of this chemical in the brain. Increased BDNF may also help brain cells to survive longer, and this may, therefore, slow down the progression of various types of dementia, such as Alzheimer's disease, and might actually help to *prevent* these brain diseases.

## Mouse Study Shows Exercise Slows Down the Aging Process

Not only do we, subjectively feel younger, when we have a regular exercise routine, as well as have less risk of serious health issues that tend to age us, but research has found a significant slowing of aging of our bodies in every way. One such study was one that was conducted with mice. In 2011, *The Proceedings of the National Academy of Sciences* published a study that had been conducted by Dr. Mark Tarnopolsky and his colleagues at McMaster University in Ontario, Canada. In this study, several mice were genetically programmed to grow old at an accelerated pace. It was then found that exercise reduced or eliminated almost every detrimental effect of aging in the mice. The researchers were actually surprised by the magnitude of the impact that exercise had on the animals' aging process. They expected to find exercise would affect the health of muscles, including the heart, since past research had shown such a connection. They had not expected, however, that exercise would affect *every tissue and bodily system studied*. Tarnopolsky's conclusion was that, "unquestionably, exercise alters the course of aging."

# Chapter 25

# Time to Hit Your Mat!

*"Yoga is the fountain of youth. You're only as young as your spine is flexible."*

~ Bob Harper, of *The Biggest Loser*

Yoga has been one of my practices on and off throughout my life since my teens. My high school was a little ahead of its time and offered yoga as a physical education class. I loved it from the first time I learned the practice. I can't say that I've been doing yoga regularly ever since, but it has been something that, whenever I've re-started practicing, has welcomed me "home" with a feeling of peacefulness and an open heart.

I've tried all different varieties of yoga throughout the years, starting with the very popular form of hatha yoga, venturing into a little bit of vinyasa and then falling in love with Kundalini. When I moved to Austin in 2003, I discovered a yoga studio that offered several different forms of yoga, and I decided to give Kundalini a spin. After the first class, I was hooked, and I attended so many classes in a week that the staff of the studio asked if I wanted to be trained as a teacher. I didn't end up doing that because I didn't want to turn this enjoyable obsession into something that I had to turn into work. I enjoyed remaining a student. Later, when I had gotten away from yoga for a while, I was reintroduced to Kundalini through several of the DVD's by Ravi Singh and Ana Brett, known as RaviAna (be sure to read my interview with Ravi Singh later in this chapter).

Sometimes, I practice yoga specifically to relax. As the yoga teacher, Steve Kane, spoke about in our interview (see Chapter 29, "Mindfulness to Break the Pain Cycle), yoga can be a very powerful form of mindfulness meditation that has the benefits of calming anxiety and improving mood. And Kane is the real deal, as I found out when I took one of his yoga classes in Tarrytown, New York. While his class had the components of strengthening and increasing flexibility, the main benefit was that I felt like a weight had been lifted off of my shoulders by the time the class was done and that sense of calmness stayed with me for the several days that followed.

At other times, I practice yoga as a workout. My "go to" for my home practice is Kundalini yoga with the RaviAna DVD's. They have released about thirty different DVD's and downloadable streams. My favorites change all the time, but, right now, I prefer their *Kundalini Yoga Cardio, Stretch, and Strengthen All-In-One Workout and Solar Power* DVD's. I find that I get a good work out from this form of yoga, and that I feel peaceful afterward, as well.

I'm not faithful to one type of yoga and take a variety of classes, when I have the chance. I've found that, if I like the teacher, the type of yoga almost doesn't matter. I've had the opportunity to interview several yoga teachers on my radio program, all with a slightly different perspective and variation of style.

One guest whom I interviewed was Peggy Cappy, who has been teaching yoga for over forty years and whose show, *Peggy Cappy's Yoga for the Rest of Us*, can be seen nationwide on Public Broadcasting Stations. When Cappy was on my program, we talked about yoga as an exercise that has many benefits at any age.

# YOGA IS BENEFICIAL AT ANY AGE

Peggy Cappy, *Yoga For the Rest of Us*

We know is that, as we get older, we lose muscle strength. It's just a fact of aging, and we begin having more difficulty with balance. We now realize that we can increase strength, particularly in the thigh muscles, which I call, "our muscles of independence." If we have strong legs, then we have the ability to get up and down, in and out of cars and chairs. So, those muscles have to be worked on every week. You have to be actively doing something.

When we're in our twenties and thirties, our normal activities take care of the strength. But, over the decades, there's a steady decline, so people have to be proactive if they want to maintain an active lifestyle. What we find is that, when people do work on strength, and when they do practice balance, they really regain confidence in moving and that translates to being more active, in general. Again, being able to do the things that you love to do helps the quality of life to be very high.

▶

> ▶ As for someone who is physically challenged in any way, there are yoga poses that will help every kind of challenge that someone has. For example, for those who are unable to get onto the floor for yoga, chair yoga can be just as valuable.

On a recent trip to Puerto Vallarta, I was taking a more strenuous and intensive yoga class in the Vinyasa style, which involves flowing from one pose to another, with yoga teacher, Anna Laurita, at her studio, Davanna Yoga. I also interviewed Laurita for a video that I was taping. During this interview, she told me that the population of retirees, both Baby Boomers and seniors, who were enrolling in her classes in Puerta Vallarta, had been increasing over the previous few years and that many of these mature students had never tried yoga before. "I've witnessed both emotional and physical transformation in these new students," Laurita told me, "including improved mood and increased confidence, as well as increased balance and flexibility and decreased aches and pains."

Using yoga as a form of exercise has the advantage of increasing strength, stamina, flexibility, and balance, as well as aiding in weight loss and increasing muscle mass, while imposing very low stress to the joints, so that it can be practiced all the way into very advanced ages. Another advantage of yoga over other exercises is that, while we receive the many physical benefits of this exercise, we're also using various breathing techniques that oxygenate our blood, cleanse our brain, and calm our nervous system. Kundalini yoga uses some rapid movement in and out of poses, rather than holding a pose. Unique breathing techniques and the chanting of certain vibrational sounds are also incorporated. It has the added advantage of balancing our glandular system and strengthening our nervous system.

---

# YOGA AS ENERGY WORK

Ravi Singh, Kundalini Yoga Teacher, Co-Founder with Ana Brett of *RaviAna* Co-Author, with Ana Brett, of *The Kundalini Yoga Book: Life in the Vast Lane*

Most traditional yoga systems are derivations of hatha yoga, which are the typical yoga poses that you'll see in most books. Hatha yoga is very good for flexibility, and it's very good for health, overall. It's a really good adjunct to various other forms of fitness. Kundalini encompasses that approach, but also picks up where other practices leave off.

The way that Kundalini yoga picks up where others leave off is that it's energy work. It takes into account the fact that we're more than just a physical body. We're actually many bodies. We're the glands, the nerves, the chakras, the meridians, and energy flow. So, all of these things determine our health, well-being, and state of mind. Kundalini

▶ operates on the premise that we don't have all the time in the world. You know, everyone is busy, so we need to maximize our effort and multitask. Kundalini is the ultimate multitasking fitness. It works on all levels at once.

One big way is its use of breathing along with the exercises. That speeds up the benefits and accelerates the healing on so many levels. It's also very dynamic. Most yoga systems use static poses, but Kundalini incorporates movement along with the poses, which makes it very powerful.

Kundalini also uses sequences called *kriyas*. The yogis in ancient times figured out that, if you do things in certain combinations, then certain benefits will occur beyond linear processes and that's what makes it so powerful and profound.

The medical doctor, Dr. Dharma Singh Kalsa, explains in his book, *Meditation as Medicine: Activate the Power of Your Natural Healing Force*, the sound waves created in our own head and body when we chant the various ancient sounds during Kundalini yoga, actually stimulate the pituitary gland to trigger the production of the neurotransmitters in our brain that have calming and mood-elevating effects. He found that Kundalini yoga not only decreases anxiety and depression, but also increases mental sharpness in older adults.

Dr. Joseph Mercola, co-author of *Effortless Healing: 9 Simple Ways to Sidestep Illness, Shed Excess Weight, and Help Your Body Fix Itself,* has reviewed several of the research studies looking at the benefits of yoga for mind and body health. The outcomes have been even more significant than expected. Multiple scientific studies found that a regular practice of yoga can significantly increase the abilities to focus attention and multitask, increase speed and accuracy of comprehension and problem-solving, improve mood and decrease anxiety, help with getting better sleep, improve immune functioning, decrease migraine headaches in those who suffer from migraines, lower the risk of hypertension and heart disease, and increase sexual functioning and satisfaction.

All of the different forms of yoga have several common benefits, as well as some that are unique to each of the different yoga types. I recommend trying a few styles of yoga and finding the one, or ones, that you enjoy the most. If you've practiced one type of yoga before, then try a new form of yoga that you've never done. You might discover a new passion. However, with whatever style of yoga you try, its essential to take a class with a teacher for the first few times because it's possible to injure yourself, even with yoga, if you're doing the postures wrong.

# Chapter 26

# Are We There Yet?

*"Moderate exercise is indispensable; exercise till the mind feels delight in reposing from the fatigue."*

~ SOCRATES

You can walk, bike, swim, do yoga, go dancing, take a Zumba class, lift weights, or try any other exercise that you enjoy and are able to do. There are many types of exercises that can be modified for those who have limitations. Try a few different types of exercise and figure out which ones you enjoy. If you enjoy it, you're more likely to stick to it. As Health Coach Quentin Vennie told me, "Being healthy and happy doesn't have to be a job. It's something you can enjoy doing. Go have a good time." If you mix it up a little and don't do the same form of exercise all the time, you'll likely benefit different muscle groups, have less chance of injury, and will be less likely to become bored, and, therefore, lose interest.

When asked how much exercise is the right amount of exercise, Vennie responded, "If you're engaging in strenuous exercise, I'd say three times per week is ideal. However, it's important, not only for your physical health, but also for your mental health, to do some form of physical activity every day. It could be as simple as going for a walk in the park. You don't need to track your mileage or get wrapped up in the statistics or the data. Just get out and enjoy the day."

Common sense says to start slow and increase to more strenuous exercises and a longer time, as you build strength and stamina. In addition, it's important to have a complete medical examination before beginning any new exercise program. Also, if you're starting a new form of exercise, meet with a trainer in order to make sure that you're doing the exercise or using any equipment correctly and to customize the right exercise program for you. And, as I mentioned, even with yoga, you can injure yourself, if you don't do the poses correctly, so that having a teacher is very important.

The most recent research shows that the more hours in the week that we spend in moderate exercise (such as walking, dancing, bike-riding, more strenuous forms of yoga, or even gardening), the longer and healthier our lives will likely be. In fact, studies have found that an hour per day of brisk walking, for example, can reduce rates of mortality by 24 percent. "A meta-analysis of physical activity, dose and longevity found that the equivalent of about an hour a day of brisk (4 mph) walking was good," wrote Greger, in *How Not to Die*, "but ninety minutes was even better." In this case, more seems to be better, as long as we're able to handle it.

A couple of years ago, I spoke with Austin fitness trainer, Jeremy Robinson, about how long it would take me to get back into my best fitness. I had gone through a pretty stressful year, leaving my exercise consistency to fall by the wayside and adding a little extra padding around my middle. I was particularly concerned because, now in my fifties, it suddenly seemed to be impossible to see results, as I was working out frequently at the gym but finding that the scale wasn't moving. His response was reassuring, and helped me to be determined to stay with the program. (More in our interview!)

# IT'S NEVER TOO LATE

Jeremy Robinson
Owner, *Austin Holistic Fitness*

It's amazing how many people think that they're "going downhill" or that they've missed their chance to be in their prime. I've been training for almost sixteen years and I've seen people in their forties, fifties, and sixties make significant progress in their fitness. Many get to see that after a good year of putting in the hard work of exercising and eating well, they can feel ten to twenty years younger. Many of them have become more athletic and in better shape at fifty than they were at thirty. Life starts all over and everything is new again. You can go into your eighties holding onto that great health. If at fifty, you have become more healthy and aware of your body, you have another life to live. Many of my clients end up saying to me, "Thank you. I never knew this could be a possibility for me."

If you come in and out of fitness and are not staying on top of it, then it will take about one solid year to turn it around. You can get some great results in four or five months, and in about one year, you will see the change really stick.

▶ I want people to understand that hard times do happen in life and there are a lot of responsibilities. There are going to be times when you say, "I'm not going to get to the gym for awhile." It's not the end of the world. You can do healthy things along the way such as make healthy food choices. And then you come back to the routine of exercising when you can. At any time, you can read a book, get inspired, find a trainer, and decide that health is for you.

Here are two final pieces of advice given to me by Quentin Vennie: "You can't out-train a bad diet. If you constantly go to the gym, but your diet is unhealthy, then you won't get good results from the gym. And, if you *over-train*, doing too much, instead of building muscle, you will be damaging muscles and joints."

Now that I'm getting back into feeling more fit, I've noticed that I have more energy, I don't catch as many colds, and my mood is better. I feel more excited about life, once again feeling enthusiastic to follow my dreams. Come join me on my journey toward even better health. On this path, we'll just walk for the sake of walking. In this situation, more than any other, the adage that "the goal of the journey is the journey itself" is the most accurate.

As Jeremy Robinson told me, "If you don't have a reason to get up and move, then it's time to seek out someone who can mentor you and inspire you to give it a chance. You might find that your life opens up because you suddenly have more energy."

# Chapter 27

# Getting Your ZZZs

*"He would lie in bed and finally, with daylight, he would go to sleep. After all, he said to himself, it is probably only insomnia. Many must have it."*

~ Ernest Hemingway, *A Clean Well-Lighted Place*

Have you ever had periods in your life when you were persistently unable to get a good night of sleep? If so, you're definitely not alone. Insufficient sleep has been declared by the Center for Disease Control (CDC) as a public health epidemic in the United States. I've certainly had my share of sleepless nights, when I tried to grab onto increasingly elusive sleep, watching it drift away from me the harder I tried to catch it. Maybe you're dealing with this very issue right now. How do you feel when you haven't been able to sleep? I usually feel more stressed out over even small conveniences when I haven't had a full night of Z's, as well as trouble thinking clearly or solving problems. I tend to feel irritable and sad, my body aches, and I feel uncoordinated, making me more likely to trip or stub my toe. If my difficulty sleeping persists for an extended period of time, I can be sure that I will catch a cold.

## Insufficient Sleep—Public Health Epidemic

There are many reasons for lack of sleep, which I will talk about in a bit. But, here's a question for you to ponder. How often have you said to yourself that there just aren't enough hours in the day to do everything? "Today much of our society is still operating under the collective delusion that sleep is simply time lost to other pursuits, that it can be endlessly appropriated at will to satisfy our increasingly busy lives and overstuffed to-do lists," wrote Ariana Huffington in her book, *The Sleep Revolution: Transforming Your Life, One Night at a Time.* "The combination of a deeply misguided definition of what it means to be successful in today's world—that it can come only through burnout and stress—along with the distractions and temptations of a 24/7 wired world, has imperiled our sleep as never before." In our fast-paced world, for many of us, our lifestyle tends to not be very conducive to taking time to relax and restore. This even causes us to cut into our hours of sleep, believing that we can borrow these hours and then pay them back when we've reached our goals. (See Chapter 5, "Know When to Pause.")

As I mentioned, the CDC recently declared lack of sufficient sleep to be at epidemic proportions in the U.S. Insufficient sleep has been linked to higher risks for chronic illnesses, such as hypertension, diabetes, obesity, and even cancer, as well as emotional conditions, such as depression. Sleep deprivation also decreases productivity at our jobs, as well as in our creative endeavors. Without sleep, our quality of life suffers dramatically and it can lead to a shorter life span. A recent collaborative study conducted by the CDC and the National Center on Sleep Disorders looked at sleep patterns in the U.S. An estimated fifty to seventy million U.S. adults were found to be reporting disorders of sleep and wakefulness, including significant difficulties with falling and staying asleep at night, as well as difficulty staying awake during the day. The National Department of Transportation has found drowsy driving to be responsible for approximately 1,550 fatalities and 40,000 nonfatal injuries every year in the U.S.

## Sleep, Health & Mood

Getting enough restful sleep is essential for physical and emotional health, no matter our age. Two recent studies demonstrated the emotional effects of lack of sleep, the first showed these effects for long-term poor sleepers, while the second showed detrimental affects on stress management and mood after missing just one night of sleep. The Great British Sleep Survey, conducted between 2010 and 2012, surveyed almost 21,000 people, representing wide-ranging ages and lifestyles, throughout Great Britain about their sleep. For those who reported having poor sleep over a long period of time, they tended to be more likely to feel helpless in their lives, significantly more lonely, and have two times the likelihood of having relationship problems, than those who reported good sleep. In addition, the poor sleepers tended to feel more fatigued during the day and to have difficulty with concentration. A study by the American Psychological Association in 2012 found that poor sleep leads to more quickly feeling stressed out, angry, and anxious in situations that would, otherwise, not be considered particularly stressful.

The emotional experiences of stress, anxiety, anger, and depression consequently have negative affects on our ability to fall asleep or to have good quality, restful, sleep. So, this can become an endless cycle and a downward spiral with regard to our quality of life.

## Common Causes for Insufficient Sleep

- Anxiety or sadness can keep us from getting a good night's sleep. This, in turn can lead to increased anxiety and/or more serious depression.

- Poor habits, such as keeping erratic hours for going to sleep and waking up, can interfere with our circadian rhythm (our twenty-four hour biological clock), which is tied closely to our sleep-wake cycle. Interference with the circadian rhythm causes significant disruptions in our ability to obtain enough restful sleep.

- Drinking alcohol before going to bed will interfere with staying asleep and receiving good quality sleep, even if we sleep through the night. (See Chapter 23, "Alcohol: The Good, Bad, and Ugly.")

- Physical pain can often interfere with our ability to sleep. (See Chapter 29, "Mindfulness to Break the Pain Cycle.")

- Medications can often be the culprit for not getting a good night of sleep. If you're taking medication for a medical issue and you're having trouble sleeping, it would be advisable to check with your doctor to see if this is a side effect of the medication. If so, see if it's possible to replace this medication with a different one that may not have such a side effect. This isn't always possible. Some of the other tips given here and in the next section might help to compensate for the effects of the medication.

- Lack of exercise can increase the risk for poor sleep. Obviously, the antidote to that is to exercise regularly. The recommendation is to do some aerobic exercise during the day, but at least three hours prior to going to bed, as exercising too close to bedtime can cause more difficulty falling asleep. I always feel more energized after working out and this is great during the day, but not when I want to go to sleep.

- Caffeine too late in the day will often interfere with sleep. (See Chapter 21, "I Love Coffee.")

- Organic disorders, such as restless leg syndrome or sleep apnea, may be culprits for poor sleep. Treatment for these conditions will help with getting better sleep.

- Hormonal fluctuations, especially in women at the time of peri-menopause and menopause, can wreak havoc with sleep.

---

# A KEY IN THE COG

Dr. Bruce Meleski, Neurosensory Performance
Specialist Founder, *Intelligent Sleep*

Sleep allows your body to restore, physiologically and neurologically. There are recent studies that sleep serves to clear and detoxify the brain in a nightly fashion. Also, your REM sleep helps you to reorganize your thoughts and to solidify memories. There have been many studies in the past few years, showing how important sleep is and how it impacts all types of chronic diseases. If you just lose one night of sleep, there will be an impact on you, to some extent. It will cause you to feel irritable and short-tempered. If you continue with that pattern, in the long-term, it will cause a decrease in your memory, your energy, and your ability to perform.

▶

▶ When I sleep well, I have great dreams and it's like a whole adventure. And this experience reorganizes my life because it gives me energy, completeness, and the ability to live a fuller life. Restorative sleep is key for performing at your best during the day, for manifesting and living your dreams. Getting good sleep is the key in the cog. If you get that, then everything else will flow. And there's a feedback loop, so that, when you're happy and living your dreams, you're going to have less anxiety and you'll be able to sleep better.

There are two types of insomnia, onset insomnia and latent insomnia, those who have trouble falling asleep and those who have trouble staying asleep. Having routines in your life is key for dealing with this. If you have trouble falling asleep, then you need to have a routine for going to bed that includes turning off all electronics (two hours before going to bed is appropriate), as those disrupt your circadian rhythm. The next step is to change your lights to amber lights, taking away the blue lights. All white lights in your house have a spectrum of blue that disrupt your brain and interfere with circadian rhythm. Your brain thinks its daylight. This is particularly a problem when you wake up at 3:00 a.m. and you turn on the light in the bathroom. Immediately, your brain says, "Good morning!" And this is one

▶

▶

of the reasons that you might have trouble falling back to sleep. The lights trick your brain, signaling that it's morning.

If you have chronic insomnia, and then can't sleep because of stress and anxiety about not being able to fall asleep, cognitive-behavioral therapy is recommended to help break that cycle. If you are a chronic insomniac, you likely engage in *negative sleep talk*, saying things to yourself such as, "If I don't sleep well, I'm going to be tired tomorrow," and have all kinds of negative thoughts about not sleeping, and worry yourself so much that you don't sleep. So that therapy would consist of restructuring how you think about sleep and how you talk to yourself about it. That's really important because people who have chronic insomnia always have those types of negative thoughts about sleep.

The other problem is that people are so wired these days they've forgotten how to relax. Relaxation and meditation is very important and very effective. Biofeedback is a very good relaxation technique, using breathing and a heart rate monitor, which is a good indicator of how much stress you have. Nutrition is also important.

As for medication to help with sleep, a lot of the sleep medications, shorten deep sleep and

▶

▶ shorten REM sleep. So, they help you get to sleep, but it's not really full sleep. There are notorious stories about people on Ambien, where people get up, sleep walk, and do various activities in their sleep.

Sleep is extremely sensitive to everything else that's going on in our life and how well we're handling our life. In fact, all of the topics discussed throughout this book, whether we're following our dreams and finding meaning in our lives, detoxifying from stress, establishing positive relationships with others and with ourselves, maintaining mindfulness about what we ingest and when we ingest these foods and drinks, getting enough exercise, and, coping with pain, all have an effect on our sleep. Therefore, if you're having trouble sleeping, putting into practice some of the suggestions made in the other chapters of this book might help you to significantly improve the quality and quantity of your sleep.

# Chapter 28

# The Quality and Quantity of Our Sleep

*"Sleep is the best meditation."*

~ Dalai Lama

The optimum amount of sleep needed for us to function at our best is different for every person, although, on average the consensus is that somewhere between seven and nine hours per night is ideal for most people. More important than the actual number of hours you've slept, though, is how you feel after a night of sleep. If you wake up feeling tired or you feel sleepy during the day, it's likely that you haven't had enough "good sleep."

In order for all of the benefits of sleep to occur—the regeneration of cells, the strengthening of our immune system, the feeling of being rested, the sharpening of our brains, the boosting of our mood, and so on—we need to have approximately four to six complete cycles of sleep during the night. A complete cycle of sleep consists of having what's called REM or Rapid Eye Movement sleep (that time during sleep when we dream), as well as four stages of non-REM sleep or N-REM sleep.

Typically, when we fall asleep, our brain goes into the four stages of the N-REM sleep, each lasting anywhere from five to fifteen minutes. Stage 1 consists of a very light sleep, when we're just falling asleep; Stage 2 is still a light sleep, when our body prepares for deeper sleep;

and Stages 3 and 4 consist of deeper levels of sleep, with Stage 4 being the deepest. These N-REM stages of sleep are then followed by a brief period of REM sleep. Interruption of these stages or the flow from one stage to another will cause us to miss out on the benefits of sleep, even if we've slept a total of nine hours in one night. As I wrote about in Chapter 22, "Alcohol: The Good, Bad, and Ugly," alcohol, for example, can be very disruptive of the quality of sleep, even if it knocks us out and causes us to sleep longer, because it often leads to skipping some of these sleep stages in the cycle.

If your sleep is light and fragmented, with frequent awakening during the night, you may need to spend a little more time in bed in order to obtain the needed hours of sleep. A nap during the day may help to make up for lost time during the night, as long as that nap is not longer than thirty minutes or past three o'clock in the afternoon. Longer and later naps can further interrupt sleep that night, causing the need for more naps, and thus, resulting in a vicious cycle.

## Getting Better Sleep

The many issues that I've touched on throughout this book all have an impact on our ability to get enough good quality sleep in order to receive all of the many benefits of sleep. For example, if we are not taking the steps we need in order to follow our dream, our soul's calling, and our purpose, this can wake us up in the middle of the night with a feeling that something is not right. Some might refer to this as an existential crisis or a "dark night of the soul." I've experienced many sleepless nights throughout past years, wondering what I was supposed to be doing with my life. For some, these sleepless nights serve as a catalyst to search for their purpose, so that they can sleep more soundly. Others might just find ways to numb themselves, so that they don't have to do the work. I believe that the latter method always catches up with us and bites us in the butt when we're least expecting it, or at the very least, causes chronic emotional and physical malaise during our waking hours.

In addition, if we're stressed out and anxious or we're not getting proper exercise nor eating a healthy diet, our sleep at night will likely suffer. Therefore, the tips and suggestions, given in the other chapters of this book, will be helpful in our quest for better sleep. If you're following your dreams, finding satisfaction and meaning in your life, reversing stressful habits of thinking, eating a healthy diet, implementing healthy routines of relaxation and exercise, and staying away from too much sugar, caffeine, alcohol, and other drugs, you're likely sleeping better, or at least you're on the road to better sleep.

In Chapter 25, "Time to Hit Your Mat!" I pointed out that yoga can be helpful for better sleep. More specifically, yoga has a positive affect on sleep because it decreases physical pain that often interferes with sleep, it leads to relaxation of mind and body, and if it's a strenuous form of yoga, the exercise early in the day will help with feeling sleepy at night. There is an additional benefit that is unique to yoga with regard to sleep. There are certain yoga poses and yogic breathing techniques, which can trigger greater sleepiness and more sound sleep. For example, poses that consist of holding a forward bend position causes the nervous system to calm down and can be very effective in helping us to fall asleep, if done right before bed. They can also be used if we wake up during the night and can't fall right back to sleep. One pose that is commonly recommended by yoga teachers to trigger sleep is the "Legs-Up-The Wall" pose. This is exactly as it sounds, lying either on a matt on the floor or on your bed with your butt up against the wall and your legs straight up the wall. Five minutes of holding this position, if you're able to do it, will increase sleepiness and the ability to fall asleep.

In Chapter 11, "Reducing Stress," I gave instructions for the alternate nostril breathing technique in order to induce the relaxation response. To get to sleep, you might try this same technique right before bed, except, this time, keep holding your right nostril closed throughout. Take ten long slow breathes in and out through your left nostril. This is a form of yogic breathing that has been found to induce sleep. Just go on-line and you will find a plethora of yoga videos demonstrating specific poses to do right before bedtime in order to help with falling asleep. *Raviana.com* has some specific bedtime routines.

## More Tips for Getting Better Sleep

- Be active and engaged, physically and socially, during the day, as well as take action to follow your life's purpose.

- Become an optimist in order to decrease racing thoughts of stress, worry, and sadness when your head hits the pillow. (See Chapter 7, "Realistic Optimism.")

- Get at least two hours of sunlight during the day. This has the effect of increasing melatonin—a natural hormone produced by our brain to help us fall asleep and to regulate our sleep-wake cycle.

- Avoid all forms of caffeine after 2:00 p.m. and decrease all caffeine, in general, if you're having a sleep problem. (See Chapter 21, "I Love Coffee.")

- Refrain from alcohol close to bedtime and limit alcohol usage, in general. (See Chapter 22, "Alcohol The Good, Bad, and Ugly.")

- Discontinue using any nicotine. Nicotine is a stimulant that will keep you awake. Quitting smoking is the number one piece of advice to benefit your health if you're a smoker, no matter what health condition you might have. Increasing your sleep will be an added bonus of kicking the habit.

- If you're having trouble falling asleep, it might be because your brain is sensitive to artificial lighting at night, as it can have the effect of stimulating and waking your brain, tricking it to think it's daytime. Therefore, avoiding bright lights in your home, as well as turning off your television, computer, smartphone, and back-lit e-reader devices, for two to three hours before going to bed, might be the key to falling asleep more easily, as Dr. Meleski recommended in the previous chapter.

- Keep your bedroom as dark, quiet, and cool as possible.

- Take a hot shower or bath about two hours before bed.

- If you're unable to fall asleep within twenty minutes of getting into bed, get out of bed and do something relaxing in another room, such as reading (the reading material should not be exciting, so that you don't have the desire to stay awake and read more), or playing solitaire (with an actual deck of cards and not on the computer), until you feel sleepy. I like to crochet, as knitting and crocheting have some of the relaxation benefits of meditation.

The reason that it works best for you to go into another room to do these activities, if you cannot fall asleep within twenty minutes, is that this is a form of brain training, leading your brain to associate your room and your bed with sleep and not with sleeplessness. If you wake up during the night and can't quickly fall back to sleep, perform this series of behaviors again. Keep repeating the routine as many times as necessary, if you don't fall asleep within twenty minutes. It may take a few nights of this form of *behavior modification*, or brain behavior training, before it starts to work, but within a few nights, you'll likely find that you fall asleep quicker, as long as you're also following the other recommendations.

## Natural Remedies

There are many natural remedies for sleep, including herbs, such as chamomile tea and valerian root tea. I recommend, before trying any herbal remedy, consult with your medical practitioner. Herbs are very powerful substances, and just as they can be powerfully effective in helping us, they can also have severe negative interactions with medications that you might be taking or any medical conditions that you might have.

Some people find melatonin to be a helpful supplement for bringing about better sleep. This is, again, different for everyone. For example, when I once tried melatonin, I felt as if I had just ingested an entire pot of coffee and was up for the whole night. On the other hand, some of my friends, family members, and clients find melatonin to be ideal to help them, not only fall asleep, but also get good quality sleep throughout the whole night. Melatonin is a hormone that we already naturally have, produced by the pineal gland in our brain. It controls our circadian rhythm or sleep/wake cycle. However, we sometimes don't produce enough of it and, therefore, have difficulty maintaining sleep. Thus, supplementation can be helpful to some. But, since melatonin is a hormone, it's important to speak with your medical practitioner, once again, before taking this supplement to see if it's safe for you. As mentioned earlier, you might just go out into the sunshine for two hours during the day for a more natural approach for triggering the production of melatonin.

I've found, for myself, the best results for sleep are when I take magnesium supplements. Magnesium is a mineral that plays a very important role in the human body, helping with hydration, muscle relaxation, energy production, regulating heart rate and blood pressure, and the deactivation of adrenaline. It turns out that most people are deficient in magnesium, especially if they drink a lot of coffee, which can flush it from our body. A deficiency in magnesium is likely to cause difficulty sleeping, as well as muscle tension, anxiety, hypertension, irregular heart rate, and can even cause seizures.

Dr. Mark Hyman, author, medical director of Cleveland's Clinic for Functional Medicine, and founder of the Ultra-Wellness Center, recommends that most people benefit from 400 to 1000 milligrams of magnesium per day of supplementation. He also advises taking a chelated form (such as citrate, ascorbate, orotate, glycinate, or a mixture of these forms). Oxide salts can tend to cause stomach upset. In fact, you may find that some of the other forms cause some stomach upset for you. It's best to start with a much lower dose and gradually increase to see how much your stomach can tolerate.

Yet, as much as we all need magnesium, before taking it as a supplement, I still caution you to do the research and check with your own health care practitioner to make sure that it doesn't have a negative interaction with any medications you're taking or with any medical conditions you have. For example, if you have kidney disease or severe heart disease, magnesium must only be taken under a doctor's supervision. Also, rather than taking supplements, there are many foods chocked full of magnesium. These foods include dark green leafy vegetables, nuts and seeds, beans and lentils, whole grains, avocados, bananas, and dark chocolate. One word of caution is to be careful with chocolate because it contains sugar and caffeine, which can backfire and keep you awake.

# THE TRYPTOPHAN TRIP FOR MOOD & SLEEP

Tryptophan is an essential amino acid, one of the building blocks of protein. It cannot be manufactured by the human body and must be obtained through diet. Tryptophan is a necessary factor in the production of the neurotransmitter, Serotonin. Enough serotonin must be present in the brain in order to obtain sufficient restful sleep, to maintain calm, and to prevent depression. Deficiencies in serotonin can lead to poor sleep, anxiety, and depression. Without the right amount of tryptophan, the optimal level of serotonin can't be produced by the brain. Many of the newer antidepressant drugs, as well as some of the sleep aids, have the action of increasing serotonin.

We have a protective barrier, called the "blood-brain barrier" (BBB). This is a semi-permeable barrier, made up of brain capillaries, to prevent some substances from crossing into the brain tissue. This protects the brain from exposure to substances in the blood that may injure the brain; it protects the brain from hormones and neurotransmitters that are present in the rest of

▶

▶

the body, but that may be harmful to the brain; and it maintains a consistent environment for the brain.

When tryptophan is consumed with a large amount of other amino acids, such as when eating animal proteins, which contain all twenty amino acids, the tryptophan has to compete with the other amino acids to cross the blood brain barrier because there are only a limited number of receptors available to aid these substances in crossing over into the brain. As it turns out, in animal proteins, there is a much smaller amount of tryptophan than there are other amino acids, and the tryptophan molecules lose out in the race to cross the BBB. They are usually left waiting at the gate and very few actually cross into the brain. For this reason, it is actually a myth that turkey or warm-milk induces better sleep because of their high levels of tryptophan. When tryptophan is consumed along with fewer of the other amino acids, such as when eating a plant-based protein, which do not contain all twenty amino acids, there will be less competition to cross the BBB and get into the brain tissue.

Also, when tryptophan is consumed with carbohydrates, the body produces insulin to metabolize the carbs and this diverts the other

▶

▶ amino acids present in the food to the muscles, while leaving the tryptophan alone. (Remember, complex carbs are always preferable to prevent a sudden spike of blood sugar.) Therefore, there is even less competition for the tryptophan to cross the BBB, allowing a greater amount of this amino acid into the brain tissue to do its thing in creating that lovely mood-elevating, sleep-inducing, relaxation-enhancing neurotransmitter, serotonin.

In *How Not to Die,* Greger recommends, "such seeds as sesame, sunflower, or pumpkin, may fit the bill" as good sources of tryptophan, along with a high complex-carbohydrate, low protein, meal for the best absorption and resulting synthesis of serotonin in our brains.

Again, difficulty in sleeping could be caused by hormonal imbalances, especially in women who are experiencing peri-menopause and menopause. So, having your hormones checked and then speaking with your practitioner about natural ways to balance your hormones, if an imbalance is found, might be what you need to get better sleep. There are some natural supplements that can help with such imbalances, as well as dietary changes. Diets high in those green leafy vegetables can balance hormones. I direct you back to the section on "Food for the Soul," to learn about the many benefits of increasing plant-based foods in your diet. Finally, check out the recommended reading list at the back of this book for some additional information.

To get better sleep, we have to take a look at how we're taking care of ourselves, overall. It's worth the effort in order to increase our restful sleep because sleep also affects every other aspect of our life. If we're not sleeping enough hours, or well enough, we will not be able to follow our dreams and enjoy our lives with the same enthusiasm and vitality. So, turn off the television and your social media and whatever else you're doing that's keeping your brain "wired." Take some time to deeply relax and let yourself drift off to a deep sleep. Sweet dreams, my friend, we have continued adventures and pleasant surprises ahead along our journey. We will all need our rest.

# Chapter 29

# Mindfulness to Break
# the Pain Cycle

*"Pain is inevitable.*
*Suffering is optional."*

~ BUDDHA

We've all experienced pain from time to time—a wrenched back, a sprained ankle, tooth pain, or even a headache. Yet when pain becomes chronic (lasting for longer than three months with little or no relief), it often leads to the *pain cycle:* Pain causes lowered activity and increased use of medications with side-effects of drowsiness and fatigue; this leads to further decreased activity and, subsequently, social isolation, boredom, less flexibility, strength, and stamina, and lowered ability to cope with daily stressors of life, spiraling us into depression and anxiety. This culminates in a lower tolerance to pain, greater sleep disturbance, and increased fatigue and muscle tension; and all of this cycles around to more pain and a repeat of this pain cycle, with even greater intensity, as well as emotional suffering.

The mind adds to this downward spiral when the body is experiencing pain that doesn't go away. In his book, *Full Catastrophe Living: Using the Wisdom of Your Body and Mind to Face Stress, Pain, and Illness,* Dr. Jon Kabat-Zinn writes, "If you have a chronic illness or a disability that prevents you from doing what you used to be able to do, whole areas of control may go up in smoke. And if your condition causes you physical pain that has not responded well to medical treatment, the distress you might be feeling can be compounded by emotional turmoil caused by knowing that your condition seems to be beyond even your doctor's control."

You may notice thoughts such as, "My body is broken," "I will never feel better," "I will never feel happy," or "This will never end." When we struggle like this in the face of pain, although it may be the "natural" thing to do, we are creating more emotional suffering, subsequently leading to greater physical pain and suffering.

In order to break this pain cycle, we need to approach it from several different angles. First, relaxation techniques can be extremely beneficial. They can reduce the stress caused by the pain. Relaxation reduces pain by releasing endorphins, which are those wonderful natural pain relievers and mood elevators in the brain. Furthermore, relaxation decreases symptoms caused by stress, such as sleep disturbance, fatigue, and muscle tension, which all tend to aggravate pain.

Mindfulness meditation, consisting of fully noticing the sensations of pain and illness as they rise and fall, without judgment, as strange as it sounds, has been shown to be more powerful in relieving pain than medication. In fact, this type of meditation has been found to reduce chronic pain by as much as 57 percent in newcomers to this technique and by more than 90 percent in seasoned mindfulness meditators, says Dr. Danny Penman, author of *Mindfulness: A Practical Guide for Relieving Pain, Reducing Stress, and Restoring Well-Being*.

As I mentioned in Chapter 12, "Finding Our Way to Happiness with Meditation," mindfulness meditation has been shown to change the structure of the brain so that meditators experience less intense pain over time, sometimes to the point of barely feeling the pain at all. These findings have inspired hospital clinics to prescribe mindfulness meditation for pain and discomfort stemming from a variety of conditions, instead of over-prescribing pain medications with their myriad of side effects. It has been suggested for coping with the pain of cancer and the physical side effects of chemotherapy, for heart disease symptoms, symptoms of diabetes and arthritis, as well as chronic back pain, migraine headaches, fibromyalgia, celiac disease, chronic fatigue, irritable bowel syndrome, and even multiple sclerosis. The research has consistently found that it's also a powerful reliever of stress, anxiety, and depression. And, in addition, it can improve memory, focus, and physical stamina, helping our overall sense of well-being and happiness.

One technique of mindfulness meditation that is frequently used for coping with physical pain and is also powerful for reducing anxiety and stress is called the Body Scan Meditation. According to Dr. Penman, the Body Scan "allows you to see your mind and body in action, to observe painful sensations as they rise, and to let go of struggling with them. When you do this, something remarkable happens: your suffering begins to melt away of its own accord."

## THE BODY SCAN

*Lie on your back, close your eyes, and feel your body sinking into the surface beneath you. Focus your attention on your breathing. There's nothing to change, nothing to control. Just notice the feeling of your breath as you inhale and exhale. Notice your*

*belly rising and falling with each breath. Notice the sound of your breath, as it comes in through your nose and as it goes out through your mouth. Feel the cool, healing breath come in through your nose, feel it as it moves through your body, and notice how it feels as it leaves your body, taking pain and tension with it.*

*Gently bring your awareness to each part of your body, slowly one by one, focusing attention on each part for two or three breaths, noticing the sensation in that part of your body without judgment and without trying to change it, just noticing. Take note: Is this body-part warm or cold, tense or relaxed, is there pain or is it pain-free? If there is pain, notice the quality of the pain, without judgment, if it's a sharp pain or a dull pain, if it's numb or intense. For example, "my left wrist has a dull achy pain, my right wrist is pain-free." Notice the sensations in each body part without judging, without telling yourself that this is good or bad. Just notice it.*

*Start with the top of your head, moving gradually through your face, your forehead, your eyes, your nose, your tongue, your throat, your lips. Move down through your throat, your neck, your right shoulder, your left shoulder, your chest, your upper back, your stomach, and your lower back. Move through each arm, one by one, down from the upper arm, through*

▶

*your elbows, your wrists, and each of your fingers. Again, settle on each area for two or three breaths, just noticing the sensations without judgment, even if you notice pain. Then notice each of your hips, your thighs, your knees, your calves, your ankles, your feet, and your toes, one by one.*

*After you've scanned each part of your body, separately, become aware of your whole body and again focus your attention on your breathing. Has it changed? Has it become deeper and slower? Allow yourself to enjoy the feeling of your breath, once again, bringing in healing energy, letting out tension and pain. When you're ready, slowly open your eyes and begin to notice where you are.*

*This has been adapted from the original by Dr. Jon Kabat-Zinn in his book, Full Catastrophe Living: Using the Wisdom of Your Body and Mind to Face Stress, Pain, and Illness. For a free audio version of the above meditation, recorded by me, especially for your use, go to: www.drmarakarpel.com.

Essentially, when pain cannot be controlled, what you resist persists. When you begin to allow yourself to go with the flow rather than fighting the pain, you will feel more in control of your life, instead of being ruled by your pain. This will ultimately break the cycle of pain and help you, once again, to have joy in your life. This goes for emotional pain, as well. "When we see other human beings suffering, it touches our capacity to feel pain," said Jan Bidwell, author of *Sitting Still*, "When we can hold that space for them, they can walk themselves out of that situation, but not if we're hiding from our internal struggle with it. And it really does just shake through. It comes through us."

This also applies to our own personal emotional pain, Jan Bidwell, author of *Sitting Still*, told me, when I had the opportunity to interview her. "When we suffer a loss, when somebody dies that we love, or something happens to our child that's difficult, it's the same thing in the sense that, if we can tolerate feeling it, it will just wash through us. It's the running from the pain that causes the problem, not the pain, in my experience." Bidwell explained our capacity to allow the pain to wash through us is strengthened by meditating regularly.

When I've found myself feeling emotionally out of balance or have lost sight of my desired goals and dreams, I remember the wisdom passed along to me by a friend during graduate school. "My grandma always told me," he said, "it's not how many times you get knocked down on the mat that counts. It's how long you stay down." We all get knocked off balance from time to time in our lives. Sometimes we can catch ourselves from falling or can get ourselves back up quickly. But, there are times when we may need to ask for help. Most important is that we get back up before too much time passes.

The bottom line is that what happens outside of us is the story of our life. It's not who we really are. Of course, we have emotional reactions to the events in our lives. But, if we can stay mostly calm, understanding that our true nature is peace, then the storms that happen around us, the ups and the downs, do not shake us to our core, and we can ride these waves without feeling sick, and perhaps even enjoying them.

As the Barefoot Doctor reminded me, when my first try at interviewing him on the radio, during a workshop he was teaching in Italy, was foiled by technical difficulties while we were live on the air (and I, admittedly, was *freaking out*), "Life is fun in spite of the hassles."

# A NEW VIEW OF HAPPINESS

Steve Kane Yoga Instructor and Teacher of *"The Art of Happiness"* Workshop

We all have happy moments, but I'm interested in a more lasting sense of well-being. I believe that's something that we can cultivate. Let's step back and look at the way society views happiness. Research has shown that in most of the United States, people need as little as $35,000 as a base income in order to no longer have an impact on happiness. That's contrary to what we see in our culture. Typically, there's a push to believe that if we do better financially, we'll be happier. The research has disproved that. So, this got me thinking about how we really cultivate happiness, rather than chasing the almighty dollar.

In many ways, happiness is a choice, and it has a lot to do with the way that we look at the world and how we react to life's challenges. And we all have life challenges. But, it's how we think about them and react to them that determine our level of well-being. In my experience, yoga is suited to help people become more present and to develop a sense of peace and equanimity that leads to the kind of true and lasting sense of happiness that I was talking about.

Essentially, yoga's approach is that we move our body and work the kinks out, and this helps us to quiet our mind and become more present. What that does is help us to develop a sense of being at peace in the present moment just the way it is. Nothing needs to change. We are comfortable in our own skin. We are resting into a sense of well-being.

This leads to the idea that bliss is actually our resting state. This idea goes all the way back to the beginning of yoga, the idea that underneath the clutter of the mind, there's a sense of bliss, a joy of being alive. So, happiness is not something we need to achieve, rather, it's something we need to remember. Inside us is a profound joy of just simply being, but it's covered up with a lifetime's accumulation of junk. It's been sometimes referred to as polishing a mirror to clean the grime away and let the light shine through.

There's also a right-brain/left-brain issue, where our thinking mind is dominant and there's this constant chatter, bringing us out of the present

▶

▶

moment. It's pulling us into the past and it's pulling us into the future. But, this joy of being that we're talking about happens in the present moment. So, that the extent that we can't quiet our mind, we are always being pulled away from this sense of well-being. It was Lao Tzu that said that if you live in the past, you have depression, and, if you live in the future, you have anxiety.

If we allow ourselves to get into a relaxed state, that's really when the body cleans itself and gets rid of the chemical stressors. And, as you start a yoga practice, you realize that this is your normal state of being. It's also useful in coping with stress. We're not really looking for shelter from the storm. We're looking for shelter within the storm because we can't just hide in a cave and meditate all the time.

Yoga, by tethering us back to the present moment and connecting us to this sense of inner peace and assisting us to cultivate that state of inner peace as our resting state of being, helps us to gain resilience during moments of stress. Then we blossom into enjoying life more as it's happening because we're more present. Everything then becomes an act of meditating on the present moment and brings about the joy of being alive. So, with this we're less knocked around by life and, when things are good, we're better able to enjoy life.

Earlier I discussed the benefits of yoga as a form of exercise that helps to improve strength, stamina, and flexibility. And I appreciate Kane's discussion here of yoga as also being a form of moving mindfulness meditation. Often after a yoga routine, I don't just feel better physically, I feel calmer and more present. When holding poses, our mind tends to slow down, we are focused on the intricacy of holding the pose, as well as on our breath, bringing us into the present moment and into our body, which is mindfulness meditation. And, if done on a regular basis, this can break the physical and emotional pain cycle.

# Epilogue

This book has been a four-year journey and a labor of love. The chapters within it emerged as I navigated the twists and turns, and the ebb and flow, of my own life, sometimes having to dig deep to find the strength and determination to continue on this path and, even, at times having to make the steep climb back up onto the path after having been slammed by life into the deepest and darkest crevices below.

During the writing of this book, I've lost several friends, including one particularly close friend, to untimely deaths; I've supported my mom during traumatic health scares and wept with relief at her return to good health each time; I've lost places to live; and I've had fortunate and thrilling quantum leaps in my career and in my personal life. By far, my father's death has been the one event that has effected me the deepest. I still have moments when the grief pops up out of seemingly nowhere and hits me so hard that it knocks the wind right out of me. I've learned that I can be still and catch my breath through each wave of pain and that it will soon move on—for a time. I've learned that picking myself back up, perhaps pulled up onto the path by my desire for purpose, has helped me to find joy and vitality once again in my life.

As I've discussed in Section One, *Follow Your Dreams*, having a dream to follow is often the beacon that lights our path during the darkest of times. I'm grateful for having *The Passionate Life* to work on, the opportunity to ask whatever my heart desired of those experts who inspire me, and the ability to share their wise words with you throughout the pages of this book. This has given a much deeper motivation for me to discover what the most difficult or most confusing of times could teach me.

It seems rather synchronistic that while writing this book, I've traveled to some of the highest peaks and the lowest, darkest, of valleys I've ever traversed in my life. But, perhaps, this is just life. Certainly, we're witnessing those high peaks and valleys in a more profound way, more than we've ever seen before in the world around us right now. But as the Barefoot Doctor, Stephen Russell, reminded me, everything appears magnified when we put a frame around it and this book is such a frame.

Now that I've had a chance to write about my experiences and share my lessons with you, I'm more aware that life is often filled with excitement, disappointment, fear, and triumph—all wrapped up together into enormous life-changing events that can lead us to tremendous personal growth, if we let them. Ironically, this is usually followed by very flat, uneventful terrain, when we find ourselves itching for another adventure. If we can use the more intense experiences, as well as the quieter times, to deepen our understanding of our true selves, including our strengths, areas where we have room for improvement, our desires, and our fears, then we will be way ahead of the game toward creating the life we choose—a passionate life— strengthening the resilience to withstand the disappointments, and embracing all that life has to offer us in its entirety with vitality, no matter what our age. One of the lessons that I've learned, on a very deep level, is that, both, grief and pain can coexist, paradoxically, alongside joy. And that is what makes our lives so rich and so valuable every fragile moment of every day. I know that grief and pain will always live within me. They're now part of who I am. But they are not all of who I am—or all of who you are either. Anyone whom we love and lose would not want that to be all that we become. Life inevitably contains deep painful loss if we allow ourselves to love and to risk putting ourselves out there, making ourselves vulnerable. It's worth the risk, with the prize being a fuller, richer life.

I feel that you've been with me along my journey, my friend. I'm grateful for your company, bearing witness for me, and I hope that some of my experiences, and the lessons I've learned from them, along with the sage words of those whom I've quoted in this book, have resonated with you and helped you on your own path. And, now that we're better prepared to create more joyful lives, filled with vitality, let's spread the joy and create a kinder world. See you in the next book. Until then, remember, in the words of the great artist, Pablo Picasso, "Youth has no age."

By embracing the grays of the journey –
Past the "rightness" and "wrongness" –
Through the ups and downs,
Whatever life gives us – even the losses-
We uncover the brilliant hues in our connection to a
Universal peace

# Acknowledgments

This book has been a labor of love, with all of the blood, sweat, and tears that go with such an undertaking. There are so many people to thank for helping me, supporting me, and reminding me why I've needed to stay on this path. First, I'd like to thank you, dear readers, as your presence has been with me throughout this journey, helping me to keep my eye on my North Star, through the clear and stormy weather, sunshine and dark nights. Thank you, thank you, thank you!

Next, with my deepest heartfelt appreciation and love, I want to thank my Mom and Dad, both of whom are very much woven into the pages of this book. Dad, thank you for advising me throughout my life to "just let your imagination run wild." Because of allowing my wild imaginings, I've manifested this book! Not long before you left this upside-down world, you held my hand in yours and said, "Mara, I know you're going to do *great things*!" I've been borrowing your surety in me to give me the ability forge forward toward creating such great things. I'm pretty sure that I have been feeling your eyes twinkling down at me as I've gotten closer to those great things. And Mom, thank you for always being there for me, whenever I've needed an ear or a shoulder, and for pointing out my accomplishments even when I've felt that I've been on shaky ground. With your abiding love and your shining example, you've taught me to be the woman that I am today. I only hope that I can continue to grow and become as strong as you are. Thank you to my brothers and your families for having my back—even if you might have worried about my head being too far into the clouds, at times.

Thank you to all of my friends who have kept me going, with your excitement for me and continued encouragement. Your belief in me has helped me more than you can possibly imagine. And, for those who read and commented on the rough draft, your comments were vital in the coming-together of this book.

To Art Mendoza, thank you for just *so much*. You've been there, holding my hand, whenever I've taken a leap of faith, sometimes pulling me and sometimes pushing me off the cliff toward my dreams. You made me realize that, even if I failed, it would be a crazy fun ride that we would one day look back upon and laugh about. Thank you for creating and producing *Dr. Mara Karpel & Your Golden Years*, with your production company, Accomplice Entertainment. Art, I hope you're wearing your running shoes because I'm getting ready for some more quantum leaps!

For Kathy Sparrow, I cannot express the depth of my appreciation. Thank you for seeing the potential in me and spending the time to be my coach, helping me to find my writing voice, and for being my mentor, guiding me in the world of the written word. And thank you partnering with me to get this book published. There will be more!

Thank you to Rob Kosberg of Best Seller Publishing for having the faith in my message to take my writing and put it into the final product of a beautiful published book. And thank you to the staff at BSP, Elizabeth Barnes, Austin Broom, Sydney Hubbard, and Steve Fata for all of your awesome work in creating the final product.

Of course, thank you to all of my radio show guests for changing my life in so many ways, mind, body, and spirit, and for advice so wonderful that I had to share it twice, by writing about many of your interviews in this book.

Thank you to Huffington Post and Thrive Global, Ariana Huffington's publications, for giving me a platform, so that I've had the opportunity to dip my toe into the writing world to see what works.

Many of the blogs on those platforms have served as the springboard for the chapters in this book and others will turn up in future books.

Thank you to my clients, the many veterans whom I meet with, and to the veterans and staff at Hero's Night Out, for keeping my feet on the ground.

And, finally, to all of the joyful dreamers whom I've met while working in senior communities, thank you for your unending inspiration. You have created the spark that has ignited my own fire.

I hope you all will continue with me through the twists and turns of the journey ahead, reading my future books, joining me for some of my workshops, classes, and radio show interviews. I look forward to meeting you and to being even more inspired by you.

With the deepest of gratitude,

*Mara*

# Appendix A

# Sources and Recommended Resources

The following is a list of the sources cited in the book. Many of these are also resources that I highly recommend. In addition, I'm including a few extras that are some of my favorites that I just want to share with you. I have listed all by category.

## Follow Your Dreams

- Canfield, Jack. *The Success Principles: How to Get From Where You Are to Where You Want to Be.* Harper Collins, 2005, 2015.

- Chopra, Deepak. *The Seven Spiritual Laws of Success: A Practical Guide to the Fulfillment of Your Dreams.* Amber-Allen Publishing, 1994.

- Farrell, Chris. *Unretirement: How Baby Boomers are Changing the Way We Think About Work, Community, and the Good Life.* Bloomsbury Press, 2014.

- Frankl, Viktor. *Man's Search For Meaning: An Introduction to Logotherapy.* Simon and Schuster, 1959.

- Gilbert, *Elizabeth. Big Magic: Creative Living Beyond Fear.* Riverhead Books, 2015.

- Hendricks, Gay, Ph.D. *The Big Leap: Conquer Your Hidden Fear and Take Life to the Next Level.* HarperCollins, 2009.

- Leftenant, *Tresa. Reinventing Her: Helping Women Plan, Pursue, and Capitalize Their Next Chapter.* Tresa Leftenant LLC, 2014.

- Levy, Naomi. *Einstein and the Rabbi: Searching for the Soul.* Flatiron Books, 2017.

- Russell, Stephen, The Barefoot Doctor. *Barefoot Doctor's Handbook for the Urban Warrior: Spiritual Survival Guide.* Piatkus Books, 1998.

- Russell, Stephen, *The Barefoot Doctor. Barefoot Doctor's Guide to the Tao: A Spiritual Guide for the Urban Warrior.* Three Rivers Press, 1998.

- Silver, Tosha. Outrageous *Openness: Letting the Divine Take the Lead.* Atria Books, 2014.

## Women and the Power to Dream

- Hughes, Aralyn. *Kid Me Not: An Anthology by Child-Free Women of the '60s Now In Their 60s.* Violet Crown Publishers, 2014.

- Janeway, Elizabeth. *Between Myth and Morning: Women Awakening.* William Morrow, 1974.

- Leder, Jan. *Women in Jazz: A Discography of Instrumentalists, 1913-1968.* Greenwood Publishing Group, 1985.

- Sandburg, Sheryl. *Lean In: Women, Work and the Will to Lead.* Knopf Publishing Group, 2013.

- Shaw, Clare. *Sageism: How to be an Older Woman.* Indigo Dreams Publishing, 2015.

# Emotional Well-being

## Healing with Humor

- Cousins, Norman. *Anatomy of An Illness: As Perceived by the Patient—Reflections on Healing and Regeneration.* New York: Bantam, 1981.

- Hoare, Joe and the Barefoot Doctor, *Awakening the Laughing Buddha Within.* Lulu.com, 2013.

## Be Still and Feel Peaceful With What Is

- Bidwell, Jan. *Sitting Still: Meditation as the Secret Weapon of Activism.* Friesen Press, 2015.

- Brach, Tara. *Radical Acceptance: Embracing Your Life with the Heart of a Buddha.* Bantam, 2003).

- Brown, Brenè. *The Gifts of Imperfection: Your Guide to a Wholehearted Life.* Hazelden Publishing, 2010).

- Chodron, Pema. *Comfortable with Uncertainty: 108 Teachings on Cultivating Fearlessness and Compassion.* Shambhala Publications, 2003.

- DeMaria, Michael Brant. *Peace Within: Clear Your Mind, Open Your Heart, Embrace Your Soul, and Heal Your Life.* Ontos World Press, 2016.

- Hanh, Thich Nhat. *Peace is Every Step: The Path of Mindfulness in Everyday Life.* New York: Bantam, 1991.

- Hay, Louise. *You Can Heal Your Life.* Hay House, 1984.

- Hershey, Terry. *The Power of Pause: Becoming More by Doing Less.* Loyola Press, 2009.

- Kabat-Zinn, Jon. *Wherever You Go, There You Are: Mindfulness Meditation in Everyday Life.* Hyperion, 1994.

- Kornfield, Jack. *No Time Like The Present: Finding Freedom, Love, and Joy Right Where You Are.* Atria Books, 2017.

- Kornfield, Jack. *The Wise Heart: A Guide to the Universal Teachings of Buddhist Psychology.* Bantam, 2008.

- Tolle, Eckhart. *Stillness Speaks.* New World Library & Namaste Publishing, 2003.

## Optimism

- Seligman, Martin. *Learned Optimism: A Leading Expert on Motivation Demonstrates That Optimism is Essential for a Good and Successful Life—and Shows How to Acquire It.* Knopf Doubleday Publishing Group, 1991.

## Coping With Grief

- Devine, Megan. *It's OK That You're Not OK: Meeting Grief and Loss in a Culture That Doesn't Understand.* Sounds True, 2017.

- Harris, Stephanie. *Death Expands Us: An Honest Account of Grief and How to Rise Above It.* Lioncrest Publishing, 2017.

- Kornfield, Jack. *A Lamp in the Darkness: Illuminating the Path Through Difficult Times.* Sounds True, 2011.

## Love and Relationships

- Ellis, Albert. *Dating, Mating, and Relating: How to Build a Healthy Relationship.* Citadel, 2003.

- Pransky, George. *The Relationship Handbook: A Simple Guide to Satisfying Relationships.* Pransky and Associates, 2013.

- don Miguel Ruiz, *The Mastery of Love: A Practical Guide to the Art of Relationship.* Amber-Allen Publishing, 1999.

- Shubhraji, *In the Lotus of the Heart: The Essence of Relationships.* Namah Inc., 2015.

## Forgiveness

- David Richo, *The Five Things We Cannot Change: and the Happiness We Find by Embracing Them.* Shambhala, 2005.

## Nature

- Louv, Richard. *The Nature Principle: Reconnecting with Life in a Virtual Age.* Algonquin Books of Chapel Hill, 2012.

## The Power of Generosity & Kindness

- Chopra, Deepak. "3 Essential Practices for Gratitude: Experience More Fullness of Heart With These Gratitude Exercises," *Spirituality & Health,* November 20, 2012.

- Ferrucci, Peiro. *The Power of Kindness: The Unexpected Benefits of Leading a Compassionate Life.* TarcherPerigee, 2007.

- Keyes, Corey L. and Jonathan Haidt, *Flourishing: Positive Psychology and the Life Well-Lived.* American Psychological Association, 2002.

- Parami: The Buddhist Home, *Compassion and Loving Kindness.* Parami.org.

- Smith, Christian & Hillary Davidson, *The Paradox of Generosity: Giving We Receive, Grasping We Lose.* Oxford University Press, 2014.

**Self-Love**

- Ellis, Albert and Robert A. Harper, *A New Guide to Rational Living.* Prentice Hall, 1975.

- Ellis, Albert, Melvin Powers, and Irving Becker, *A Guide to Personal Happiness.* Wilshire Book Co, 1982.

- Ellis, Albert. *How to Stubbornly Refuse to Make Yourself Miserable about Anything—Yes, Anything!* Lyle Stuart Inc., 1996.

- Flaxington, Beverly. *Self-Talk for a Calmer You: Learn How to Use Positive Self-talk to Control Anxiety and Live a Happier, More Relaxed Life.* Adams Media, 2013.

- Parkin, John. *F\*\*k It: The Ultimate Spiritual Way.* Hay House UK Ltd., 2012.

- Ruiz, don Miguel. *The Four Agreements: A Practical Guide to Personal Freedom.* Amber-Allen Publishing, 1997.

## Mind and Body

**We Are What We Eat**

- David, Marc. "The Simple Psychology of Habits," *Institute for the Psychology of Eating.* psychologyofeating.com, 2014.

- DeMarco, Venus. *Fearless: My Journey That Healed Breast Cancer—and My Life Through Faith, Food, & Fun.* Aspenhill Publishing Group, 2015.

- Fuhrman, Joel. *Eat to Live: The Amazing Nutrient-Rich Program for Fast and Sustained Weight Loss, Revised Edition.* Little, Brown and Company, 2011.

- Fuhrman, Joel. *The End of Diabetes: The Eat to Live Plan to Prevent and Reverse Diabetes.* HarperOne, 2014.

- Greger, Michael. *How Not to Die: Discover the Foods Scientifically Proven to Prevent and Reverse Disease.* Flatiron Books, 2015.

- NutritionFacts.org. For the latest research.

- Korn, Leslie. *Nutrition Essentials for Mental Health: A Complete Guide to the Food-Mood Connection.* W. W. Norton & Company, 2016.

- Lipman, Frank and Danielle Claro. *The New Health Rules: Simple Changes to Achieve Whole Body Wellness,* Artisan, 2015.

- Mercola, Joseph. *Effortless Healing: 9 Simple Ways to Sidestep Illness, Shed Excess Weight, and Help Your Body Fix Itself.* Harmony, 2015.

- Saltworks. seasalt.com/epsom-salt-uses-and-benefits

- Stoll, Scott. *Alive!: A Physician's Biblical and Scientific Guide to Nutrition.* Creative Enterprises Studio, 2011.

## Delicious Foods & Healthy Recipes

- Carr, Kris and Chef Chad Sarno. *Crazy Sexy Kitchen: 150 Plant-Empowered Recipes to Ignite a Mouthwatering Revolution.* Hay House, 2012.

- Castoria, Elizabeth. *How to Be Vegan: Tips, Tricks, and Strategies for Cruelty-Free Eating, Living, Dating, Traveling, Decorating and More.* Artisan, 2014.

- Mascha, Michael. *Fine Waters: A Connoisseur's Guide to the World's Most Distinctive Bottled Waters.* Quirk Books, 2006.

- Sarno, Chad, Derek Sarno, and David Joachim. *The Wicked Healthy Cookbook: Free. From. Animals.* Grand Central Life & Style, 2018.

## Yoga

- Jude Boccio, Frank. "Calm Within," *Yoga Journal,* April 2018.

- Brett, Ana and Ravi Singh. *The Kundalini Yoga Book: Life in the Vast Lane.* RaviAna Productions, 2018.

- raviana.com. Kundalini yoga DVD's and yoga streams for a home practice.

- Cappy, Peggy. *Yoga for the Rest of Us.* DVD series at PeggyCappy.com.

## Meditation for Health and Pain Relief

- DrMaraKarpel.com. Body Scan meditation and Guided-Meditation for Inner Peace, Joy, and Vitality. Go to: DrMaraKarpel.com/free-guided-meditation.

- Kabat-Zinn, Jon. *Full Catastrophe Living (Revised Edition): Using the Wisdom of Your Body and Mind to Face Stress, Pain, and Illness.* Bantam, 2013.

- Kalsa, Dharma Singh. *Meditation as Medicine: Activate the Power of Your Natural Healing Force.* Pocket Books, 2001.

- Penman, Danny. *Mindfulness for Health: A Practical Guide for Relieving Pain, Reducing Stress, and Restoring Well-Being.* Piatkus Books, 2013.

## Sleep

- Huffington, Ariana. *The Sleep Revolution: Transforming Your Life, One Night at a Time.* Harmony, 2016.

# Appendix B

# Guest Interviews

The following is a list of guests interviewed on my radio program, *Dr. Mara Karpel & Your Golden Years*, who have been cited in this book, along with the dates of the those interviews. I've also included information about each of the guests and the dates of any additional times they were interviewed on the program. You can check out *all* of the many other guests who have appeared on my program, as well, at my website: www.DrMaraKarpel.com.

## Chapter 1

- **Tresa Leftenant,** Financial advising/coaching. www.MyFinancialDesign.com.
  Author of *Reinventing Her: Helping Women Plan, Pursue, and Capitalize Their Next Chapter.* Date of interview transcribed in the text: June 8, 2014. More interviews on the radio show: August 7, 2016; April 30, 2017

- **Quentin Vennie,** Speaker and Health Coach: www.QuentinVennie.com
  Co-Author of *A Memoir of Addiction and Redemption Through Wellness.* Dates of interview transcribed in the text: May 17, 2015. More interviews on the radio show: November 2, 2014; July 10, 2016

- **Chris Farrell,** Host of American Public Media's, *Marketplace.* www.marketplace.org/people/chris-farrell Podcast Host at: www.apmpodcasts.org/unretirement/

Author of *Un-Retirement: How Baby Boomers Are Changing the Way We Think About Work, Community, And The Good Life*. Dates of interviews: December 14, 2014; January 10, 2016

- **Ben Gibson,** Co-founder of *The UnIncubator*.
  www.theuninc.com.
  Dates of interviews: January 11, 2015; July 31, 2016; December 3, 2017

# Chapter 2

- **Aralyn Hughes**, Performance artist and storyteller.
  www.Aralyn.com
  *Kid Me Not: An Anthology of Child-Free Women of the 60's Now In Their 60's*. Date of interview transcribed in the text: March 20, 2016. More interviews on the radio show: May 5, 2013; April 27, 2014

- **Kathy Sparrow,** Leadership Expert, Message Strategist, Writing & Publishing Consultant. Certified Canfield Trainer of The Success Principles. Master RIM Facilitator.
  www.KathySparrow.com.
  Co-Author of *Ignite Your Leadership: Proven Tools for Leaders to Energize Teams, Fuel Momentum, and Accelerate Results,* by Kathy Sparrow, Neel Raman and Nine International Thought Leaders.
  Author of *On the Mother Lagoon: Fly Fishing and the Spiritual Journey*. Date of interview transcribed in the text: February 2, 2014. More interviews on the radio show: October 27, 2013; August 21, 2016; July 30, 2017

- **Jan Leder,** Jazz Flutist, Creator of *Making a Living in Music Wellness: A Workshop for Professional Performers*.
  www.JanLeder.info

Author of *Women in Jazz: A Discography of Instrumentalists, 1913-1968*. Date of interview transcribed in the text: September 4, 2016. More interviews on the radio show: March 26, 2017

## Chapter 3

- **don Miguel Ruiz,** Renowned Spiritual Teacher. www.MiguelRuiz.com.
  Internationally Bestselling Author, the *Toltec Wisdom Series,* including: *The Four Agreements, The Mastery of Love, The Voice of Knowledge, The Four Agreements Companion Book, The Circle of Fire, and The Fifth Agreement*. Date of interview: March 11, 2012

- **Jihan Barakah,** Founder *Global Quantum Shift*. https://www.facebook.com/Jihan-Barakah-Founder-of-The-Global-Quantum-Shift.
  Date of interview cited in text: September 21, 2014. More interviews on the radio show: August 27, 2017; September 24, 2017

- **Naomi Levy,** Rabbi and founder/leader of Nashuva www.RabbiNaomiLevy.com and www.Nashuva.com
  Bestselling author of *To Begin Again, Talking to God, Hope Will Find You,* and *Einstein and the Rabbi*. Date of interview: April 8, 2018

## Chapter 5

- **Terry Hershey,** Speaker and Founder of *Sabbath Moment* . www.TerryHershey.com
  Author of *The Power of Pause: Becoming More by Doing Less, Sanctuary: Creating a Space for Grace in Your Life,* and *Soul*

*Gardening.* Date of interview transcribed in the text: March 6, 2016. More interviews on the radio show: April 2, 2017

## Chapter 7

- **Megan Devine,** Therapist and Founder of Refuge in Grief. www.RefugeInGrief.com
  Author of *It's OK That You're Not OK: Meeting Grief and Loss in a Culture That Doesn't Understand.* Dates of interviews: April 10, 2016; October 8, 2017

- **Stephanie Harris,** Speaker and Grief Coach. www.StephanieHarrisCoaching.com
  Author of *Death Expands Us: An Honest Account of Grief and How to Rise Above It.*
  Date of interview: March 25, 2018

## Chapter 8

- **The Barefoot Doctor, Stephen Russell,** Taoist master, Therapist, Speaker, Workshop Leader, Musician, www.BarefootDoctorWorld.com
  Author of *The Barefoot Doctor's Guide to the Tao: A Spiritual Handbook for the Urban Warrior, Manifesto: The Internal Revolution, Supercharged Taoist: An Amazing True Story To Inspire You on Your Own Adventure.* Date of interview: February 5, 2017

## Chapter 9

- **Beverly Flaxington,** The Human Behavior Coach™. www.the-collaborative.com

Author of *Self-Talk for a Calmer You: Learn How to Use Positive Self-talk to Control Anxiety and Live a Happier, more Relaxed Life.* Date of interview: December 7, 2014

## Chapter 11

- **Michael Brant DeMaria,** Psychologist, Poet, Speaker, Grammy® Nominated Recording Artist. www.MichaelDeMaria.com
Author of *Peace Within: Clear Your Mind, Open Your Heart, Embrace Your Soul, and Heal Your Life.* Date of interview transcribed in the text: March 26, 2017. More interviews on the radio show: March 24, 2013

- **Dara Kelly,** Certified Integral Yoga Instructor, Energy Worker, & Occupational Therapist. www.DaraKelly.com. Date of interview transcribed in the text: March 19, 2017. More interviews on the radio show: January 17, 2016

- **Dave Richo,** Psychotherapist, Teacher, Workshop Leader, Writer. www.DaveRicho.com
Author of *The Five Things We Cannot Change: and the Happiness We Find by Embracing Them,* by David Richo. Date of interview: June 26, 2016

## Chapter 12

- **Cathy Bonner,** Austin's *Meditation Bar.*
www.MeditationBar.com Date of interview: February 21, 2016

## Chapter 13

- **Jonathan Troen,** *Austin Yoga Tree.* www.AustinYogaTree.com. Date of interview: September 11, 2016

# Chapter 14

- **Carol Polcovar,** Poet, Author, Playwright, Producer, Teacher. www.facebook.com/candrwrite. Date of interview: December 18, 2016

- **Crista Beck,** Love Coach. www.CristaBeck.com. Date of interview: February 14, 2016

- **Gigi Sage,** Communication Expert, Founder of *Happy, Health, Wealthy & Free.* www.GigiSage.com. Date of interview transcribed in the text: December 6, 2015.
  Other interviews on the radio show: February 1, 2015

# Chapter 19

- **Scott Stoll,** Board Certified Specialist in Physical Medicine and Rehabilitation, Team Physician at Lehigh University, U.S. Bobsled and Skeleton team, Former member of 1994 Olympic Bobsled team, National Speaker, Member of the Whole Foods Scientific and Medical Advisory Board, Co-Founder of the *Plantrician Project, The International Plant Based Nutrition Healthcare Conference, The International Cardiovascular Summit.* www.DrScottStoll.com
  Co-Author of *Alive!: A Physician's Biblical and Scientific Guide to Nutrition.* Date of interview transcribed in the text: September 29, 2013. More interviews on the radio show: November 15, 2015

- **Michael Greger,** Physician, International Speaker, Founder of www.NutritionFacts.org
  Founding Member and Fellow of the American College of Lifestyle Medicine. www.DrGreger.org
  Best-Selling Author of *How Not to Die* and *The How Not to Die Cookbook.* Date of interview: May 22, 2016

# Chapter 20

- **Joel Fuhrman,** Board Certified Family Physician, International Speaker, President of the *Nutritional Research Foundation,* Faculty at Northern Arizona University – Health Sciences Division. www.DrFuhrman.com

  Best-Selling Author of *Eat to Live: The Amazing Nutrient-Rich Program For Fast and Sustained Weight-Loss, The End of Diabetes: The Eat to Live Plan to Prevent and Reverse Diabetes, The End of Heart Disease, Super Immunity, The End of Dieting, Disease-Proof Your Child, Fast-Food Genocide.* Date of interview: August 25, 2013

# Chapter 24

- **Michael Mascha,** Water Connoisseur, Artist, Photographer. www.FineWaters.com

  Author of *Fine Waters: A Connoisseur's Guide to the World's Most Distinctive Bottled Waters.* Date of interview cited in the text: October 2, 2016. More interviews on the radio show: July 20, 2014

- **Venus DeMarco,** National Speaker on "Wellness, Prevention of Disease, and Keeping the Cancer Switch Off," Health Coach, Healthy Cooking Teacher. www.VenusDeMarco.org

  Author of Fearless: *My Journey That Healed Breast Cancer—and My Life, Through Faith, Food, & Fun* and *My Healing Kitchen.* Dates of interviews on the radio show: February 9, 2014; July 20, 2014; December 21, 2014; June 21, 2015; December 13, 2015; July 17, 2016

## Chapter 25

- **Peggy Cappy**, Creator of the PBS's *Yoga For the Rest of Us* DVD Series, Founder of Gentle Stretch Yoga www.PeggyCappy.com Author of *Yoga for All of Us: A Modified Series of Traditional Poses for Any Age and Ability.* Date of interview: June 29, 2014

- **Ravi Singh,** Co-Founder, with Ana Brett, of *raviana:* Kundalini Yoga Workshops, Retreats, Teacher-Training, 25+ DVD's and Streaming Videos of Kundalini Yoga. www.raviana.com Co-Author, with Ana Brett, of *The Kundalini Yoga Book: Life in the Vast Lane.* Date of interview: January 26, 2014

## Chapter 26

- **Jeremy Robinson,** Fitness and Nutrition Coach, Founder, *Austin Holistic Fitness.* www.AustinHolisticFitness.com. Date of interview transcribed in text: July 31, 2016. More interviews on the radio show: February 8, 2015; May 31, 2015; July 12, 2015; November 8, 2015; May 1, 2016; October 30, 2016; February 19, 2017; June 18, 2017; September 10, 2017

## Chapter 27

- **Bruce Meleski,** Neurosensory Performance Specialist, Founder, *Intelligent Sleep,* Date of interview transcribed in text: May 3, 2015, More interviews on the radio show: December 4, 2016

# Chapter 29

- **Steve Kane,** Yoga Teacher and Teacher of *The Art of Happiness.*
  KaneSteve@me.com
  Date of interview transcribed in text: June 19, 2016. More
  interviews on the radio show: April 3, 2016; October 16, 2016;
  March 5, 2017; May 7, 2017; June 4, 2017; October 15, 2017;
  April 29, 2018

# Appendix C

# Research Studies Cited

## Chapter 2

- Raymond, Joan. "Men, Women and IQ," *Newsweek, U.S. Edition,* January 22, 2008.

## Chapter 6

- Emmons, Robert A & Michael E. McCullough. "Counting Blessings Versus Burdens: An Experimental Investigation of Gratitude and Subjective Well-being in Daily Life." *Journal of Personality and Social Psychology,* 84, no. 2 (2003). 377-389.

## Chapter 7

- Levy, Becca R., et al. "Longevity Increased by Positive Self-perceptions of Aging." *Journal of Personality and Social Psychology,* 83, no 2 (2002): 261-70.

- Seligman Martin E. P. "Learned Helplessness." *Annual Review of Medicine.* 23 (1972): 407-412.

## Chapter 9

- Kross, Ethan, et al. "Self-talk as a Regulatory Mechanism: How You Do It Matters." *Journal of Personality and Social Psychology,* 106, no. 2 (2014): 304-324.

- Moser, Jason S., et al. "Third-person Self-talk Facilitates Emotion Regulation without Engaging Cognitive Control: Converging Evidence from ERP and fMRI." *Scientific Reports,* 7 no. 1 (2017).

## Chapter 12

- Holzell, Britta K., et al. "Mindfulness Practice Leads to Increases in Regional Brain Gray Matter Density." *Psychiatry Research: Neuroimaging,* 191 (2011): 36-43.

## Chapter 14

- Park, Lora E., Ariana F. Young, Paul W. Eastwick "(Psychological) Distance Makes the Heart Grow Fonder." *Personality and Social Psychology Bulletin,* 41 no. 11, (2015): 1459-1473.

## Chapter 18

- Carter, Sherrie Bourg. "Helper's High: The Benefits (and Risks) of Altruism. *Psychology Today,* September 2014.

- Layous, Kristin, et al. "What Triggers Pro-social Effort? A Positive Feedback Loop between Positive Activities, Kindness, and Well-being." *The Journal of Positive Psychology,* 12, no. 4 (2017): 385-398

- McClelland, David C. & Carol Kirshnit. "The Effect of Motivational Arousal through Films on Salivary Immunoglobulin-A." *Psychology and Health,* 2 no. 1 (1988): 31-52.

- The Saguaro Seminar: Civic Engagement in America, *John F. Kennedy School of Government: Harvard University.* "Social Capital Community Benchmark Survey."

## Chapter 19

- Lee, Yu-Mi et al. "Effect of a Brown Rice-based Vegan Diet and Conventional Diabetic Diet on Glycemic Control of Patients with Type 2 Diabetes: A 12-week Randomized Clinical Trial. *PLoS One,* 11 no. 6 (2016).

- Oyebode, Oyinlola, et al. "Fruit and Vegetable Consumption and All-Cause, Cancer and CVD Mortality: Analysis of Health Survey for England Data." *Journal of Epidemiology and Community Health,* 68, no. 9 (2014): 856-862.

## Chapter 22

- Robinson, Jennifer, et. al. "Role of Self-medication in the Development of Comorbid Anxiety and Substance Use Disorders: A Longitudinal Investigation." *Archives of General Psychiatry,* 68 no. 8, (2011): 800.

- Stampfer, Meir J. et al. "Effects of Moderate Alcohol Consumption on Cognitive Function in Women." *New England Journal of Medicine,* 352 (2005): 245-253.

## Chapter 24

- Safdar, Adeel, et al "Endurance Exercise Rescues Progeroid Aging and Induces Systemic Mitochondrial Rejuvenation in mtDNA Mutator Mice." *Proceedings of the National Academy of Sciences,* 108 no. 10 (2011): 4135-4140.

## Chapter 27

- Centers for Disease Control and Prevention: Morbidity and Mortality Weekly Report (2011). *Unhealthy Sleep-related Behaviors – 12 states*, 2009, 60, no 8.

- *Drowsy Driving Prevention Week: Facts and Stats*, DrowsyDriving.org/about/facts-and-stats/

- Minkel, Jared D, et al. "Sleep Deprivation and Stressors: Evidence for Elevated Negative Effect in Response to Mild Stressors when Sleep Deprived." *Emotion*, 12 no. 5 (2012): 1015-1020.

- *The Great British Sleep Survey*, www.sleepio.com/2012report/

## Chapter 29

- Zeidan, Fadel, et. al. "Mindfulness-Meditation-based Pain Relief is not Mediated by Endogenous Opioids." *Journal of Neuroscience*, 36, no. 11 (2016): 3391-3397.

**Mara Karpel, Ph.D.** is a clinical psychologist, working with adults of all ages for over 26 years, and having a specialty of working with older adults and caregivers. For the past several years, Dr. Mara has also been evaluating veterans for service-connected mental health conditions. She is a speaker, the host of the Internet radio show, *Dr. Mara Karpel & Your Golden Years*, and a regular contributor to Ariana Huffington's, *Thrive Global* and contributor to *Huffington Post*. Born and raised in New York City, Dr. Mara currently resides in the "Live Music Capital," Austin, Texas, where she's been enjoying the music and following her dreams.

Dr. Mara is available for keynotes and workshops on a variety of topics including living a passionate life, finding meaning well into our golden years, caring for elderly parents, and much more. Find out more at: www.drmarakarpel.com.

# Living the Passionate Life
## An online course with Dr. Mara Karpel

No matter our age, we all want to live a joyful vital life. Having a dream and passionately following it, gives our life direction and meaning. Without this, it's easy to feel that we're stuck in a rut.

In this course, we'll discuss strategies to find the joy in discovering and following our own North Star, get "un-stuck," face our fears, and love and nurture ourselves to enhance the quality of our life.

And when those inevitable obstacles appear, we'll address them with tried and true methods for forging ahead with our dreams—no matter what may lay across our path--other people's opinions, practical logistics or even our own inner critic.

Participants will also discover how to:

- Stay healthy through better food choices and exercising
- Nurture healthy relationships
- Create positive thought habits
- Laugh to invoke vitality and joy

You'll leave this six-module course inspired to find a new dream or renew an old one--and with the tools to love yourself right now in this present moment.

### For more information, visit:

# www.drmarakarpel.com/course

Made in the USA
Middletown, DE
15 September 2018